Classroom Discipline and Management

Clifford H. Edwards
Brigham Young University

Macmillan Publishing Company
New York

Maxwell Macmillan Canada
Toronto

Maxwell Macmillan International
New York   Oxford   Singapore   Sydney

Cover art: © Nancy Doniger
Editor: Robert Miller
Production Editor: Mary M. Irvin
Art Coordinator: Lorraine Woost
Cover Designer: Cathleen Norz
Production Buyer: Patricia A. Tonneman
Artist: Jane Lopez
Electronic Text Management: Ben Ko, Marilyn Wilson Phelps

This book was set in Transitional 511 by Macmillan Publishing Company and was printed and bound by R. R. Donnelley & Sons. The cover was printed by New England Book Components.

Macmillan Publishing Company
866 Third Avenue
New York, New York 10022

Macmillan Publishing Company is part of the
Maxwell Communication Group of Companies.

Maxwell Macmillan Canada, Inc.
1200 Eglinton Avenue East, Suite 200
Don Mills, Ontario M3C 3N1

Library of Congress Cataloging-in Publication Data
Edwards, Clifford H.
  Classroom discipline and management / by Clifford H. Edwards.
    p. cm.
  Includes bibliographical references and index.
  ISBN 0-02-331630-6
  1. School discipline—United States. 2. Classroom management—
United States. I. Title
LB3011.E34 1993
  371.1'024   92-19792
                                                           CIP

Printing: 2 3 4 5 6 7 8 9   Yes: 3 4 5 6 7

For Deanna, Shon, Steve, Jeff, and Eric

Preface

Discipline, along with drug abuse, remains the single most common and pernicious problem educators face in their day-to-day teaching. Because discipline problems are so prevalent and difficult to solve, many educators and specialists in related fields have attempted to provide help for teachers. Their suggestions come from a variety of perspectives and are based on different assumptions about the purposes of schooling and the capabilities of students. Rarely do teachers scrutinize the assumptions on which these discipline approaches are based or measure them against their own values and educational philosophy. Teachers commonly use a procedure simply if it works. The extent to which a discipline approach works is, of course, a critical concern. However, there are other considerations, such as the teacher's own philosophy, that must be included in decisions about discipline.

Knowing a successful method of discipline is essential to teaching; so are a teacher's own values and beliefs about discipline. This book is designed to help teachers thoughtfully examine various approaches to discipline along with their personal philosophy and then either to choose an existing approach or to create one. To make decisions about discipline, teachers must have a thorough understanding of the assumptions that undergird various discipline approaches in addition to knowledge of theory and practical applications. Otherwise, informed choice is impossible.

Identifying basic assumptions is important for two reasons. First, teachers need to consistently follow their own educational philosophy, not only in matters of discipline but in the overall instructional program as well. Teachers who are guided by a consistent philosophy are able to teach with integrity and avoid hypocrisy. Second, teachers who carefully examine their educational practices in terms of personal philosophy are able to achieve a level of commitment unattainable by those who are less systematic and sure of themselves. Committed teachers are more inclined to devote themselves to the profession and achieve success.

One aspect of discipline often ignored is the extent to which a particular theory or approach is designed to prevent or correct discipline problems. Most models claim to correct discipline problems. Few are deliberately designed to prevent them. This important consideration is raised for each discipline approach presented. Another important topic covered is the question of whether a particular discipline model is appropriate for schoolwide application or is limited to classroom use.

The sequence of chapters is arranged to help teachers make consistent, rational decisions about discipline. Chapter 1 is an introduction to the effects as well as the sources of discipline problems in the schools. Chapter 2 provides a model for determining a personal discipline approach. In Chapters 3 through 10 various discipline models are discussed. The models selected cover a wide spectrum of possible approaches.

In Chapters 11 and 12 the various models are considered for inclusion in a comprehensive discipline program. Chapter 11 shows how to compare various discipline approaches with one another and to select the one that most closely corresponds to one's personal philosophy. Chapter 12 provides an example to illustrate the development of a comprehensive, personal approach to discipline that is consistent with specified criteria and is based on verifiable assumptions.

The focus in Chapters 13, 14, and 15 is on classroom management. Chapter 13 is designed to help teachers ensure that their discipline approach is consistent with their overall instructional program. Chapter 14 demonstrates the importance of having good student-teacher relationships and shows teachers how to improve these relationships. Chapter 15 shows teachers how to properly manage the various aspects of the classroom—teacher-student relationships, time, the physical environment—so that students will stay on-task and maintain their interest in learning.

The following professors provided timely and helpful reviews of the manuscript, for which I am grateful: Leslie Chamberlin, Bowling Green State University; Dorothy L. W. Dobson, Utah State University; Rey A. Gomez, Arizona State University; Nancy Lourie, San Jose State University; and Bruce D. Smith, University of Cincinnati.

Contents

UNIT 2
Discipline Models   34

CHAPTER 6
Transactional Analysis: Eric Berne and Thomas Harris   99

C H A P T E R 7
Reality Therapy/Control Theory: William Glasser   121

C H A P T E R 8
The Ginott Model: Haim Ginott   145

CHAPTER 9
The Kounin Model: Jacob Kounin   159

CHAPTER 10
The Jones Model: Fredric H. Jones   179

CHAPTER 15
Managing the Classroom   277

Classroom Discipline
and Management

1

Problems and Issues
in Discipline

The sources of school discipline problems are many and varied. Home, society, and school all play a role. Educators often contend that problems in school stem from children's experiences at home or in society at large. Schools, however, must take responsibility for some of these problems. Some home and social problems do carry over into the schools, but many difficulties are created through various school practices and conditions.

For schools, creating an appropriate learning environment is critical. Learning is what schools are about. An improper learning environment strikes at the very heart of the school's purpose. Because good learning conditions are critical and because discipline problems are a constant threat to learning, classroom discipline is very important. The need for good discipline has stimulated educators and others to create and promote a variety of approaches to ensure that a proper learning environment is maintained. These different approaches are based on various assumptions about human beings and how they should be treated in the schools. They also produce different outcomes.

Because teachers have many different discipline options available to them and because there is no one generally accepted theory of discipline, individual teachers must decide for themselves which discipline approach to use. This decision requires teachers to examine the various assumptions on which each discipline theory is built, as well as its principles and practices, and compare them with their own personal values and beliefs. The purpose of Unit 1 is to help readers to begin this important process.

CHAPTER

1

Discipline Problems and Their Causes

OBJECTIVES

This chapter is designed to help you
1. understand the nature of discipline problems and their causes
2. recognize the roles of home, society, and school in creating discipline problems
3. identify some common mistakes teachers make when they discipline their classes

Introduction

▼ Mr. Haskell looked up as Marcia sauntered into the room. He watched out of the corner of his eye as Marcia swaggered down the aisle between the first two rows of desks and took a seat in the back of the room. After a similar incident the day before, Mr. Haskell had appealed to the class to help him solve the problem. Earlier in the year the class had agreed to rules and consequences regarding misbehavior in class. They had decided then that students who disrupted class had to forfeit their right to sit where they wanted and instead be placed in a designated seat near the front of the room. Confronted with Marcia's recent disruptiveness, they had together agreed that she should sit in the front row seat next to Mr. Haskell's desk until further notice. Obviously Marcia was ignoring these directions and provoking a confrontation. Mr. Haskell shuddered as he contemplated the scene that would probably result if he tried to get Marcia to cooperate. Marcia was always picking fights with other students and routinely threw spit wads and paper airplanes around the room. Mr. Haskell could not remember the last time Marcia had not disrupted the class by talking loudly to other class members. Then there was that arrogant smirk whenever she misbehaved. It was easy to see that she was just issuing a challenge. Mr. Haskell hated to confront Marcia because she always seemed to prevail. Most of the class was assembled now. Mr. Haskell knew that the bell was going to ring any minute and he still had not decided how to deal with the situation. Marcia was looking at him with a big smile on her face. The other students were looking on expectantly, wondering how their teacher would handle Marcia this time. Mr. Haskell stepped reluctantly to the front of the room and, looking at Marcia, asked, "Class, what did you decide the consequences should be for anyone who disrupts class?"

Amanda quickly replied for the class, "They were to be moved to the front of the class."

Looking directly at Marcia, Mr. Haskell said, "Marcia, you can either take your seat here near my desk or be excused to talk to Mr. Pugmire in the counseling department about finding a new English class."

The entire class was now looking at Marcia. She slowly rose to her feet and, making her way to the front of the class, picked up the hall pass and defiantly walked through the classroom door. Mr. Haskell was suddenly aware that he had been holding his breath. He silently exhaled and filled his lungs again. "Thank heavens she's gone," he thought. "I wonder what she will do now." Coupled with his desire to get Marcia out of his class was a tinge of regret that he had been unable to reach her. He knew of Marcia's family situation—that her father had been convicted of drug possession and was currently serving a prison term. He knew also that Marcia was actively involved in one of the local street gangs.

Forcing these thoughts from his mind, Mr. Haskell turned to the class and said, "All right, class, let's get started with our lesson for the day." For about 30 minutes Mr. Haskell involved the class in a spirited discussion. Just before he was about to close the discussion and give the class a few minutes to start their homework assignment, the classroom door opened and in walked Mr. Pugmire, directing Marcia ahead of him. Walking straight up to Mr. Haskell he said, in a voice the entire class could hear, "Mr. Haskell, you're just going to have to take Marcia back in your class. The other eleventh grade English classes are filled. There is nowhere else she can be placed." Mr. Haskell looked at Mr. Pugmire's determined face and then back at Marcia. He anticipated what he would see—the telltale smirk was slowly forming on Marcia's lips. Without waiting for further direction Marcia boldly turned and strutted to the back of the room, where she defiantly took her seat.

Causes of Discipline Problems

Teachers can often be overwhelmed by the discipline problems with which they have to deal. They cause some of these problems themselves, of course. However, many of the problems they face are an outgrowth of problems at home and in society or of conditions and administrative procedures in the school. As illustrated in the story about Mr. Haskell and Marcia, teachers can sometimes be confronted with a combination of these problems all at once. Their combined effects may sometimes make it nearly impossible to handle disruptive students effectively. When these difficulties persist despite one's best efforts to solve them, it is common for a teacher to blame other contributing factors. Mr. Haskell could well have blamed parents, the society at large, or the ineffective performance of counselors and administrators. Such recrimination, of course, does little to change conditions and solve problems. Certainly teachers can work with administrators and counselors in an attempt to alter school policies and procedures that impede effective discipline. They can do little, however, to change influences outside the school that promote children's misbehavior. But, by understanding these outside influences, they can be better prepared to manage the discipline problems that result.

along with the crowd and put little effort into their studies; nearly every large high school has such a group, universally recognized but rarely acknowledged. If students place great value on conspicuous consumption, they may feel compelled to keep up with the latest styles. An increasing number of students are carrying and listening to portable tape players, which often interfere with their attentiveness in class. Even the kind of music children play may be a source of conflict between them and their teachers. Students' schoolwork—and their attitudes—may suffer if they work long hours at part-time jobs to earn money for clothes, music, or electronic equipment. (Some students, of course, have to work because their families need the money.) If students feel that their interests lie elsewhere, they may drop out of school.

THE ROLE OF THE SCHOOL

Teachers usually consider students to be the source of school discipline problems. However, many behaviors should be looked upon as normal reactions by children to deficiencies in the school as an institution and to teachers and administrators as directors of the educational enterprise. In fact, the school may not only promote misbehavior in students; it may also help create conditions that put children at risk generally. Teachers and administrators can invite discipline problems if they

1. misunderstand learning conditions and require students to learn information that is not meaningful to them

2. fail to encourage the development of independent thinking patterns in students

3. establish rigid conditions for students to meet in order to feel accepted

4. sponsor a competitive grading system that prohibits success for the majority of the students and erodes their self-concepts

5. exercise excessive control over students and fail to provide an environment in which children can become autonomous and independent

6. use discipline procedures that promote misbehavior (Edwards, 1989)

Instruction Without Context.   Educators may fail their students if they teach concepts as though they were abstract, self-contained entities. Outside the school, children learn by acquiring information in a real-life context and applying it to new situations and experiences. In school, however, students may be expected to manipulate symbolic information and to apply it in ways that are detached from the real world. Under such conditions, children fail to make proper associations and are unable to apply what they learn to the problems they face each day (Resnick, 1987). Because they are unable to readily comprehend the usefulness of what they are taught in school, they are frustrated. They see school as unrelated to real life. They are required to attend, but they find no meaning there. They repeatedly ask why they have to learn what teachers offer and often sabotage the learning of classmates.

   A number of things can be done to alleviate this problem. Considerable emphasis is currently being placed on school reform in America. One of these reform movements is an effort to involve students in community service. These service experiences, designed as outgrowths of academic programs, are intended to give students an opportunity to learn in practical settings. Commonly these service experiences help students learn civic responsibility, but they also provide a means of acquiring important social, scientific, and communication skills.

For example, students in Salt Lake City have been responsible for the cleanup of a hazardous waste site, the passage of two crucial environmental laws, the planting of hundreds of trees, and the completion of several neighborhood improvement projects (Lewis, 1991). In the south Bronx, students have been involved in the restoration of a building to be used for homeless people. In Chicopee, Massachusetts, middle schools have saved the city $119,500 by helping to solve sewage problems. Students in Brooks County, Georgia, were responsible for establishing a day care center that has been in operation since 1981 (Nathan & Kielsmeier, 1991). Researchers have concluded that these activities not only have enhanced and broadened students' academic performance but have contributed greatly to the social and psychological development of participants (Conrad & Hedin, 1991).

In science education, a similar new approach has been advanced in a program called Science Technology Society (STS). In this program, students identify a social problem that can be studied both scientifically and technologically. They may, for example, choose to work on a specific pollution problem, using their science skills to take measurements of various pollutants and track their effects. When the problem has been carefully studied, the students make their recommendations to appropriate community groups. In some cases, when they have received little or no response, groups of students have been given free legal services to initiate litigation in order to correct the problem (Bybee, 1985).

Students can also gain academic experience that is less abstract through work-study programs in which they spend part of the school day working for various community agencies. Each student may work in a doctor's office, insurance company, factory, or other location to learn how school is related to the world of work and to explore various career opportunities. When students are involved in service- and project-based curricula, far fewer discipline and personal problems can be anticipated.

Failure to Teach Thinking Skills.   When children are consistently unable to solve their problems, they often seek to escape them through alcohol or other drugs or various thrill-seeking activities. Some drop out of school or even commit suicide (Frymier, 1988). Some children fail to find satisfactory solutions to their problems because they have difficulty thinking through them. Some have trouble organizing their lives and responding appropriately to life's demands. Others are unable to set priorities for themselves. If higher-order thinking skills were regularly taught in the schools, a good deal of frustration and failure, as well as behavioral problems, could be avoided. Learning these skills would also help children deal with conflicts at home and elsewhere.

Traditional methods of teaching make learning a passive endeavor. Students are just expected to assimilate information. Recently, cognitive psychologists have proposed that learners be allowed to generate their own conceptual structures (Jones, 1988). Children actually resist knowledge assimilation; instead, they insist on adding to their present conceptual structures only that knowledge that makes sense to them personally

(Osborne & Wittrock, 1983). In other words, they tend to learn only what fits in with what they already know. Teachers must introduce children to higher-order thinking so that they can make more valid conceptual structures of the world. Failure to do so dooms children to the frustration of taking simplistic lessons memorized in school and trying to apply them to the complex problems of the modern world. It is unfortunate, and ironic, that the children who most lack advanced thinking skills are considered at risk because they also lack basic skills. They are assigned remedial work while their more advanced counterparts are given more meaningful and integrated learning experiences (Shavelson, 1985), experiences from which they too might greatly benefit.

There are a number of excellent programs currently available for teaching children how to think and make valid decisions. Most have sets of materials that can be used as supplementary lessons in nearly every classroom. Chance (1986) has reviewed eight different programs and made comparisons of their characteristics, goals, methods, underlying philosophy, and target audiences. The eight programs include sample exercises, along with research data and staff development requirements. These programs are:

- CoRT Thinking Lessons
- Productive Thinking Program
- Philosophy for Children
- Odyssey
- Instrumental Enrichment
- Problem Solving and Comprehension
- Techniques of Learning
- Thoughtful Teaching

Teaching thinking skills can provide a means of improving students' motivation and help solve the perennial problems of failure, disillusionment, and unmet potential in students. In the process, many discipline problems can be avoided (Marzano et al., 1988).

Nonacceptance.   Without realizing it, many teachers convey nonacceptance to some of their students. For example, when teachers force students to do a task in a prescribed way, they implicitly show a lack of confidence in the students' ability to make decisions about their own work. In an attempt to show approval, a teacher may say to a student, "You have done good work, but I know you can do better" or "It really helps a lot when you clean up your work area." Such praise carries with it implied criticism; it rewards students for conformity but leaves their need for acceptance unfulfilled. Children do need to grow and therefore to change. However, they also need to feel that they are acceptable as they are.

The simplest way to avoid conveying nonacceptance is to permit students to evaluate themselves more and to establish their own directions and expectations. Allowing self-evaluation does not mean simply letting students give themselves a grade. Children must compare their own performances over time to achieve a sense of their own growth and to learn and accept the true value of their efforts.

Competitive Grading.   Many schools foster competition between children through the use of grades. Only a few students, however, are consistently good at taking tests. The rest must find other means of bolstering their sense of worth. Unfortunately, many of them conclude that they are less able—they would say "dumber"—than more successful classmates and are therefore less valuable.

Thus, in an effort to motivate them, schools can demoralize students with the implicit threat of possible failure. They virtually ensure that many students will fail and feel the sense of incompetence that comes with failure (Englander, 1986).

Some teachers make sincere efforts to reduce the impact of school competition by giving more high grades or refusing to give students failing grades. Many teachers realize the detrimental effects of grading on their students but feel powerless to change the system. Some school districts actually impose grade quotas on teachers, who are not allowed to give too many high grades for fear that grade inflation will erode academic standards.

Making evaluation less traumatic for students may be one of the most difficult problems teachers have to face. The system of norm-based grades, in which the performance of each student is compared with that of others, may have to be set aside in favor of other systems. Such changes certainly merit consideration. Many teachers who recognize the negative effects of grades have already made some adjustments to lessen their impact. Nevertheless, competition for grades, with all its attendant problems, continues.

One adjustment some teachers have made is to evaluate students' progress individually and grade them accordingly. Others have involved their students in the evaluation process. This practice has the added advantage of helping students become more self-directed. The problem with most of these adjustments is that letter grades are given as a consequence of the evaluations. These grades, which still carry the connotation that students are being compared with one another academically, are likely to promote some of the same problems as grades given in the regular norm-based system. This problem will continue until universities and employers begin to accept forms of evaluation other than comparative grading and school professionals and parents begin to recognize fully the negative impact of grades and make appropriate changes.

Excessive Coercion.   Much is said by teachers and school administrators about teaching children to be more responsible. This "responsibility" often consists of completing assignments on time and accomplishing other tasks as directed. Students judged to be the most responsible and mature are those who comply exactly with expectations. Responsibility, however, requires the exercise of free will and the opportunity to make choices. Ironically, a common assumption behind many school practices is that children are unable to govern themselves or even to learn how to be self-regulating. Students, therefore, are given few opportunities to make decisions. Teachers fear that students will behave improperly—get "out of control"—if they are allowed "too much" freedom. Undoubtedly, some children appear to have little ability to direct their own lives. This apparent inability prompts teachers to give them excessive guidance and to exercise too much coercive control. The result is increased rebellion by students. When children rebel, teachers believe that they have made correct assumptions about the students' irresponsibility. More control is the usual remedy. Unfortunately, rebellion cannot be subdued by coercion and control. Perhaps some children can be broken in this process, but many others rebel all the more. These "incorrigible" children usually end up being expelled.

Happily, responsibility can be taught by providing children with more real opportunities to make decisions. Responsible actions will replace rebellious ones when children are taught to make valid decisions within a context of free choice and when they are held personally accountable for the decisions they make. This is how true responsibility is fostered. A balance must be struck between the teacher's control and students' self-determination. Students should not simply be turned loose to do as they wish. They must be involved with the teacher in responsible decision-making.

Punishment.   The method of discipline used by teachers and administrators may itself contribute to discipline problems. Historically, punishment is how society has dealt with infractions. It is still the most common way to deal with discipline problems in school. Eighty to ninety percent of the rule violations in schools are dealt with punitively (Englander, 1986). The long tradition of punishment in schools has been supported by general child-rearing practices, court decisions, and public opinion. Part of this tradition includes corporal punishment. The use of corporal punishment has been upheld by the U.S. Supreme Court, but by 1989 nineteen states had forbidden its use in the schools (Hyman, 1990). Despite the fact that corporal punishment is increasingly being abolished by state laws, Chase (1975) reports that the majority of teachers and parents believe in its use. Perhaps in time it will be universally considered unacceptable for use in schools.

Although punishment is still the most prevalent means of dealing with problems in the schools, most of the research on punishment is dated. There seems to be little current interest in the subject. In addition, most of the research that is done in this area focuses on the extent to which punishment can be successfully used to enforce students' compliance. Little attention has been given to other effects of punishment.

One aspect of punishment that has received some attention is the effect of timing. Some important conclusions can be drawn from the studies that have been made. First, the effects of punishment are greatest before the act is carried out. Delays of even six seconds greatly limit the effects of punishment. Second, seeing others go unpunished tends to nullify the effects of punishment. If several students are breaking a rule and classmates see that only those who are caught get punished, the effectiveness of punishment as a deterrent is reduced (Englander, 1986).

Although it is intended to reduce misbehavior, punishment instead routinely increases misbehavior. When teachers treat their students in a rough, angry, and punitive way, children's disruptive behavior, apprehension, and restlessness increase and their involvement in school tasks decreases (Kounin & Gump, 1961). Students react in a similar way to teachers' directives. In one study, for example, when teachers told their students more often to sit down, students spent more time out of their seats (Becker, Engelmann, & Thomas, 1975).

If punishment tends to be ineffective and produces unexpected negative results, what can be done to replace it? Most of the discipline approaches outlined in this book are punishment-free. Among them teachers will find a number of ways to deal with misbehavior in nonpunitive ways.

▼

SUMMARY

Discipline problems experienced in school may have their origin in the family or in society at large, but many problems are aggravated and sometimes caused by school policies and procedures as well as by teachers and other school personnel. To reduce the number of discipline problems, teachers need to make learning more relevant and meaningful, foster independent thinking, show greater acceptance of diversity, encourage cooperative learning, avoid excessive control, and discontinue the use of punishment to discipline children.

CENTRAL IDEAS

1. School discipline problems can be created at home if parents do not provide their children
   a. the support they need to develop a healthy self-concept,
   b. adequate attention,
   c. unconditional love, and
   d. an opportunity to develop responsible independence.
2. Certain aspects of society can cause discipline problems in the school. Peer pressure plays a strong role in shaping children's behavior. Gangs in particular often recruit members from among children who have experienced adjustment problems at school and at home. Gangs often create problems for schools by pushing drugs and encouraging delinquency and violence in their members, especially participation in illegal acts as a sign of their allegiance to the gang. Other significant factors, such as the drive to earn money to buy the latest styles of clothing, can also affect students' participation in and attitudes toward school.
3. Schools create their own discipline problems by
   a. failing to provide children relevant, meaningful learning,
   b. failing to help children learn to think independently,
   c. exercising too much coercion,
   d. forcing children to compete with one another and thereby limiting the number who can be successful, and
   e. disciplining with punishment.

REFERENCES

Becker, W. C., Engelmann, S., & Thomas, D. (1975). *Teaching: Classroom management.* Chicago: Science Research Associates.

Biehler, R., & Snowman, J. (1982). *Psychology applied to teaching.* Boston: Houghton Mifflin.

Bybee, R. (Ed.). (1985). *Science Technology Society: 1985 yearbook of the National Science Teacher's Association.* Washington, DC: National Science Teacher's Association.

Chance, P. (1986). *Thinking in the classroom: A survey of programs.* New York: Teacher's College Press.

Chase, N. F. (1975). *A child is being beaten: Violence against children, an American tragedy.* New York: Holt, Rinehart and Winston.

Conrad, D., & Hedin, D. (1991). School-based community service: What we know from research and theory. *Phi Delta Kappan, 72,* 543–549.

Edwards, C. H. (1989). Self-regulation: The key to motivating at-risk children. *The Clearing House, 63*(2), 59–62.

Englander, M. E. (1986). *Strategies for classroom discipline.* New York: Praeger.

Frymier, J. (1988). Understanding and preventing teen suicide: An interview with Barry Garfinkel. *Phi Delta Kappan, 69,* 290–293.

Glasser, W. (1984). *Control theory: A new explanation of how we control our lives.* New York: Harper and Row.

Harris, T. A. (1967). *I'm OK—You're OK.* New York: Avon Books.

Hyman, I. A. (1990). *Reading, writing, and the hickory stick.* Lexington, MA: Lexington Books.

Jones, B. F. (1988). Toward redefining models of curriculum and instruction for students at risk. In B. Z. Presseisen (Ed.), *At-risk students and thinking: Perspectives from research* (pp. 76–103). Washington, DC: National Education Association and Research for Better Schools.

Kounin, J. S., & Gump, P. V. (1961). The comparative influence of punitive and non-punitive teachers upon children's concepts of school misconduct. *Journal of Educational Psychology, 52,* 44–49.

Lewis, B. (1991). *The kids' guide to social action.* Minneapolis, MN: Free Spirit.

Marzano, R. J., Brandt, R. S., Hughes, C. S., Jones, B. F., Presseisen, B. Z., Rankin, S. C., & Suhor, C. (1988). *Dimensions of thinking: A framework for curriculum and instruction.* Alexandria, VA: The Association for Supervision and Curriculum Development.

Nathan, J., & Kielsmeier, J. (1991). The sleeping giant of school reform. *Phi Delta Kappan, 72,* 729–742.

Osborne, R. J., & Wittrock, M. C. (1983). Learning science: A generative process. *Science Education, 67,* 489–508.

Purkey, W. W. (1970). *Self-concept and school achievement.* Englewood Cliffs, NJ: Prentice-Hall.

Resnick, L. B. (1987). Learning in school and out. *Educational Researcher, 16,* 13–20.

Shavelson, R. J. (1985). *Schemata and teaching routines.* Paper presented at the annual meeting of the American Educational Research Association, Chicago.

2

Making Decisions About Discipline

OBJECTIVES

This chapter is designed to help you
1. understand the value of theory in school discipline
2. recognize the fundamental emphasis different approaches to discipline place on the amount of control the teacher exercises or the amount of autonomy students have
3. use criteria to evaluate different discipline approaches
4. identify and validate assumptions on which discipline approaches are based
5. select or create a discipline approach that is most appropriate for you
6. determine not only whether a discipline approach corrects and prevents discipline problems in the classroom but also whether it can be applied to schoolwide discipline

Introduction

To be successful in the classroom, teachers need a well-planned, individual approach to discipline. They must understand various psychological theories of discipline and the assumptions on which they are based, they must understand their own values and educational philosophy, and they must take an approach to discipline that is in harmony with their convictions. Unfortunately, some teachers unwittingly discipline their students in ways contrary to their own beliefs without considering the inherent conflicts. When teachers' behavior is incompatible with their beliefs, they not only experience personal conflict but confuse their students as well. Teachers must clarify objectives, both for themselves and for their students, and then ensure that learning experiences and discipline procedures are consistent with these objectives.

Educational Philosophies and Child Development Theories

Different educational philosophies dictate different school purposes, and within these different philosophies are a number of child development theories designed to achieve these purposes. Educational philosophies have been variously categorized, mostly according to the relative amount of freedom or control to be exercised by teachers and students. These philosophies emphasize the role either of the teacher in transmitting knowledge and culture to students in an orderly and controlled manner or of students in determining for themselves what is important to learn from the teacher. Theories of child development and discipline follow a similar pattern. Generally these theories can be arranged into three categories:

- management theories
- nondirective intervention theories
- leadership theories

MANAGEMENT THEORIES

Management theories assume that children's growth and development is a consequence of external conditions over which they may have little control. Children, according to this point of view, are born as "blank slates" and are "written upon" by the environment. These theories hold that human development can be explained essentially in terms of observable human behaviors and the environmental stimuli that promote or reinforce these behaviors. Changing children's behavior is simply a matter of arranging environmental conditions (e.g., giving rewards) to influence desired responses.

The leading proponent of management theories is B. F. Skinner. His work has become very popular and enjoys considerable support in the schools and in other institutions. Teachers who use management theories believe that the behavior of children must be controlled because, they assume, children are unable to adequately monitor and control themselves and without supervision their behavior will be erratic and potentially destructive. Therefore, teachers must control the students' environment to elicit only desirable behaviors.

NONDIRECTIVE INTERVENTION THEORIES

Nondirective intervention theories are based on the assumption that children develop from an inner unfolding. Children contain within themselves the necessary "blueprint" for complete rational self-determination. Intervention in the form of control or directed interaction is unnecessary for children to reach their fullest potential. Children achieve the best possible growth only if they are allowed to direct themselves. From this perspective, children have a natural inclination to learn and become self-directed and self-actualized. Actualization is a process of personal growth that only the individual can properly direct and achieve.

The role of the teacher in this process is to provide conditions that promote self-growth and help to clarify life experiences for the individual. Carl Rogers is the most popular proponent of this child development approach. In the school setting, he advocates considerable freedom for children. So long as children are able to direct their own school experiences, Rogers argues, there is little cause to fear that they will make inappropriate choices.

LEADERSHIP THEORIES

Leadership theories are based on the assumption that children develop from an interaction of both inner and outer influences. From this viewpoint, behavior is the product of a multitude of factors, each of which is vital. Children can only be understood insofar as all these factors and their relationships are properly taken into account. Growth is believed to come from a constant interplay between children and their social experiences.

The role of teachers from this perspective is one of leadership. It is assumed that children can achieve a state of responsible self-determination if the teacher uses appropriate intervention strategies. Children, it is believed, want to control their own lives and can eventually do so responsibly if teachers and other adults teach them how. Children continually try to gain greater competence and achieve more control over their lives, but they often fail to understand that their behavior is a hindrance to their own growth and development. They need to recognize the consequences of their behavior and make adjustments to achieve more favorable consequences. William Glasser is a leading proponent of leadership-oriented discipline. He believes that teachers can provide valuable assistance to children as they learn to assume greater responsibility for themselves and gain more control over their behavior.

In selecting an approach to discipline, teachers first need to determine which of the general views of child development is most consistent with their personal values and educational philosophy. Then they can examine various theories and discipline models more carefully to determine which would be most appropriate to use; they may even combine features of several models to create a discipline model of their own. Child development theories and discipline models are usually categorized according to the relative amounts of freedom they give to children and control they give to teachers or parents. Management theories allow children very little autonomy and depend on teachers to carefully monitor students' behavior and control its expression. Nondirective intervention theories favor almost unlimited freedom for children. Leadership theories advocate considerable freedom for children, but only as they become able to use it responsibly. Before choosing an approach to discipline—or designing an entire educational program—teachers should ask themselves how much freedom they believe children should have in school. The answer will make it much easier to select from among the various theories and models.

Characteristics of Theories

Choosing a discipline model also depends on which one is judged to be the most powerful. Better theories provide clearer descriptions, more insightful explanations, and more valid predictions (Beauchamp, 1968).

DESCRIPTION

Description consists of ordering and organizing a jumble of facts and observations, unifying them into some scheme that makes the assembled material comprehensible. Ideas and phenomena that at first may appear unrelated are arranged in such a way that the scope and the internal relationships of the total body of information become visible. Without theory, masses of data and their complex interrelationships would be difficult if not impossible to comprehend.

EXPLANATION

Theories also account for phenomena. They can trace cause and effect, show correlations, and explain how things work. A theory of discipline may, for example, show that reinforcement increases the frequency of the behavior with which it is associated and also explain how it does so. Theory not only can clarify meaningful relationships between areas of knowledge; it can show how various areas of knowledge can be applied in the practical world. Theory makes the connection between abstract concept and concrete act; good theories provide clear explanations and produce explicit applications.

PREDICTION

Finally, theory has the quality of predictability, which is perhaps its most powerful feature. Prediction in the area of discipline helps teachers anticipate the effect their strategies will have on the behavior of their students. Some theories also predict behavior in

FIGURE 2.1
Theoretical bases for eight models of discipline.

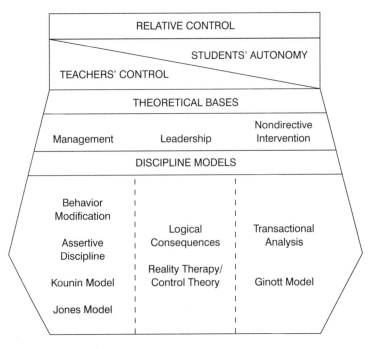

a more general sense. For example, William Glasser's Reality Therapy/Control Theory may be used to predict not only the effects of interpersonal and intrapersonal relationships but also what can be expected from different family interactions, social relations, conflicts at school, political behavior, and so on. Teachers who apply theory appropriately in their classrooms can predict outcomes in advance with some assurance that their predictions will be correct.

In each of the three general approaches to child development—management, nondirective intervention, and leadership—there are a number of discipline theories or models to choose from. Eight of these discipline theories and models are presented in detail in the next eight chapters: Behavior Modification, Assertive Discipline, Logical Consequences, Transactional Analysis, Reality Therapy/Control Theory, the Ginott Model, the Kounin Model, and the Jones Model.

Behavior Modification, Assertive Discipline, the Kounin Model, and the Jones Model are based on management theories. The Logical Consequences model and Reality Therapy/Control Theory are based on leadership theories. Transactional Analysis and the Ginott Model are based on nondirective intervention theories (see Figure 2.1).

Comparing Four Approaches to Discipline

The discussion of a single discipline problem can illustrate the distinctive characteristics of four of the discipline models:

- Behavior Modification
- Assertive Discipline
- Logical Consequences
- Reality Therapy/Control Theory

You can then see how these theories differ from or coincide with your own educational philosophy.

The Problem: Clair and Jo continually disrupt classes by talking to neighbors, yelling across the room, and throwing objects at other students.

BEHAVIOR MODIFICATION

When Mr. Condie observed Jo talking and throwing objects in class, he decided to set up a token economy to help Jo improve her behavior. Mr. Condie explained to Jo the behavior he expected of her and the rewards she could receive for demonstrating them. He gave her a folder inside of which were listed the various expected behaviors. Next to this list were boxes in which Mr. Condie could mark the points Jo received for each appropriate behavior. Mr. Condie would ignore all of Jo's inappropriate behavior. A second list in the folder contained the rewards possible for behaving appropriately and the number of points needed to receive each of these rewards. Jo was allowed to decide which of the rewards she wished to receive and when she wanted to earn them.

ASSERTIVE DISCIPLINE

When Clair yelled across the room, Ms. Adams, his teacher, wrote his name on the board as a warning for Clair to refrain from any further misbehavior. Later when Clair threw his pencil at James, Ms. Adams put a check mark by his name. Before the end of the class period, Clair's name had three check marks by it. The rules as well as punishments for misbehavior had been given to the class at the beginning of the year; a poster outlining this information hung in the front of the room for ready reference. The punishment to be received for each check mark was carefully explained. Clair's punishment for getting three check marks was to be sent to the principal's office and to have a conference with his parents and the principal. He could not return to class until this conference had been held and appropriate action taken.

LOGICAL CONSEQUENCES

After Ms. Taggert had observed Jo's habitual misbehavior, she tried to decide what her motives were. She realized that Jo's misbehavior was primarily an attempt to satisfy her needs, an attempt based on mistaken goals—Jo was either seeking attention, power, or revenge or struggling with feelings of inadequacy. Unable to determine Jo's exact motives herself, Ms. Taggert decided to talk directly to Jo. She first asked Jo whether she thought that her talking and throwing objects were related to a need for attention. Jo replied that she did not know why she had talked out in class. Ms. Taggert then asked whether Jo felt anger toward her. She said that, no, she just liked to talk with friends. Ms. Taggert concluded that Jo talked out in class for the attention she received. She explained this conclusion to Jo and told her that she could better satisfy this need for attention by assuming a leadership position in class. Ms. Taggert asked Jo whether she would like to be the class president for the next month. Jo agreed. Ms. Taggert explained that one of Jo's responsibilities would be to help ensure that the classroom was quiet.

REALITY THERAPY/CONTROL THEORY

When Mr. Ronowski observed Clair disturbing the class by talking excessively and throwing objects, he motioned him up to his desk and, out of earshot of the rest of the class, engaged him in the following conversation:

Mr. Ronowski	Clair, what were you doing during class discussion today that disturbed others around you?
Clair	I was just talking to Owen.
Mr. Ronowski	What did you along with the rest of the class decide would happen to anyone who disturbed the class by talking?
Clair	We decided we would be kicked out of class and not be allowed back until we made a written plan about how we planned to avoid these problems.
Mr. Ronowski	When will you get your plan to me?
Clair	I'll try to get it by tomorrow.

Mr. Ronowski   Where must you go until you have your written plan prepared?

Clair   The counselor's office.

Mr. Ronowski   I will anticipate hearing from you tomorrow before class, then.

Deciding on a Personal Approach to Discipline

How does one decide what discipline approach to use, given the various options available? There are a number of considerations that must be taken into account in this process. The following steps are useful in making this determination (see Figure 2.2):

1. Make a thoughtful examination of your personal philosophy of education. Decide how much emphasis you feel is appropriate to place on *the teacher's control or students' autonomy*. Examine the various discipline models to see which one most closely fits your philosophy.

2. Establish a set of *criteria* and use them to evaluate each discipline model.

3. Identify the *assumptions* on which each discipline model is based and determine their *validity*. The validity of assumptions can be determined by using

   a. *personal experience*

   b. *empirical evidence*

   c. *logical exposition*

4. From the various discipline options you examine

   a. *select* an existing option that meets the bulk of your expectations

   b. *synthesize* components of two or more options

   c. *create* your own discipline model

5. Consider also the extent to which the discipline approach you plan to use provides adequately for the *functions* of

   a. *correction* of discipline problems

   b. *prevention* of discipline problems

   c. *schoolwide discipline*

6. Determine the *orientation* you prefer:

   a. a *theory-based* approach

   b. an *eclectic* approach

   c. a *shifting* approach

7. Keeping all these factors in mind—your personal values, the criteria you used, their relative strengths and weaknesses, the assumptions on which various approaches to discipline are based, their functions, and your preferred orientation—make a *decision* about your approach to discipline.

Now let's go through the process of choosing a discipline approach one step at a time, illustrating what must be done to make wise choices.

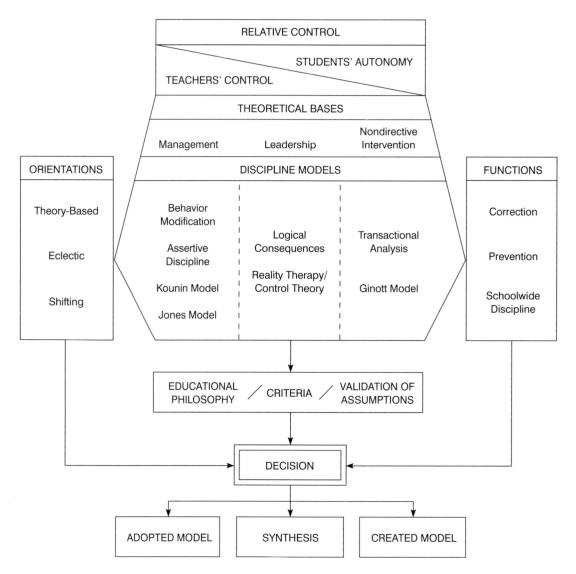

FIGURE 2.2
Deciding on a discipline approach.

EXAMINING ONE'S PERSONAL PHILOSOPHY

In deciding on a discipline approach, teachers must not only understand the underlying psychological and philosophical consequences of that choice but also ensure that what they decide is consistent with their own beliefs and values. As Wolfgang and Glickman (1980) indicate,

All too often, we unwillingly practice behaviors that are contrary to our own beliefs. Unless we behave towards children in ways that are reasonably compatible with our own values and ideals, we find ourselves working at cross purposes with our inner selves. In other words, what we desire in students' behavior will not materialize until we choose those strategies that are most consistent with our own beliefs in achieving those ends. We cannot possibly know what is most congruent in these contexts until we understand the psychological basis for each of our actions. (p. 9)

When you choose an approach to discipline, the most important philosophical consideration is the relative importance you give to teachers' control and students' autonomy. You must decide whether or not children can learn to be responsibly self-determined, that is, whether you believe that children assert themselves as persons having a will of their own or are essentially controlled by the environment. Theorists who believe in human self-determination conclude that children can be controlled only to the extent they allow themselves to be. Theorists who discount human will believe that controlling others simply involves finding a compelling reinforcer or exerting enough force. They believe that systematic control is necessary to help children behave appropriately. If these outside controls are neglected, children will be adversely affected by the indiscriminate influences of the environment. Clarifying your attitudes about students' autonomy helps determine which general theory of child development most closely reflects your own views: (1) development is completely determined by external conditions, (2) development is an inner unfolding of potential, as some developmental psychologists believe, or (3) development is a consequence of an interaction of both internal and external forces.

Another important philosophical consideration is the role motives are believed to play in human behavior. Behaviorists, for example, believe that children are motivated by external rewards. In the Logical Consequences approach, children are thought to seek attention in an effort to determine how well they are accepted by others. In Control Theory, children seek not only to obtain acceptance and affection but also to satisfy their needs for control.

The philosophical considerations identified here will be elaborated in subsequent chapters in connection with the various discipline approaches with which they are associated. As you explore your own beliefs about these critical matters, you should begin to formulate your own personal views.

ESTABLISHING CRITERIA FOR MAKING DECISIONS

Criteria provide the basis on which decisions are made. They are standards of judgment, crystalized from one's educational philosophy. The following list is an example of criteria a teacher could use to decide among a number of discipline models. You, of course, will want to construct your own list. The particular criteria used have an enormous bearing on the decisions made.

Which of the discipline approaches

1. is most likely to help children become more self-disciplined and responsible?

2. is consistent with the view that children's motives are based on a self-directed effort to achieve autonomy, gain control of themselves and their environment, and achieve a high level of acceptance by others?

3. can be most easily implemented?

4. can be readily learned?

5. is most consistent with an instructional program involving self-determined learning projects?

6. is most effective in achieving good classroom behavior?

7. will help promote good self-concept in students?

8. is most likely to help prevent discipline problems?

9. can be applied in a schoolwide discipline program?

Now let's see how you could apply some of these criteria in deciding between several possible approaches to discipline. For convenience, use the models discussed in the section of this chapter entitled "Comparing Four Approaches to Discipline." The teacher who uses Behavior Modification monitors Jo's behavior and rewards her when she behaves appropriately. Behavior Modification obviously does not contribute toward the development of self-discipline. A similar conclusion may be drawn about Assertive Discipline. In this case, Clair is not consulted regarding the rules in the class nor the punishment he can expect. When the Logical Consequences approach is used, Jo is consulted about her behavior. Her teacher tries to help Jo analyze her misbehavior and make appropriate changes. In the Reality Therapy/Control Theory approach, Clair has already been involved with his classmates in making decisions about classroom conduct and the consequences of misbehavior; students also have the right to decide how to correct their own misbehavior. Obviously Reality Therapy/Control Theory promotes more self-discipline in students.

Reality Therapy/Control Theory also more readily satisfies criterion #8: It has a better prevention component not only because it defines behaviors and consequences in advance but also because it involves students in making this determination. Both Assertive Discipline and Behavior Modification have limited preventive elements. In Assertive Discipline, the teacher determines rules and punishments in advance. Because students are not involved in their determination, these rules and punishments have less preventive power. In Behavior Modification, the teacher may reward students for appropriate behavior as a deterrent to misbehavior. Behavior Modification may prevent problems to some extent; students may anticipate receiving rewards and behave appropriately. However, just as with Assertive Discipline, students are not directly involved in the process and consequently the prevention aspect is not as strong.

IDENTIFYING AND VALIDATING ASSUMPTIONS

When making decisions, you should examine the assumptions on which your options are based and attempt to judge their validity. Teachers often make decisions without identifying the assumptions behind the alternatives being considered. More often the assumptions are recognized but their validity goes unquestioned. Nearly everyone has failed to identify and validate assumptions in daily living. Many people lock themselves out of their car or house, confidently assuming that they took their keys with them. When common, everyday assumptions are checked, fewer problems can be anticipated in life. When the assumptions behind the various discipline options are carefully identified and validated, better decisions can be expected.

What are the assumptions for the different discipline models and how can they be validated? Lists of assumptions will be provided for your consideration at the beginning of each of the chapters dealing with models (Chapters 3 through 10). In Chapter 11 you will be given an example of how to compare these assumptions and determine their validity. At this point, however, attention will be focused on the basic process of identifying assumptions and determining their soundness. A few assumptions from several of the discipline theories will be used as illustrations.

Sometimes, in the writings of discipline theorists, assumptions are explicitly stated and defended. More often you must sift through what is written and discover them for yourself. You will occasionally find inconsistencies between the assumptions of a particular theory and the way in which it is actually put into operation. For example, responsibility is presented as a necessary component of the Jones Model. You might expect, then, that the model would help students become more responsible. However, it is almost entirely teacher-directed, with little opportunity for students to achieve responsibility. Another application of the Jones Model intended to help students become more responsible is Preferred Activity Time. In reality, preferred activities are allotted through a program of negative reinforcement, an aspect of the Jones Model that also fails to promote responsible behavior in students. These inconsistencies must be identified, for often they make a great deal of difference in a model's attractiveness.

The best way to identify assumptions about various discipline theories is to look for statements about

- the nature of children
- how children grow
- how children learn
- whether children are capable of self-control or need to be directed
- how children react to different situations and treatments
- how children interact with others
- what children's needs are

Reference has already been made to what different theories say about children's needs and their ability to be self-directed. Remember that leadership theories and nondirective intervention theories believe in self-direction; management theories do not. Each type of theory focuses on a significantly different set of needs.

Let's look now at different sets of assumptions. If we compare what the various discipline models say about children's reactions to their teachers, we see a marked contrast:

1. In Assertive Discipline, it is assumed that children like to be in classrooms where the teacher controls their behavior rigidly. Students supposedly realize the necessity of teachers' punishment as a deterrent to bad behavior and think positively of their teachers when they punish misbehaving students.

2. However, according to Reality Therapy/Control Theory, punishment will only create rebellion. From the Reality Therapy/Control Theory perspective, it is assumed that children want to control the various situations in which they find themselves and to be free from the control of others.

3. The assumptions of Transactional Analysis are similar to those of Reality Therapy/Control Theory: The influence of the teacher is more positive when control by the teacher is absent.

4. The Jones Model relies on nonverbal techniques to control children's behavior. The role of teachers is an intimidating one. Their imposing physical presence is used to force children to behave.

5. The Kounin Model depends more on teachers' having eyes in the backs of their heads. They are able to control students by being aware of everything taking place in the classroom and reacting to it according to its relative seriousness. Students respect teachers who are able to skillfully manage the class in this way.

6. In the Logical Consequences approach, it is assumed that children will react positively toward their teachers only when a democratic environment is provided. The consequences for misbehavior are spelled out in advance in consultation with students.

7. In the Behavior Modification model, it is assumed that if teachers provide desirable reinforcers, then students not only will reach a higher level of academic achievement but will also have higher regard for the classroom.

There are obvious differences in the assumptions of different discipline models regarding the effects of student-teacher interactions. Once teachers have identified these differences, they must examine them and determine which they believe to be most valid or true. The validity of assumptions can be checked by evidence gained in any of at least three ways—that is, assumptions can be validated from at least three evidence bases:

- experience
- empirical research
- logical exposition

Greater assurance of validity is possible when all three types of evidence are examined.

Experience.   You can validate assumptions from an experience base, that is, check them against your own experience and that of others. If, for example, you wanted to examine assumptions about the effect teachers' control has on student-teacher relationships, you could simply try out all the techniques from various models over a period of time to see what happens. You could also share in the experiences of other individuals by talking to them, corresponding with them, or reading their professional writings.

Empirical Research.   To validate from an empirical base, examine research. Unfortunately, most discipline models have not been studied extensively. Hardly any research is available that compares different models. More often than not the validity of assumptions for the different models is held to be self-evident. Assumptions usually are not even explicitly stated, so readers themselves must identify them. Because it is not always possible to locate research to validate assumptions directly, interpretations may have to be made with what little information is available.

Logical Exposition.   Logical exposition is a method of validating assumptions perhaps more commonly used by beginning teachers, who usually do not have enough experience to validate assumptions directly or to wade through the body of research or engage in research on their own. The bulk of the data they use for validation must come from personal judgment—they make an educated guess.

ADOPTING, SYNTHESIZING, OR CREATING A MODEL

After you have examined your own educational philosophy, created a defensible set of criteria, and validated the assumptions behind the different discipline options, your next step is to use all this information to decide which of the models is most acceptable to you. In making this decision, you can go in any one of three directions (see Figure 2.2). First, you may decide that one of the models meets your expectations sufficiently to be adopted without substantial adjustment. Second, you may decide to synthesize compatible components of two or more models. Third, you may discover that none of the models is satisfactory and decide to create your own discipline approach.

What is involved with each of these courses of action? It is obviously simplest just to adopt a single existing approach to discipline. All that is necessary then is to master its use.

It is more difficult and complicated to combine components from several approaches. Each of the models has some incompatible elements. The task of synthesis is to include only compatible elements. For example, if you decided to use Glasser's Reality Therapy/Control Theory as your basic model with the addition of some components from Behavior Modification, you would have to be careful to avoid those aspects which detracted from the self-determination emphasized by Reality Therapy/Control Theory. In fact, the only aspects of Behavior Management likely to be compatible are the practices of ignoring bad behavior and avoiding punishment. If you considered including elements of the Logical Consequences approach, you would have to be sure to avoid the practice of publicly determining motives so as not to encourage students to make excuses. You would also have to decide whether you wanted to have students personally explore a wide range of possible consequences for misbehavior, as Reality Therapy/Control Theory advocates, or just give them a choice between two designated options, as the Logical Consequences model requires.

Creating your own discipline model is the most difficult of these three options. You might have to construct an entirely different approach, or you might combine some components of your own creation with compatible components of other models. If you construct a personal model, the first step is to formulate basic principles. Then you would describe discipline practices. An example of how to create a personal discipline approach is discussed in Chapter 12.

CONSIDERING FUNCTIONS OF A COMPREHENSIVE DISCIPLINE PROGRAM

An adequate discipline model should include

1. techniques for correction of misbehavior,
2. procedures for prevention of classroom discipline problems, and
3. applications for a schoolwide discipline program. (See Figure 2.2.)

Correction.   Most discipline models are designed primarily to correct discipline problems. In fact, little is usually said about how they may be used either to prevent problems or to create a schoolwide discipline program. Usually the focus is on existing problems in the classroom and how to eliminate them once they appear.

Prevention.   Prevention involves steps taken in class to avoid potential discipline problems. Students are commonly involved in determining preventive discipline procedures. The Logical Consequences and Reality Therapy/Control Theory models incorporate preventive discipline in this way. When the model emphasizes control by the teacher, preventive discipline usually takes the form of deterrence. For example, in Assertive Discipline, the threat of punishment is designed to act as a deterrent.

Schoolwide Discipline.   Schoolwide discipline is the least common discipline function to find in any particular discipline model. It involves procedures used for discipline in hallways, the library, the cafeteria, and on the school grounds. This feature has been added to Reality Therapy/Control Theory in Glasser's latest work, *The Quality School* (Glasser, 1990), and is included in a very limited way by Canter in Assertive Discipline (Canter & Canter, 1981). Explicit statements about schoolwide discipline are decidedly lacking from the other approaches, although this aspect could possibly be added to any of them. Specific prevention and schoolwide discipline procedures are discussed for each model in Chapters 3 through 10.

CHOOSING A DISCIPLINE ORIENTATION

The orientation of a discipline program refers primarily to the consistency with which it is applied. Some theorists emphasize the importance of using a single set of internally consistent principles and believe that discipline practices should conform as much as possible to these principles. Others contend that teachers should be encouraged to choose freely from among a variety of techniques or discipline models as the situation dictates, despite their being based on disparate principles. There are three possible orientations for a discipline program:

- theory-based
- eclectic
- shifting (see Figure 2.2)

Theory-Based Discipline Programs.   A theory-based discipline program is one in which a single theory or model is used to prevent and correct all discipline problems in the school as well as in the classroom. This theory could be one that is already in use or one that has been newly created. Any discipline procedures used must conform to the principles of the theory. Teachers who find a theory-based approach attractive usually have a well-organized and carefully articulated set of values to which they are committed. The principles they live by professionally are the same as those governing their private lives.

Eclectic Discipline Programs.   In the eclectic orientation to discipline, components of various discipline theories and models are synthesized. As Charles (1989) explains, teachers select components from various discipline models that suit them best and recombine them into an "effective approach that is satisfactory to all." Charles claims that this recombination is necessary because one approach may work well with one student whereas another approach works better with others. Combining approaches helps teachers discipline various students in different circumstances. Eclectic teachers are less concerned about possibly causing confusion to their students with a conglomeration of various theories and more concerned about maintaining the flexibility of their approach.

Shifting Discipline Programs.   The shifting orientation to discipline is similar to the eclectic approach. However, instead of combining various theories or theory components, advocates of this approach favor changing from one theory to anther as circumstances dictate. Wolfgang and Glickman (1980) provide an excellent example of this orientation. Instead of settling on one approach created out of various pieces, as does Charles, they recommend using all the valuable elements contained in all the models. In the discipline procedure of Wolfgang and Glickman, teachers make decisions on the spot as circumstances demand and follow one of three possible procedural pathways. These three pathways incorporate different levels of autonomy for students and control for the teacher. On one pathway, the teacher moves from discipline techniques that provide a lot of autonomy for students (such as Transactional Analysis) to those that involve more control by the teacher (such as the Logical Consequences approach) and then finally to even more controlling techniques (such as Behavior Modification) as conditions warrant. The second pathway provides for movement in the opposite direction; the teacher begins with strong control and gives up power to students as they appear more able to regulate themselves. On the third pathway the teacher starts with a discipline model that advocates sharing power with students (such as Reality Therapy/Control Theory) and can move toward either more autonomy for students or more control by the teacher as the situation demands.

The defense made for using the eclectic and shifting orientations is about the same. The following are the essential elements of that defense:

1. Some theories work better than others with children of different ages, children with different personal and social aptitudes, children from different home situations or social environments or ethnic and racial groups, and children involved in different school situations. All these elements create considerable complexity and, to be properly managed, require a full range of discipline approaches. As Charles (1989) indicates, Behavior Modification may work better with young children and students with developmental disabilities than with older children or students with more severe behavior disorders. Assertive Discipline, he claims, may control misbehavior at all levels but be too cumbersome for primary grades. It may also fail to help students gain a proper value orientation because it focuses exclusively on students' obedience.

2. It may be difficult for some teachers to use some techniques successfully with some groups of students. For example, a teacher may be able to apply Reality Therapy/Control Theory so long as students do not become too unruly. However, if students get too far out of control, more teacher-directed discipline may be necessary.

3. Some groups of students may be so difficult to handle that initially they have to be controlled more vigorously by the teacher, even though the teacher wants them eventually to achieve greater self-control. The teacher must then change tactics as students become more able to govern themselves.

4. If a discipline approach does not seem to work, for whatever reason, it makes sense to change to some other technique that holds more promise of success. If, for example, students are not achieving greater responsibility through the use of Reality Therapy/Control Theory, a change may be appropriate.

Teachers who use one discipline approach based on a single set of principles present arguments counter to those set forth by proponents of eclecticism:

1. Teachers who advocate changing discipline theories assume that such a change is warranted by different or changed circumstances in the classroom. These circumstances may be related to children's growth and development or to students' inclinations to be more or less disruptive. Younger children, for example, are considered less able to deal intellectually with the rational problems implied by discipline theories that emphasize self-determination. They are also thought less able to accurately express their personal thoughts and feelings and to construct the responses necessary to engage in meaningful communication. However, the level at which children of elementary school age can function has proven adequate for techniques such as Reality Therapy/Control Theory and Transactional Analysis. Perhaps the only exceptions are very small children or children with conditions such as autism.

2. A second reason given to change discipline theories periodically is that the approach currently being used does not successfully limit students' misbehavior. It is assumed that changes in classroom circumstances have promoted more misbehavior and that more misbehavior dictates the use of a more control-oriented discipline theory. However, there is no evidence to suggest which theory is best to use

in any particular set of circumstances or change of circumstances. Without such evidence, it is better to select one theory and stay with it.

Some discipline theories routinely and effectively used in a wide variety of classroom situations have also been useful in a number of other settings. For example, Behavior Modification has been successfully applied to persons with mental illness, children with autism, individuals with social and behavioral disorders, and individuals with a host of everyday problems such as smoking and eating disorders. Reality Therapy/Control Theory has been used not only in teaching children but also in treating people with nearly all types of mental illness, in counseling individuals who are socially maladaptive, and in helping inmates in penal institutions regulate their behavior. Both Behavior Modification and Reality Therapy/Control Theory have been applied in a variety of special schools for children who have been unsuccessful in regular school situations. The wide use of these theories in various difficult circumstances attests to their suitability for use in most situations that might be encountered in school classrooms.

3. Another problem with using multiple discipline theories is that many teachers have difficulty learning them well enough to apply them all properly, particularly those theories that require considerable interpersonal skill, such as Reality Therapy/Control Theory, the Logical Consequences model, and Transactional Analysis. In addition, most teachers have trouble switching between discipline approaches because of differences in their application, assumptions, and expected results. The educational philosophies of many teachers would also prevent them from applying such a divergent array of discipline tactics.

4. The use of multiple theories may also be confusing for students. Because the one variable that is likely to be in a constant state of flux is autonomy, teachers may never be sure what level of autonomy is acceptable. Even if it is made clear that students' autonomy and the teacher's control depend on how responsibly students use the freedom they have, students will certainly view increased control by the teacher as undermining their desire to become more self-determined.

MAKING A DECISION

In making a decision about which discipline approach to use, it will be very helpful to follow the steps outlined earlier in this section of the chapter. The steps are not sequential, although step #1, examining your personal philosophy, should probably be done first. This examination allows you to eliminate quickly some discipline approaches that are too incompatible with your most important values. Eliminating possible models, of course, simplifies your work. You may also want to decide at this point whether or not you plan to use a theory-based, an eclectic, or a shifting orientation to discipline. You could then create and apply criteria to the remaining models and decide whether or not the assumptions for each model are valid.

When you have carefully examined the different models outlined in Chapters 3 through 10, compared them with your philosophy, and judged them in terms of your criteria, you should be prepared to make a decision about the discipline option you prefer. You should remember to examine and validate the assumptions associated with each model and then decide to what extent each of the models meets your expectations. At this point you will also need to decide (1) whether a single model satisfies your requirements, (2) whether you need to make a synthesis of two or more models, or (3) whether you need to create your own discipline approach (see Figure 2.2). Be sure that the approach you choose can be applied to preventing classroom discipline problems as well as to solving them and that your approach has potential beyond your classroom alone.

Chapter 11 gives you an example of how to use this decision-making process. As you make your decision, you should think carefully about the relative strengths and weaknesses of the models presented. A list of the strengths and weaknesses of each model may be found near the end of its chapter.

▼

SUMMARY

Deciding which discipline approach to use is an extremely important task for teachers. Many approaches are available to choose from. The best discipline theories provide the most insightful descriptions and explanations of phenomena as well as the most powerful predictions. You should carefully weigh the various choices against your own educational philosophy and personal values. The most significant aspect of your personal philosophy of discipline is the relative importance you place on the teacher's control or students' autonomy. You can make better decisions about which model of discipline to use if you first establish criteria for making these decisions and then carefully examine and validate the assumptions underlying each model.

After you have evaluated the various discipline models in this way, you can decide whether to accept a particular model, synthesize two or more models, or create your own. Whatever you choose to do, it is imperative that your model correct and prevent discipline problems and have schoolwide applications. You must also determine whether your approach to applying discipline in the classroom should be consistently based on one particular set of principles and practices, created eclectically from the components of a number of models, or allowed to change from one discipline model to another according to various circumstances and conditions.

CENTRAL IDEAS

1. Theory provides useful descriptions of phenomena and their operations, along with predictions of what will happen when associated principles are applied in real situations.
2. Using theory simplifies and provides a more consistent approach to classroom discipline.
3. Personal values and philosophy should provide the basis for selecting or creating an approach to discipline.
4. Choosing an approach to discipline involves the application of an appropriate set of criteria.
5. Before a particular discipline model is accepted, its assumptions should be identified and validated.

6. A chosen approach to discipline should prevent as well as correct discipline problems in the classroom, and it should be applicable to schoolwide discipline.

7. The orientation of a discipline approach can be theory-based, eclectic, or shifting.

8. Teachers must decide whether to use an existing model of discipline, synthesize one from components of two or more models, or create their own.

QUESTIONS AND ACTIVITIES

QUESTIONS TO CONSIDER

1. What are the essential elements of an adequate theory of discipline?

2. What basic questions must a theory of discipline answer?

3. What are the considerations involved in deciding whether or not to use a particular theory of discipline?

CLASSROOM ACTIVITIES

1. Debate the issue of whether to follow a single theory or multiple theories for handling discipline problems in the schools.

2. As a class, prepare a list of concerns about discipline for which a theory should provide explanations and procedures.

REFERENCES

Beauchamp, G. A. (1968). *Curriculum theory* (2nd ed.). Wilmette, IL: Kagg Press.

Canter, L., & Canter, M. (1981). *Assertive Discipline follow-up guidebook*. Los Angeles: Canter and Associates.

Charles, C. M. (1989). *Building classroom discipline: From models to practice* (3rd ed.). New York: Longman.

Glasser, W. (1990). *The quality school*. New York: Harper and Row.

Wolfgang, C. H., & Glickman, C. D. (1980). *Solving discipline problems: Strategies for classroom teachers*. Boston: Allyn and Bacon.

UNIT

2

Discipline Models

There are a number of classroom discipline options available for teachers. In Unit 2 you will learn about several discipline theories or models that have been created for classroom use. These theories have been selected to cover a broad spectrum of values and educational philosophy so that you can compare divergent discipline approaches and the assumptions on which they are based. The underlying principles of each model are presented, along with an explanation of how the model is applied in the classroom. The extent to which each theory can be used to prevent as well as correct discipline problems is discussed. The model's usefulness for a schoolwide discipline program is considered, and its strengths and weakness are identified.

3

Behavior Modification: B. F. Skinner

OBJECTIVES

This chapter is designed to help you
1. understand the difference between positive and negative reinforcement
2. explain the mistake teachers make of reinforcing students they intend to punish
3. discover the applications of Behavior Modification in the classroom
4. understand the technique of extinction
5. explain the procedures and purpose of providing students time-out
6. identify the negative effects of punishment
7. describe the effects of using different schedules of reinforcement
8. explain the role of conditioned reinforcers in the classroom
9. recognize the various kinds of reinforcers that may be used in the classroom
10. explain the use of a token economy

ASSUMPTIONS

1. Human beings are born as "blank slates." They have no will.
2. Human beings are essentially responders to external stimuli. They are regulated by environmental influences that satisfy basic needs.
3. For students to behave appropriately, they must receive guidance from their teachers.
4. Students cannot learn to be responsibly self-governing. They must be managed by someone who can arrange reinforcers appropriately.
5. If the behavior of humans is not managed, we can expect an increase of discipline problems, crime, poverty, war, and other social ills.

Introduction

B. F. Skinner, the most prominent behaviorist of our day, was born in Susquehanna, Pennsylvania, in 1904. He died in 1990. He trained and spent his professional career at Harvard University, where he worked extensively with animals, particularly rats and pigeons. But he is perhaps most widely known for his studies of human babies who were cared for inside glass enclosures called air cribs. In this environment, children were kept dry, warm, and comfortable, and all their needs were satisfied. He even raised his own daughter in an air crib. His purpose, of course, was to create an environment that could be more completely controlled.

Skinner received considerable attention after the publication of his novel, *Walden Two*, in which he envisioned a utopia brought about by social engineering (Skinner, 1948). He believed that war, poverty, and other social ills could be eliminated through the application of the principles of reinforcement he had carefully researched. Increased attention came with the publication of *Beyond Freedom and Dignity* (Skinner, 1971). In this book he rejected freedom and dignity as viable concepts for society. Instead, he claimed that our choices are determined by the environmental conditions under which we live.

From his research, Skinner formulated reinforcement strategies to be used by teachers in the classroom. He found that students' behavior could be controlled through a program of reinforcement. Many teachers now use reinforcement principles and procedures to discipline their students and manage learning in their classrooms.

▼ Jimmy Carington came into the school building after lunch and walked quickly down the hall toward Mr. Johnson's social studies room. He was followed by an entourage of seventh and eighth grade students who had accepted him as their leader. A ninth grader, Jimmy was taller and more powerfully built than the rest. As he strode down the hall, determination showed in his face. The younger children chattered noisily as they hurried to keep up with Jimmy's rapid pace. Jimmy was their hero. His heroics thus far consisted of nine infractions, nine appearances before the juvenile judge, and avoidance in each case of any punishment. He always succeeded in being released and returned to school, where he continued to ignore the same old warnings. His latest offense was to break into the school several days earlier and use a hammer to smash all the typewriters in the typing classroom. All twenty-five machines were beyond repair.

When Jimmy and his followers reached Mr. Johnson's room, they found him standing out in the hall. Jimmy went directly up to him and said, with a sneer, "I'm not going to make up any of your stupid assignments. You'd better not send me to the principal again, either." He then punched the teacher directly in the face.

The teacher grabbed Jimmy by the arm and, twisting it behind him, marched him straight to the principal's office. Dr. Stroud, the principal, was not happy to see Jimmy again. She knew that she could not send him back to Mr. Johnson's class. And the other social studies teachers had already refused to take him.

Some will say that legal officials and school administrators indulged Jimmy until he was spoiled. From the behaviorist point of view, this explanation is too imprecise. A behaviorist would explain that school officials and others mistakenly reinforced Jimmy's bad behavior. They intended to get him to stop being destructive by punishing him, but what they did to punish him acted as a reinforcer instead. It is not uncommon for teachers, parents, and other adults to make the mistake of reinforcing bad behavior (Madsen, Becker, Thomas, Koser, & Plager, 1968).

Inadvertently reinforcing unwanted behavior is common in most situations in life. In mental hospitals, for example, it was formerly believed that inmates' inability to dress, feed, or wash themselves was a symptom of mental illness. It was discovered, however, that these and other unacceptable behaviors were actually taught to patients by the hospital staff. If the patients did not perform these functions, the staff would; patients thus had little incentive to care for themselves. To correct this problem, smoking, watching television, and other privileges were made to depend upon patients' dressing, feeding, and washing themselves. Under these conditions, patients demonstrated that they could perform these tasks adequately (Ayllon & Michael, 1959).

One resident of a mental institution made a practice of stealing towels and hiding them in her room. Each time the towels were stolen, hospital workers would go to her room to retrieve them. When they realized that their attention was reinforcing her towel collecting, they decided to stop retrieving stolen towels. Over a period of several days, while staff members ignored her, the towel thief accumulated more than 400 towels. She stacked them on the floor, in cupboards, under the bed, and on the bed. When there was no longer enough space for her to occupy her room comfortably, she removed all but one towel. Because stealing towels no longer brought attention, she decided to stop (Ayllon, 1963). Inadvertent attention by hospital workers helped shape the patient's inappropriate behavior, and withdrawing attention helped reverse it.

In school, students' misbehavior may be encouraged by teachers in a similar way. Educators tend to attribute bad behavior by students to poor home environment or other causes outside the school. Outside influences do affect children's behavior. Much misbehavior in school, however, may be shaped by teachers and administrators, whose attention to the misbehavior actually reinforces it. Behavioral scientists claim that habitual misbehaviors persist because they are reinforced. When children misbehave in school, it is very common for teachers to pay attention to them in some way—by scolding, shaming, insulting, or otherwise acknowledging them. Another common tactic is to formally punish students who break rules. School personnel try to stop bad behavior by creating very aversive consequences. However, these consequences usually stimulate more bad behavior, as evidenced by the fact that a very small percentage of the student body exhibit a disproportionately large number of behavior problems and receive the most administrative sanctions. If repeated punishment were effective, children would stop their unacceptable practices. The fact that they do not is an indication that the "punishment" they receive is reinforcing.

Not all misbehavior in school comes from the misapplication of reinforcement principles. Often the complexity of the school environment creates problems that teachers find difficult or impossible to counter. Teachers are frequently required to adhere to administrative directives about discipline and other policies that are contrary to their own desires and beliefs. Sometimes community expectations, financial constraints, and other factors limit the way teachers can practice their craft. Improving discipline is, therefore, not just a matter of helping teachers learn more effective methods. School practices that limit the effectiveness of teachers must also be eliminated.

Basic Principles of Behavior Modification

Behavior Modification had its beginning in the work of psychologist Ivan Pavlov. He succeeded in getting dogs to salivate by ringing a bell. This bell had previously been rung whenever the dogs were fed meat powder. The salivating response was made in the absence of the meat powder because the bell had become associated with, or *conditioned to*, the food. The salivating response is called a *respondent* because it is controlled by stimuli that precede it. Other responses, called *operants*, are controlled by stimuli that follow them (Bijou & Baer, 1961).

Much of what we know about operant conditioning we owe to the work of B. F. Skinner. His work was primarily done with rats and pigeons, but it has often been applied to humans as well. Skinner believed that all human behavior could be explained as responses to environmental stimuli. He concluded that humans have no internal will to guide their behavior—that they are not directed toward goals but are instead controlled by their environment. Therefore, to behave properly, children need to have adults manage their behavior by arranging environmental consequences. If adults fail to properly reinforce desirable behavior, various rewarding factors in the environment may inadvertently influence children to behave in undesirable ways. Skinner even envisioned a utopia regulated by social engineers arranging contingencies of reinforcement and directing the behavior of inhabitants toward socially desirable ends. He believed that problems such as poverty, war, and rioting could be prevented in a properly conditioned society (Skinner, 1948).

Behaviorists do not make any attempt to explain human behavior in terms of will. Such expressions as *wish-fulfilling, pleasure-seeking*, and *pain-avoiding* imply that people actively seek or desire certain stimuli and that they choose certain behaviors that are likely to produce them. Behaviorists wish to avoid such implications. They simply state that behavior is controlled by consequences. In other words, any behavior can be reinforced if a sufficiently strong reward is provided following the behavior.

To modify behavior, behaviorists provide either reinforcement or punishment. Reinforcement increases the strength or frequency of a particular behavior; punishment reduces it. It has been noted that some teachers inadvertently reinforce bad behavior when they intend to punish. It must be concluded, therefore, that neither teachers' intentions nor the nature of their actions determines whether or not punishment has taken place. Whether an action is punitive is determined instead by the responses students make to these stimuli. It is more appropriate, then, to refer to the influence of teachers' actions by their consequences than by their intentions. It is correct to say that Stephanie found the teacher's actions to be reinforcing or that Jeff found the teacher's actions to be punishing. It is incorrect to say that the teacher reinforced Ray or that the teacher punished Jane.

Correction Strategies

▼ Ms. Ropp was a young, new teacher who had very little understanding of classroom management. The noise level in her sixth grade classroom had become intolerable. This noise consisted mainly of visiting between children, yelling across the room, and whistling. There was also an occasional fight, and several students made a habit of throwing spit wads and paper airplanes. Sometimes children chased one another around the room and climbed over desks to catch other children or avoid being caught by their pursuers. Ms. Ropp routinely dealt with these situations by issuing threats and loudly directing students to be quiet and take their seats. These efforts usually reduced the noise level temporarily, but within minutes students' misbehavior increased. One day Ms. Ropp could take it no longer. Utterly exasperated, she fled from the room, determined never to go back again. She spent a couple of hours in the main office, resisting the principal's efforts to have her return to the classroom. She finally consented to go back to class if the principal agreed to spend a couple of hours each day in her classroom for a week or so and also to help her develop successful management techniques.

The principal taught Ms. Ropp the following three procedures:

1. *Specify rules clearly.*   Specify the desired behavior. Make your rules clear, so that children will know what is expected. Explain the rules periodically, so that they are always understood.

2. *Ignore disruptive behavior.*   Do not attend to the behavior you wish to eliminate. Call attention to the behavior of children who are following the rules. Praise behavior that is distinctly different from disruptive behavior. Ignore inappropriate behavior.

3. *Praise the children for following rules.*   Look for instances when students are following the rules and praise them for doing so. Provide special privileges to children who are following the rules (Becker, Engelmann, & Thomas, 1971).

It was difficult at first for Ms. Ropp to resist her natural tendency to call attention to the misbehavior of her students. It seemed wrong not to inform misbehaving students that they were disrupting the class. She felt that it was her responsibility to control the class and was constantly tempted to continue with her threats and admonitions. With the principal present, however, she held her tongue and ignored the antics. After two or three days, it was agreed that the principal would no longer remain in her class. When the principal had left, the children immediately began behaving as they had before. Ms. Ropp, determined to follow through with her new management approach, continued to ignore inappropriate behavior and praise those students who were following the rules. After a week she could see a noticeable difference in her students. Encouraged, she remained faithful to the management procedures. Before long her students were reasonably well-behaved.

REINFORCEMENT

There are two kinds of reinforcement, negative and positive. Negative reinforcement is often mistakenly thought of as a negative act on the part of the teacher designed to suppress undesired behavior. Although it is often confused with punishment, negative reinforcement actually involves withdrawing a stimulus, not providing negative experiences. The student wishes to avoid the withdrawal of the stimulus. For example, at the beginning of a term students may be given 100 points that can be applied toward their citizenship grade. Points are then taken away for each previously defined inappropriate behavior. If students increase good citizenship to avoid having points taken away, they are said to have been negatively reinforced.

Positive reinforcement, on the other hand, occurs when stimuli are presented. For example, if children are given points when they display good citizenship and they then demonstrate better citizenship behavior, they have been positively reinforced.

Notice that, in these two examples, good citizenship is the object of providing reinforcement. In the case of positive reinforcement, points are given when acceptable behavior occurs. With negative reinforcement, students avoid having points taken away by behaving in a proper way. Both positive and negative reinforcement stimulate an increase in the response with which they are associated.

Another approach to reinforcement is to focus attention on academic performance. When good academic behavior is reinforced, disruptive behavior is correspondingly reduced (Edwards, 1975). Obviously, when one increases, the other must decrease.

Some research on behavior management has involved teaching students to shape the behavior of their teachers (Klein, 1971). When their teachers' behavior improved, the behavior of students also improved. Researchers trained several students with very disruptive behavior to react positively to their teachers. In the process teachers behaved better, had better attitudes, and made comments that were more supportive of students. As a result, students' disruptive behavior decreased (Sherman & Cormier, 1974).

EXTINCTION

When inappropriate behavior that was once reinforced is resolutely ignored, it is often extinguished, that is, weakened to the point of disappearing. Extinction is particularly effective when desired behaviors are reinforced at the same time. While teachers are ignoring disruptive students and paying attention to their well-behaved classmates, they should be on the lookout for any sign that the disruptive students are changing their behavior patterns. As soon as any appropriate behavior is noticed, it should be reinforced. When extinction is combined with reinforcement, teachers can expect significant improvement in classroom discipline (Hall et al., 1971). Inappropriate behavior will be extinguished while the good behavior increases in frequency.

For example, one kindergarten child had a habit of crying and throwing tantrums on the playground. The teacher would go to the child and implore her to stop crying and carrying on. Sometimes the teacher got angry with the child. Tantrum behavior became more pronounced and intolerable. On the advice of a knowledgeable principal, the teacher started ignoring the tantrums. She brought a book or magazine with her to the playground and pretended to read it when the child threw a tantrum. Eventually the child no longer displayed tantrum behavior.

TIME-OUT

Sometimes no amount of praising good behavior and ignoring bad behavior reduces a student's misconduct. Reinforcement received from peers for behaving improperly may appear to be more powerful than reinforcement for good behavior offered by the teacher. In such cases, behaviorists may recommend that the student be placed in time-out, that is, removed temporarily from the environment in which the misbehavior is being reinforced. Time-out usually takes place in a small room away from the regular classroom. The room should be as nearly free of stimuli as possible so that students do not find being there preferable to being in the classroom. Students are usually required to stay in the time-out room for some designated time or until the undesirable behavior is terminated. For example, a child who cries uncontrollably in the classroom may be expected to remain in the time-out room until the crying has stopped for five minutes. This situation is explained as the child enters the time-out room.

It is wise to limit the use of time-out as much as possible. Students should not be traumatized by time-out experiences. For example, a child should not be imprisoned in an "isolation box" with a bolted door.

PUNISHMENT

The most common correction strategy is punishment. Sometimes teachers elect to punish children for bad behavior rather than ignore bad behavior and reinforce good behavior. Students, however, may find a teacher's actions to be reinforcing rather than punishing. When they do, their inappropriate behavior only increases. Suppose, for example, that Ralph throws spit wads at other students and that the teacher routinely lectures him in an effort to somehow get him to stop. However, if Ralph finds the increased attention reinforcing, he will not stop throwing spit wads. He gets the double pleasure of attention from peers as well as from the teacher. He may prefer more positive attention, but if his teachers have always ignored his good behavior and focused only on his misbehavior, he may find this negative attention preferable to no attention from teachers at all. Therefore, he provokes all his teachers until they react negatively.

It is very hard to predict how students will react to punishment. Some, of course, relent and behave better. Others become more disruptive. In still other cases, students may avoid a direct confrontation but still take aggressive, retaliatory actions against their teachers. They may destroy school or personal property, for example. Some students withdraw from those who punish them; these students may stop learning if they are punished. These problems with punishment are rarely encountered when acceptable behavior is reinforced and bad behavior is ignored.

Behaviorists believe that punishment may occasionally be necessary. It is recommended, however, only when a more positive approach has failed or when quick action must be taken. For example, one would not look for opportunities to use positive reinforcement during a fight. Instead, the fight would be stopped and punishment used if necessary to suppress students' inclination to continue (Charles, 1989).

Punishment is usually arbitrary. It is often given without prior notification and involves painful experiences of a nature and duration that have little to do with students' bad behavior. For example, Deanna and her friend Jasmine threw a brick through a stained glass window in a church adjacent to the school. Deanna was a star athlete in both basketball and track. Her friend did not participate in any school activities. As punishment, Deanna was forbidden to participate in basketball for the entire season. Jasmine was reprimanded. Deanna's punishment had little to do with breaking the window, and the length of time the punishment was inflicted was arbitrary. Jasmine's punishment was less severe, but it also had little to do with breaking windows. It would have been better to make the two pay for replacing the window.

Schedules of Reinforcement

A schedule of reinforcement is the frequency with which reinforcement is supplied. Reinforcement can be provided on a *continuous schedule*, in which case it is given each time the target behavior is demonstrated. If an *intermittent schedule* is desired, reinforcement is delivered at various, previously determined times. For example, reinforcement may be provided every third time a target behavior is observed or every third, ninth, and eighteenth time it appears. Usually the initial reinforcement is given on a continuous schedule. Then, when the behavior has been established, a shift is made to an intermittent schedule.

There are two advantages in using an intermittent schedule of reinforcement. First, it is more economical of the teacher's time and effort. Second, the use of an intermittent schedule of reinforcement is more likely to lead to more persistent behavior that is resistant to change (Becker, Engelmann, & Thomas, 1971). This persistence comes about apparently because reinforcement is unpredictable and therefore more elusive and enticing (Kazdin & Polster, 1973).

The use of intermittent reinforcement also has its drawbacks. Desirable behavior that is intermittently reinforced will have a greater tendency to persist than desirable behavior reinforced on a continuous schedule. Unfortunately, the same is also true of undesirable behavior. As shown in the following example, if inappropriate behavior is reinforced intermittently, as it often is, greater effort will be required to eliminate it later.

▼ Mr. Forsgren had been watching K.D. and Jinyun out of the corner of his eye for some time as they talked incessantly in the back of the room. The conversation between the two had become louder and louder as time passed. Mr. Forsgren decided not to call attention to their disruption for fear of satisfying their need for attention and promoting a worse problem. However, their talking and other disruptive antics finally could no longer be ignored. A few students were peering at him with expectant looks and others had irritated expressions on their faces. Obviously some class members felt that he should take action. Suddenly Mr. Forsgren shouted out, "K.D.! Jinyun! I've heard about enough of your talking. If I hear any more from you, I'll send you to Ms. Brenchley's office." There was general snickering around the room. Mr. Forsgren could not decide whether they were laughing at him or the two unruly students. He hoped that the threat to send them to the principal's office would deter them. He went on grading papers at his desk but occasionally shot a dour look in the direction of K.D. and Jinyun. Not more than five minutes later he heard whispering coming from where the two sat. "I'll wait them out this time," he thought. "When they have gone far enough, I'll take them both to the principal." The talking reached a crescendo as several other students joined the pair. Mr. Forsgren drew in a deep breath in preparation for another verbal assault. Before he could make a sound, the bell rang, ending the class. K.D. and Jinyun were first out the door. They knew that they had just barely missed incurring the wrath of Mr. Forsgren and a possible trip to Ms. Brenchley's office.

Some teachers recognize that paying attention to students' misbehavior only increases its frequency. This knowledge encourages them to wait until students' misbehavior becomes intolerable before responding. When they finally do react, they end up reinforcing the disruptive behavior intermittently, thus ensuring its persistence and making it much harder to curtail subsequently.

Reinforcers

Stimuli used to reinforce behavior are called reinforcers. Some reinforcers are convenient to use but lack sufficient power to alter students' behavior. Verbal reinforcers, for example, are sometimes rather ineffective; attention by peers may be far more powerful in promoting bad behavior than a teacher's praise is in influencing good behavior. In this case, the teacher may want to increase the power of praise by pairing it with some other, more powerful reinforcer. For instance, praise can be given at the same time the teacher rewards a student with a special privilege such as acting as a lab assistant. A reinforcer that is thus strengthened by association with some other reinforcer is said to have become conditioned.

TYPES OF REINFORCERS

There are several types of reinforcers. Although there is no inherent advantage in using one type of reinforcer over another, one type may be preferable depending on the resources of the school or the inclination of the teacher.

Edible Reinforcers   Edible reinforcers, such as candy and other goodies, are commonly used with preschool and early elementary school students and some exceptional children because they have immediate reinforcement value. Edible reinforcers are usually used in conjunction with various material reinforcers, particularly where a commissary has been established.

Material Reinforcers   Objects such as toys, games, personal items, and so forth have been widely used as reinforcers. The specific kind of items used varies with the age level and interests of the student. Trinkets and toys can be used effectively with small children. Older children may want recorded music, games, or tape players.

TABLE 3.1
Possible edible and material reinforcers.

Edible	Material	

Bakery items
   Cookies
   Doughnuts
	Arts and craft supplies
	   Building sets
	   Model kits
	   Modeling clay
	   Painting sets
	   Pliable dough
		Party items
		   Balloons
		   Costumes
		   Noisemakers

Candy
   Candy bars
   Chocolate kisses
   Jelly beans
   Lemon drops
   Lollipops
   Marshmallows
	Badges	Pennants
		
		Posters

Cereal (sweetened)	Books
	   Picture books
	   Comic books
		Toys and games
		   Balls
		   Bean bags
		   Blocks

Dairy products
   Cheese
   Ice cream
   Yogurt
	Decals
	
	Entertainment
	   Radios
	   Recorded music
	   Tape players
		Board games
		Computer games
		Flying discs
		Gliders
		Jacks

Drinks
   Fruit juice
   Soft drinks
	Figurines	Jump ropes
		Kazoos
		Kites

Fruit
   Apples
   Oranges
   Raisins
	Make-up
	
	Office Supplies
	   Colored chalk
	   Coloring books
	   Crayons
		Marbles
		Minature cars
		Playing cards
		Puzzles
		Stuffed animals

Gum
 	
Nuts
	Felt-tip pens
	   Paper
	   Pencils
		Yo-yos

Snacks
   Caramel corn
   Popcorn
   Potato chips
   Tortilla chips		

Often material reinforcers can be obtained quite inexpensively. For example, stores and industries in the community may furnish rejects, excess spare parts, and other odds and ends. Sometimes edibles can be obtained in the same way; some teachers have gleaned broken cookies or day-old baked goods from wholesale bakeries.

Parents and other community members can also be asked for "white elephants" such as magazines, old toys, and all sorts of objects that are of no further use to their owners. Giveaways, promotional offers, and free samples are another possible source of inexpensive reinforcers. Old special-occasion cards, playing cards, and other colorful paper items are great to use with small children. Shells, leaves, stamps, and foreign coins are available at minimal cost. Some teachers have purchased items in bulk at very low prices from companies that service vending machines. A small amount of money can go a long way in procuring such items (Sulzner-Azaroff & Mayer, 1977).

Table 3.1 lists some common edible and material reinforcers.

Activity Reinforcers   Sometimes teachers do not wish to give students edibles or toys but prefer instead to provide special privileges or activities as reinforcers. Table 3.2 gives a list of possible activity reinforcers.

GENERAL AND BACKUP REINFORCERS

To increase the power of reinforcement, teachers may employ *general reinforcers*. General reinforcers are symbols that have little or no intrinsic value to students. But they are nevertheless extremely valuable, because they can be exchanged for any one of a number of *backup reinforcers* that are desirable to students.

The best example of a general reinforcer is money. The power of money is evident in the effort most people expend to obtain it. It is almost unheard of for people to rob a store at gunpoint to obtain some particular item; they take money. Money holds such power because it can indirectly satisfy almost any need. A teacher who provides general reinforcers, along with a wide variety of backup reinforcers, does not need to decide which backup reinforcers are most satisfying. Students make this decision for themselves. In school reinforcement programs, tokens instead of money are used as a medium of exchange. Tokens may be plastic money pieces, poker chips, slips of paper, or

TABLE 3.2
Possible activity reinforcers.

Running errands	Passing out papers
Watching a movie	Watching TV
Listening to music	Playing games
Going to lunch early	Having a party
Choosing a seat	Taking care of classroom pets
Acting as team captain	Designing a test
Assisting the teacher	Using the microscope
Going to the library	Spending a period in a commons area
Having an extra P.E. period	Reading a book during class
Attending class outdoors	Going on a field trip
Choosing a game for recess	Putting up the school flag
Supervising the playground	Acting in a skit
Leading the music	Seeing a film strip
Supervising the lab	Attending/skipping an assembly
Making puppets	Going home early
Running the projector	Playing educational games
Spending a period talking to a friend	Demonstrating a hobby to the class

TABLE 3.3
Possible tokens.

Held by the Student	Maintained by theTeacher
Pennies	Marks on the blackboad
Gold stars or other stickers	Tallies on a sheet of paper
Tickets or slips of paper	Computer entries, displayed creatively
Beads for stringing	
Poker chips	
Punches on a card	

even points marked in a folder or on a chart (see Table 3.3). The common characteristic of all these variations is that they can be exchanged for some other desired reward.

TOKEN ECONOMY

When tokens are used in a system of exchange, the system is called a token economy. For tokens to be effective, teachers must be able to dispense them quickly and easily. For example, a teacher with a pocketful of plastic beads could readily dispense them while moving around the room teaching the whole class or working with individual students at their desks. The effectiveness of a token economy also depends on the desirability of backup reinforcers to students. If backup reinforcers have little reinforcing value, they will not motivate students. Sometimes it is surprising what some students will find desirable. A reinforcer's appeal usually depends to a large extent on students' age. Small children may work consistently for hours on schoolwork to earn tokens with which to buy some rather inexpensive trinket. Older students, of course, will not.

Until behavior improves, tokens need to be given out on a continuous schedule. As time goes by, a more convenient intermittent schedule can be established. In addition, praise may be given at the same time tokens are delivered so that it gains power as a conditioned reinforcer. If praise is then interspersed with tokens as reinforcement, it can be expected to have a positive influence on the behavior of students.

When a formal token economy is established in a school, a commissary is often created from which students can "purchase" rewards with their tokens. Depending on the age of the students involved, the commissary is usually stocked with items such as those listed in Table 3.1.

▼ Mr. Hansen was having trouble disciplining several students in each of his seventh grade science classes. With help from one of his university professors he created a token economy for use exclusively with these few unusually disruptive students. One thing he wanted to avoid was the practice, common in most token economy programs, of providing students with food or play materials as backup reinforcers. Instead, he wanted to provide them with special privileges, which he felt would be more in keeping with the purposes of schooling. In addition, he doubted that he could finance tangible reinforcers out of his own pocket and knew that the school budget could not accommodate this added expense. He thought that in any case parents might consider food and trinkets a bribe but that they—and others—would be less likely to object to this kind of program.

Mr. Hansen wanted to base his token economy on the curriculum used in his science classes and so sat down one day to list the things he expected of his students. In his classes, students spent most of their time working on experiments with plants. From a side desk students would pick up cards that described the experiments. They would get materials from the supply room as they needed them. They performed experiments at their desks. They could then put their experimental materials into grow tables and wait for results to appear. While they waited for the results of one experiment, they were encouraged to start new ones. Consequently, each student had several experiments to work on at any one time.

This is the list of behaviors Mr. Hansen decided to use as the basis of his token economy:

1. Listening during lecture or discussion portions of the class
2. Participating in class discussion
3. Reading appropriate materials
4. Working on one's own experiments
5. Carrying out timely, complete, and correct experiments
6. Answering the review questions on experiments
7. Answering extra questions on experiments
8. Doing extra experiments
9. Improving test scores

The next task was to decide what to use as backup reinforcers. He had developed a list of things he supposed students would find attractive, but he wanted to get their suggestions as well. He asked the target students what activities they would enjoy participating in during class. A caution was added that they should only include things that could legitimately be done in school. From his own ideas, as well as the students' suggestions, the following list was created:

1. Run the film projector   (50 points)
2. Mark the roll for a week   (50 points)
3. Be the teacher's assistant   (50 points)
4. Run errands   (25 points)
5. Play a board game during class   (150 points)
6. Be excused five minutes early for lunch   (25 points)
7. Spend a period visiting with a friend in the commons   (150 points)
8. Spend one science period in a physical education class   (150 points)
9. Spend a period in the library   (75 points)
10. Prepare a special report   (25 points)
11. Prepare a true-false quiz for the class   (50 points)
12. Use the microscope for a period   (100 points)
13. Be the supply room attendant   (50 points)

To each of the disruptive students he had identified—there were three or four in each of his six classes—Mr. Hansen gave a folder. Stapled to the inside of the folders were two sheets. One sheet contained a list of the backup reinforcers along with their point values. On the other sheet, desired behaviors were listed. At the side of each desired behavior was a series of boxes in which points could be marked. Whenever Mr. Hansen observed one of the target students exhibiting acceptable behavior, he would mark an appropriate number of points in one of the boxes. Mr. Hansen thought it important that his target students receive at least the minimum number of points each day to "purchase" some reward. He therefore attempted to give each student at least 25 points in each class period. Mr. Hansen tried to assign different point values to various behaviors in such a way that his students could learn to save their points and exchange them for more valuable reinforcers.

Mr. Hansen was very pleased with the effects of his token economy system. His most unruly students became the most conscientious ones almost immediately. In the process, Mr. Hansen discovered that some backup reinforcers were more popular than others. Being excused early for lunch was the most popular. Anyone who has been in a typical, crowded junior high school cafeteria can see why. Having an extra physical education period was very popular among the boys; the girls tended to prefer being the teacher's assistant and running errands. One student chose to present a special report. However, after he had received this reward once, it lost its appeal. Such experiences helped Mr. Hansen realize that he needed to maintain and from time to time revise a fairly large list of possible backup reinforcers to satisfy students more fully.

Sometimes teachers want to involve the whole class in a token economy. More efficient ways of dispensing tokens must then be used. Passing out plastic discs or poker chips usually works well. Some teachers print up paper money of different denominations to use as tokens. This practice is common among foreign language teachers and has the added advantage of teaching students the monetary system of the country whose language they are learning. If you plan to use a token economy, it is wise to consult with your principal beforehand. Consultation may help prevent some objections that might otherwise occur, and it also provides an opportunity to get clearance for such activities as being excused early for lunch or going to an extra physical education period. If you plan to have your students participate in an extra class or go to the library as part of your program, be sure to discuss the matter with the appropriate school personnel.

THE QUESTION OF BRIBERY

One of the criticisms often made of Behavior Modification is that it constitutes bribery. Sloane, Buckholdt, Jenson, and Crandall (1979) list the following responses commonly given by behaviorists to this criticism:

1. All educators hope that children will be encouraged to learn worthwhile things because of their intrinsic value. However, most worthwhile learning requires a minimum amount of skill or understanding before children really become drawn to it. Take reading, for example. For reading to be enjoyable, certain basic skills must be

learned. A poor reader could hardly be expected to be satisfied by attempting to read a difficult book such as *Hamlet*. In the beginning, reading must be motivated by external rewards. These external rewards, however, are only temporary. Once adequate reading skills are developed, extrinsic rewards will no longer be necessary.

2. Some individuals, such as those who have mental disabilities or psychoses, may not be motivated by the same things as most other people. They may require concrete, immediate reinforcers before they are motivated to do many of the things that make their lives more meaningful.

3. A reinforcer given to a child for schoolwork is no more a bribe than the salary earned by teachers and other adults for their services.

4. Bribery is a word used ordinarily with reference to payoffs for illegal or immoral behavior. To use it to describe tangible learning rewards is a misapplication of the true meaning of the term.

Preventing Discipline Problems

Behavior Modification has no explicitly stated strategies for the prevention of discipline problems. Correcting problems is emphasized exclusively. However, discipline problems are prevented to some extent when Behavior Modification principles are implemented. When desired behavior is reinforced, it increases in frequency. There is usually a corresponding decrease in undesirable behavior.

Schoolwide Discipline

When Behavior Modification is used on a schoolwide basis, it often involves a commissary from which a wide variety of backup reinforcers are dispensed. Teachers and other school personnel provide tokens to use as a medium of exchange. Usually the commissary is open only at predetermined times such as during lunch periods and before and after school. It is ordinarily staffed by students, under the direction of a faculty member.

Usually there is little if any punishment imposed on students in a Behavior Modification approach to discipline. Various reinforcement programs are preferred, which sometimes take the form of incentive programs. For example, students may be occupied with advancing their reading skills to obtain rewards. Charts hung in prominent places in the school often track the progress of students in such programs. Sometimes individual students are rewarded for reading achievement. At other times the school as a whole receives a reward for cumulative reading achievement. The whole school may take a special field trip, throw a party, or sponsor a dance. In some schools, the principal or teachers promise to do certain things if students achieve specified reading goals. For example, beards may be shaved, hair may be cut short, or the principal may spend the entire day sitting on top of the school building as a reward for students' achievement. Similar rewards have been given in secondary schools that remain drug-free for a year. Schoolwide incentive programs are designed to promote good behavior and have the effect of reducing negative behavior in the process.

Strengths and Weakness of Behavior Modification

STRENGTHS

1. It is simple to use.
2. Results are immediate.
3. It accommodates most teachers' desire to maintain control.
4. Students can feel successful while they obtain rewards.
5. Standards of behavior are uniform, consistent, and clear to all students.
6. Time does not have to be spent in class on discussing rules and students' conduct.
7. It can be readily employed with all students regardless of age.
8. The procedure has been well researched and found to work consistently.

WEAKNESSES

1. The results may not last long.
2. Students may not perform as desired when rewards are terminated.
3. Students may not learn how to govern their own behavior.
4. To some teachers, this approach seems too much like bribery.
5. It ignores any underlying problems caused by influences at home, in society, or at school.
6. To use so much control in a democratic society may be unethical.
7. Students do not get an opportunity to clarify emotions, weigh alternatives, decide on solutions, or develop their intellect.

SUMMARY

Teachers who intend to reduce students' misbehavior by punishing them often discover that their efforts produce an increase in bad behavior instead. This unintended result occurs because some students find the teachers' attempts to punish them reinforcing. The result of teachers' actions, not their intentions, determines whether their students have been punished or reinforced. Teachers may also confuse negative reinforcement and punishment, believing them to be one and the same thing. Actually, negative reinforcement is given to increase some behavior, whereas punishment is implemented to terminate a behavior. A student has been negatively reinforced when she or he increases a behavior in an effort to avoid something or to eliminate some aversive stimulus. When the stimulus of punishment is sufficiently painful, a student stops unwanted behaviors rather than suffer its effects.

Teachers who want to eliminate undesirable behavior in students may elect to ignore the behavior and reinforce competing behavior. In this way the unacceptable behavior is likely to become extinguished while desirable behaviors increase in frequency.

Teachers can economize their efforts by reducing the amount of reinforcement they provide after the desired behaviors become established. This reduction usually involves shifting from a continuous schedule of reinforcement to an intermittent one. An intermittent schedule of reinforcement has the advantage of providing a stronger conditioning influence than a continuous schedule—which can also be a disadvantage if the behavior that has been conditioned intermittently is an undesirable one. Such behavior will ultimately be much more difficult to eliminate. Greater economy can also be achieved by incorporating conditioned reinforcers, that is, by pairing a reinforcer that is powerful enough to elicit a desired response with one that is less powerful but easier and more convenient to use. After the conditioning has taken place, the less powerful but more convenient reinforcer can take the place of the more powerful one.

If still more powerful reinforcement is needed to influence appropriate behavior, general reinforcers can be employed. A generalized reinforcer is one that can be exchanged for a wide variety of backup reinforcers. When general reinforcers are used in a token economy, a commissary is often established from which students can make purchases with the tokens they have earned.

CENTRAL IDEAS

1.   Many teachers believe that they are punishing students only to discover that their actions promote the behavior they are trying to eliminate. They thereby reinforce rather than punish.

2.   Students are negatively reinforced when they behave in a desired way in order to avoid an unpleasant stimulus.

3.   To eliminate undesirable behaviors, teachers should stop reinforcing them (thus causing their extinction) and reinforce behavior that is acceptable.

4.   An intermittent schedule of reinforcement strengthens the effect of the reinforcer.

5.   The time and expense involved in reinforcement programs may be reduced by using praise and attention as conditioned reinforcers.

6.   Token economies increase the power of a reinforcement program by providing a greater range of reinforcers to satisfy the diverse desires of students.

QUESTIONS AND ACTIVITIES

QUESTIONS TO CONSIDER

1. How can you determine what students find to be reinforcing?
2. What do you consider to be the strengths and weaknesses of Behavior Modification?
3. What differences would there be in applying Behavior Modification techniques in elementary schools and secondary schools?

CLASSROOM ACTIVITIES

1. As a class, create a token economy for yourselves. Outline which behaviors you would provide tokens for and what you would use as backup reinforcers. In determining what reinforcers to use, consider the different values of the group. Try to reach a consensus about which reinforcers are mutually acceptable.
2. View the audio-visual materials associated with Behavior Modification that are listed in Appendix A.
3. Create a reinforcement program for someone you know who has a problem that needs to be overcome. For example, the person may be tardy frequently. Apply this program and evaluate the results.

STUDENT APPLICATIONS

1. Dan sits in his seat and sleeps most of the time. When he is awake, he spends his time talking with his friends or reading comic books he brings to class. He never does any work in class and has not turned in a homework assignment since the beginning of the year. Using Behavior Modification principles, describe what you would do to help Dan to become more involved in class and complete his homework.
2. Bianca annoys other members of the class by flipping spit wads at them and throwing paper airplanes around the room. In addition, she often talks loudly during quiet study time as well as during lectures and discussions. How could you solve these problems using Behavior Modification principles?

REFERENCES

Ayllon, T. (1963). Intensive treatment of psychotic behavior by satiation and food reinforcement. *Behavior Research and Therapy, 1*, 53–61.

Ayllon, T., & Michael, J. (1959). The psychiatric nurse as a behavioral engineer. *Journal of the Experimental Analysis of Behavior, 3*, 323–334.

Becker, W. C., Engelmann, S., & Thomas, D. R. (1971). *Teaching: A course in applied psychology*. Chicago: Science Research Associates.

Bijou, S. W., & Baer, D. M. (1961). *Child development I: A systematic and empirical theory.* New York: Appleton-Century-Crofts.

Charles, C. M. (1989). *Building classroom discipline: From models to practice* (3rd ed.). New York: Longman.

Edwards, C. H. (1975). Variable delivery systems for peer associated token reinforcement. *Illinois School Research, 12,* 19–28.

Hall, R. V., Fox., R., Willard, D., Goldsmith, L., Emerson, M., Owen, M., Davis, F., & Porcia, E. (1971). The teacher as observer and experimenter in the modification of disputing and talking-out behavior. *Journal of Applied Behavior Analysis, 4,* 141–149.

Kazdin, A. E., & Polster, R. (1973). Intermittent token reinforcement and response maintenance in extinction. *Behavior Therapy, 4,* 386–391.

Klein, S. S. (1971). Student influence on teacher behavior. *American Educational Research Journal, 8,* 403–421.

Madsen, C. H., Becker, W. C., Thomas, D. R., Koser, L., & Plager, E. (1968). An analysis of the reinforcing function of "sit down" commands. In R. K. Parker (Ed.), *Readings in educational psychology* (pp. 265–278). Boston: Allyn and Bacon.

Sherman, T. M., & Cormier, W. H. (1974). An investigation of the influence of student behavior on teacher behavior. *Journal of Applied Behavior Analysis, 7,* 11–21.

Skinner, B. F. (1948). *Walden Two.* New York: Macmillan.

Skinner, B. F. (1971). *Beyond freedom and dignity.* New York: Knopf.

Sloane, H. N., Buckholdt, D. R., Jenson, W. R., & Crandall, J. A. (1979). *Structured teaching: A design for classroom management and instruction.* Champaign, IL: Research Press.

Sulzner-Azaroff, B., & Mayer, G. R. (1977). *Applying behavior-analysis procedures with children and youth.* New York: Holt, Rinehart and Winston.

4

Assertive Discipline: Lee Canter

OBJECTIVES

This chapter is designed to help you
1. learn what it means to be assertive
2. accurately apply Canter's steps of Assertive Discipline in the classroom
3. explain the communications skills needed to apply Assertive Discipline effectively
4. list the various kinds of punishment that may be used with Assertive Discipline
5. identify the positive consequences that may be provided for good behavior
6. understand the role of Assertive Discipline in preventing discipline problems

ASSUMPTIONS

1. Students must be forced to comply with rules.
2. Students cannot be expected to determine appropriate classroom rules and follow them.
3. Punishment will cause students to avoid bad behavior and engage in good classroom behavior.
4. Good behavior can also be encouraged by positive reinforcement.
5. For proper classroom management, parents and school administrators must help to enforce rules.

Introduction

Lee Canter is a child guidance specialist who has turned his entire attention to discipline in the schools. He has established an organization in California called Canter and Associates, through which he provides training for teachers who want to become more assertive in their teaching. His wife, Marlene, who teaches people with learning disabilities, also participates actively in this endeavor. Together they lead workshops all over the country. Many school districts have accepted the Canter Model and adopted it for use by their teachers. Hundreds of thousands of teachers currently use Canter's Assertive Discipline.

The Assertive Discipline approach of Lee Canter has certain similarities to Behavior Modification strategies, but it also differs from them in significant ways. Whereas Behavior Modification emphasizes reinforcing appropriate behaviors and ignoring inappropriate ones, Assertive Discipline emphasizes punishing unacceptable behaviors and providing reinforcement for behaviors that are acceptable to teachers. The following exchange illustrates how Assertive Discipline would be applied in the case of an elementary school student who refuses to work in class and walks around the room instead:

Teacher	Chris, I want you to take your seat now and do your work!
Chris	I'm going to start in a minute. Just let me get my pencil sharpened.
Teacher	I want you to go to your seat now and start your work!
Chris	I'm going to. You don't make other students work like you do me.
Teacher	Chris, you must go to your seat immediately and start working on your assignment!
Chris	Just a minute, I have to get some paper from Jess.
Teacher	Chris, you must take your seat and go to work right now or you must come in after school and do it!

Canter believes that teachers have traditionally ignored their own needs in the classroom in favor of satisfying students' needs, assuming that as professional teachers they are expected to behave in this way. This misconception, however, contributes to many of the discipline problems teachers experience. Teachers have needs, wants, and feelings just as their students do. Teachers labor under other misconceptions as well:

- Good teachers should be able to handle discipline problems without any help from administrators or parents.
- Firm discipline may cause children psychological harm.
- Discipline problems do not persist when students are provided with activities that satisfy their needs.
- Misbehavior has deep-seated causes on which teachers can have no influence.

These misconceptions—which are promoted by such authorities as Sigmund Freud, B. F. Skinner, William Glasser, and M. M. Gordon—encourage teachers to discipline their students in wishy-washy ways that lead to additional problems (Canter & Canter, 1976).

Teachers, according to Canter, need to change their indecisive approaches to discipline. First and foremost, they must insist that their own rights as teachers are met. These rights include:

- the right to establish classroom rules and procedures that produce the optimum learning environment
- the right to insist on behavior from students that meets teachers' needs and that encourages the positive social and educational development of students
- the right to receive help in disciplining from both parents and school administrators

Students also have rights. They have the right to have teachers who will limit inappropriate behavior, who will provide positive support for appropriate behavior, and who will communicate how students should behave and what will happen if they do not.

To make sure that the needs of both teachers and students are met, teachers must learn to assert themselves. Assertive teachers clearly and firmly communicate personal wants and needs to students and are prepared to reinforce their words with appropriate actions. They attempt to get their own needs met and still take into account the capabilities of their students. Teachers need to communicate the idea that they care too much about themselves to allow students to take advantage of them. They also need to show students that they care too much about them to allow their inappropriate behavior to go unnoticed. In simple terms, assertive teachers let students know that they mean what they say and say what they mean.

Becoming an assertive teacher involves becoming forceful and self-assured with students. The assertive teacher is able to

1. identify wants and feelings in interpersonal situations
2. verbalize wants and feelings in a straightforward way
3. persist in stating wants and feelings
4. use a firm tone of voice
5. maintain eye contact when speaking
6. reinforce verbal statements with congruent nonverbal gestures

Responses to Misbehavior

Teachers may respond to students' actions in one of three ways. They may be nonassertive, hostile, or assertive.

THE NONASSERTIVE STYLE

Nonassertive teachers fail to let their students clearly know what they want and what they will not accept. They also fail to back up their words with appropriate, decisive actions. Commonly they threaten the misbehaving student but stop short of implementing their threats. Sometimes they even ignore the unacceptable behavior. The following example shows a teacher using a nonassertive response style:

▼ Ms. Tew had a particularly difficult time getting three of the students in her biology class to stop talking during quiet study time. They would sit and talk and often roam around the room playing in the aquaria and making noises with the other science equipment. One day Eric, the leader of the three, encouraged the other two, Alma and Adelaide, to accompany him to the back of the room during quiet study time, where they immediately began trying to catch the guppies in one of the fish tanks. In the beginning, Ms. Tew did not even look at them. She had long ago tired of the misbehavior of these three and tried her best not to pay any attention to them. Finally, however, their rowdy, noisy antics caused other students in the class to implore her to do something about the situation. Finally, in desperation, Ms. Tew called out to the three, "Please try to sit down and do your work. I'll bet none of you has your assignment ready to turn in."

The students looked up from what they were doing and, as though challenging Ms. Tew, just ignored the request and went back to what they were doing. Five minutes later the noise level had again reached an unacceptable level. "Look, you three," pleaded Ms. Tew, "I don't know what I'm going to do with you. You're going to have to learn to sit in your seats and do your work. You're disturbing other students. We just can't put up with this any longer." Eric made a snide remark, which most members of the class heard but which Ms. Tew could not understand. The whole class burst into laughter. Red-faced, Ms. Tew retorted, "I don't have to stand for this. You are going to get into real trouble if you don't watch it."

THE HOSTILE STYLE

Teachers who use a hostile response style address students in an abusive way. They make derogatory remarks and often lose their temper. Hostile teachers commonly "put down" their students. For example, they may tell children that they never act their age or that they are stupid. Sometimes they make overt or implied threats of violence: "I'll get you for what you did." Their mean-spiritedness violates the rights and feelings of their students. A hostile response style is illustrated in the following example:

▼ Mr. Applegate ruled his class with an iron fist. He felt that students should learn to be more responsible by strictly complying with his expectations. Several students in his third period class routinely defied him, however. They never turned in their homework on time, rarely worked on in-class assignments, and spent most of the class period disturbing students around them. One day when they were particularly rowdy, Mr. Applegate walked over to the loudest of the group and yelled, "I've taken all of the insulting behavior from you I intend! If I catch you doing just one more thing to disturb this class, you're going to be very sorry!"

THE ASSERTIVE STYLE

When teachers respond assertively, they clearly communicate their wants and feelings to their students and indicate a willingness to back up their words with actions if necessary. This approach ensures greater compliance with their demands and expectations, so long as those demands and expectations are not unreasonable. Assertive teachers establish limits for their students and enforce them. They give explicit directions to a child, such as "Stop running in the halls and walk" or "Stop writing on your desk or you will have to sand and refinish it." In the following example the teacher uses an assertive response style:

> ▼ Ms. Romero had a student named Fred in her fifth grade class who habitually picked on the other students and was involved in fighting almost every day. One afternoon Fred hit Roy and then sat back in his seat and laughed out loud. Roy was about six inches shorter than Fred and weighed at least 60 pounds less. Fred usually picked on smaller children. Ms. Romero observed Fred and firmly said, "Fred, stop fighting!" She added, "Fred, I will not tolerate your fighting in class. You have a choice: Either stop fighting or go to the principal's office." Fred said, "I don't want to be sent to see the principal. I've heard she is really tough." "The next time you fight," replied Ms. Romero, "you will have to go there."

Roadblocks to Becoming More Assertive

For most teachers, the most common roadblock to becoming more assertive is their own doubt about their ability to deal with students' behavior problems. Some students, they feel, misbehave because of emotional illness, heredity, brain damage, ignorance, peer pressure, inadequate parenting, lower socioeconomic background, or other influences. Children with these problems can create difficulties for teachers, but the problems can be managed if the teachers are assertive. First, teachers must realize that such children can be handled in the regular classroom. They then must learn to implement Assertive Discipline techniques consistently. Ordinary discipline procedures will not work with such children. With some of these children teachers will have to be firmer; other children will require more lenient treatment. Teachers must realize that they have the right to set limits and to ensure that children do not exceed them. They must get over the fear that children will develop an aversion to education if teachers set strict limits. There are indeed too many children who come to school burdened by emotionally and educationally crippling problems such as parental neglect, inadequate home life, poverty, and racism. However, teachers who allow such children to go undisciplined or allow them to act inappropriately without responding firmly to them run the risk of doing additional harm.

When students have severe behavioral problems, teachers have the right and responsibility to ask for help from school administrators and other teachers. Some teachers fear that they will be considered weak if they ask for assistance with particularly difficult children. If they do not ask for assistance, they may avoid dealing with students who are out of control. Ultimately they may have no choice but to involve others. However, it is better to seek help from other professionals sooner than later. Students should know that their teachers will act decisively to bring in other school personnel if they behave inappropriately. The assistance of parents should also be sought. Many children with behavior problems will respond more readily when parents are involved.

Applying Assertive Discipline

There are four steps to follow in applying Assertive Discipline:

1. establishing rules or expectations
2. tracking misbehavior
3. using punishment to enforce limits
4. implementing a system of positive consequences

Each of these steps has important aspects that must be kept in mind. In addition, it is critical that assertiveness be implemented consistently.

STEP 1: ESTABLISHING RULES OR EXPECTATIONS

Rules in the classroom should be based on the needs of teachers. Teachers need to specify exactly what behaviors they expect of children. These behaviors may be specified in a list such as:

1. Complete all assignments on time.
2. Do your own work.
3. Don't talk without receiving permission.
4. Follow directions.
5. Don't leave the classroom without permission.
6. Don't make any unnecessary noise in class.
7. Don't fight.
8. Don't swear.
9. Sit up straight in your seat.
10. Keep hands, feet, and objects to yourself.
11. Come to class on time.
12. Don't steal.

A longer list of rules can be made, but it is wise to limit it to perhaps only five or six rules. The rules created should satisfy the teacher's needs but not make unreasonable demands on students. For example, very young children should not be expected to sit for long periods of time without moving.

Once teachers have determined the behaviors expected, they must communicate them effectively to students, either verbally or with written instructions. A poster may also be prepared and placed in a prominent place in the classroom. When teachers explain rules to students, they should do so clearly and assertively. Instructions can be given in a straightforward manner:

"As your teacher, I insist that you follow certain rules so that I can do the best possible job. I expect the following behavior from each of you during the class period: One, do not talk in class without permission. Two, do not leave the room without permission. Three, turn in all assignments on time to receive credit. Four, do your own work. Five, stay in your seat and sit facing the front of the room. Six, follow all directions. Seven, keep your hands and feet to yourself. Eight, listen when the teacher is talking. I will let you know when you are and when you are not doing as I have directed. If you disobey the rules, I will first write your name on the board as a warning. If you continue, I will place a check mark by your name. This check mark means that you must stay after school for 10 minutes. If you get a second check mark, you must stay after school for 30 minutes. A third check mark means that you must stay after school for 30 minutes and your parents will be called. If you get a fourth check mark, you will be sent to the principal for possible expulsion from school. Now I suggest that you follow these rules. They are for your good and the good of the class."

The procedure of putting names and check marks on the board is considered by some to be an essential part of Assertive Discipline. Canter says that they are not (Canter, 1989). Their use is a convenience for teachers that allows them to discipline their students with limited disruptions. They can write names and check marks on the board without missing a beat in the presentation of their lessons. Then at the conclusion of instruction they can affirm their intentions to follow through on merited punishments. (Note: Canter uses the term *consequence* instead of *punishment*. Because Canter's idea of consequence fits the definition of punishment used by other theorists such as William Glasser and Rudolf Dreikurs, the word *punishment* is used in this chapter to avoid possible confusion over the use of *consequence*.)

Canter recommends that different types of activity periods be identified for use during the day (Canter & Canter, 1976). In an elementary classroom, for example, there may be quiet study time, discussion time, transition periods, independent work time, free time, rest periods, physical education or recess, art, music, and library time. During each of these times, teachers may have different needs that students must meet. For example, during quiet study time there may be rules that require students to work on assignments, stay in assigned seats, and refrain from talking. During free time, quiet talking may be appropriate so long as students work on their projects. It may be useful to make different signs to use during different periods. During quiet study time, a sign saying "QUIET WORK" could be posted. During discussions, a sign might be posted informing students to raise their hands for permission to talk. Initially, teachers must inform their students of the specific expectations for each type of activity.

STEP 2: TRACKING MISBEHAVIOR

Once students have been informed of teachers' expectations, teachers must follow through to ensure that their demands are met. If a system of writing names and check marks on the board is used, it is a simple matter to make sure that students receive the punishment identified for each number of check marks. These punishments may vary depending on local conditions and policies, grade level, and perhaps even the nature of the class or the particular rule infraction. In school districts where many students ride buses, for instance, teachers may not be allowed to keep children after school. Sometimes an entire school has the same set of punishments prescribed. Sometimes each teacher establishes his or her own rules. Canter gives the following examples (Canter & Canter, 1981) that show various discipline plans:

When a student at the primary level breaks a rule:

1st Instance: Name on the board — You receive a warning.

2nd Instance: One check mark — You lose 10 minutes of free time.

3rd Instance: Two check marks — You lose 20 minutes of free time.

4th Instance: Three check marks — You lose 30 minutes of free time, and your parents are called.

5th Instance: Four check marks — You lose 45 minutes of free time, your parents are called, and you are referred to the principal.

When a student at the primary level breaks a rule:

1st Instance: Name on the board — You receive a warning.

2nd Instance: One check mark — You are let out for recess 5 minutes late.

3rd Instance: Two check marks — You lose one recess.

4th Instance: Three check marks — You lose two recesses, and your parents are called.

5th Instance: Four check marks — You lose recess for a week, your parents are called, and you are referred to the principal.

When a student at the upper elementary school level breaks a rule:

1st Instance: Name on the board — You receive a warning.

2nd Instance: One check mark — You copy out 25 times the rule that was broken.

3rd Instance: Two check marks — You copy out 50 times the rule that was broken.

4th Instance: Three check marks — You copy out 50 times the rule that was broken and take the paper home for your parents to sign.

5th Instance: Four check marks — You are referred to the principal, and your parents are called in for a conference.

When a student at the upper elementary school level breaks a rule:

1st Instance: Name on the board — You receive a warning.

2nd Instance: One check mark — You spend 10 minutes cleaning up the playground.

3rd Instance: Two check marks — You spend 20 minutes cleaning up the playground.

4th Instance: Three check marks — You spend 30 minutes cleaning up the playground, and your parents are called.

5th Instance: Four check marks — You spend 30 minutes cleaning up the playground, your parents are called, and you are sent to another classroom for one hour.

When a student in junior or senior high school breaks a rule:

1st Instance: Name on the board — You receive a warning.

2nd Instance: One check mark — You receive a citation and 45 minutes of detention.

3rd Instance: Two check marks — You receive a citation and detention, and your parents are called.

4th Instance: Three check marks — You receive a citation and detention, your parents are called, and you are referred to the principal.

5th Instance: Four check marks — You receive an in-school suspension.

When a student in junior or senior high school breaks a rule:

1st Instance: Name on the board — You receive a warning.

2nd Instance: One check mark — You perform 30 minutes of campus cleanup.

3rd Instance: Two check marks — You perform one hour of campus cleanup.

4th Instance: Three check marks — You perform two hours of campus cleanup, and your parents are called.

5th Instance: Four check marks — You perform two hours of campus cleanup, your parents are called, and you are sent to the counselor.

Sometimes teachers end up putting many names on the board and adding check marks. This result can be expected when students are reinforced by their peers for daring to challenge class rules. Obviously these students are not influenced by the threat of punishment. In this case, Canter believes that tougher punishments must be applied. Teachers may have to tell their students that the first time they disobey a rule they will get their name on the board with two check marks. The severity of punishments may also have to be increased. For example, detention may be increased from 30 minutes to two hours. Teachers may have to call parents or refer students to the principal earlier if applying milder punishments first does not produce adequate results (Canter & Canter, 1981).

Teachers must not only competently employ discipline plans such as names and check marks; they must also effectively employ proper assertive language with their students. Four different methods are used to request compliance:

- Statements such as "Everyone should be working" are hints.
- "Would you please get to work?" has a question format.
- "I want you to open your books and get to work" is an "I message."
- "Get to work now!" is an example of a demand.

Whenever possible, it is best to use hints, questions, and "I messages" to request desired behavior. These three methods will work with most children most of the time. When a stronger request is needed, use a demand. Demands imply that a punishment will follow noncompliance. Remember, you should make no demands on which you are unprepared to follow through. You may, for example, demand that students stop talking and get to work. You may repeat this demand several times and indicate that if they do not quit talking immediately and get to work, they will be in big trouble. This approach is unlikely to alter the situation. The students will probably ignore you and go on with what they are doing. It is better simply to demand that students comply and tell them exactly what will happen if they do not.

Teachers can do several things to increase their effectiveness in requesting compliance with rules. The first is to use a tone of voice that is firm but not abusive. The tone of voice should never be harsh, sarcastic, or intimidating. It should, however, carry the message that you mean what you say and that you will carry out proper punishments if necessary.

Eye contact is also important in delivering requests to students. One's true intentions are often revealed more through the eyes than in any other way. Children often depend on this form of communication because they distrust verbal language. Some students may have difficulty understanding some words used by adults. Teachers can also learn how their students respond by watching their eyes.

Messages can be enhanced by hand gestures. Gesturing with the hands emphasizes the spoken word. When properly employed, gestures act as an affirmation: "I mean what I say." Teachers must, however, refrain from using gestures that are threatening or intimidating to children. For example, you should avoid shaking your finger in children's faces as you speak to them.

Using children's names as you make your requests also increases the impact of your message. It helps as well to direct what you have to say to the individual for whom it is intended. If, for example, a group of children across the room are disturbing the class, rather than giving a general directive—"You kids over there, stop talking!"—you would be better off singling out the noisy students: "Ruth, Larry, Cheryl, stop talking so loudly."

Finally, physical touch can be used to emphasize your verbal requests. Touching can also establish physical limits for students. If you want a child to turn around in his seat, a gentle nudge may be helpful. Placing your hand on a child while you speak to her adds forcefulness to your message. It indicates that you really do mean what you are saying and intend to enforce it. Touching students in ways that might be misconstrued as improper or abusive should of course be avoided.

As you apply the skills of assertiveness, it is helpful to employ the *broken record* technique: Repeat your demands several times when children either ignore you or object to your request. For example:

Teacher	Bret, I want you to go to work on your project now.
Bret	No one else has started. Why are you picking on me?
Teacher	That's not the point. I want you to begin working on your project now.
Bret	I will in just a minute.
Teacher	You are not to wait a minute. Start working on your project now.
Bret	OK, I will.

Remember as you employ this technique that you should maintain eye contact and use gestures and a suitable tone of voice. Using the child's name and touching will also emphasize your requests. In repeating your request, it is wise to limit yourself to three repetitions. You should then be prepared to tell the student what punishment will be applied if she or he does not comply. For example, Bret may be told that unless he starts his project immediately, he will have to sit in the time-out area for the rest of the period and stay in class after school until he completes it.

STEP 3: USING PUNISHMENTS TO ENFORCE LIMITS

It is important to follow through on demands. When telling students what will happen if they do not comply with a demand, teachers should make promises, not issue threats.

A promise is a vow to take appropriate actions when necessary. A threat is a statement of proposed punishment that does not have to be taken seriously, because it often is more extreme than anything children have learned to expect. For example, a new teacher who was a former Marine Corps drill sergeant met his students on the first day of class with a baseball bat in his hands. As he strutted up and down in front of the class explaining his expectations, he repeatedly smacked his palm with the bat, implying that if students did not comply, he would hit them with it. They, of course, knew better and set out then to sabotage the class. In three weeks he had decided to give up teaching.

Several methods of punishment are used in Assertive Discipline:

1. One commonly used punishment advocated by Canter is time-out. Time-out is also known as isolation. In a classroom, the isolation area is often a corner in the classroom that is screened from the view of class members. Children may be sent to the time-out area for varying lengths of time. Isolation within the classroom works best with elementary school children. If Assertive Discipline is used on a schoolwide basis, a time-out room may be available to which teachers may send their disruptive students.

2. Withdrawing a privilege is another commonly used punishment. For example, free time or recess may be taken away. Other preferred class activities may be taken away, such as physical education, art, field trips, or music. Children may be denied participation in such activities as interscholastic sports, debate, drama, cheerleading, contests, intramural athletics, student government, the school yearbook, or the student newspaper. Canter indicates that the more meaningful activities are, the more useful they are in forcing students to comply. Therefore, teachers should be sure that activities denied are particularly desirable ones.

3. Detention, or staying after school, is also a recommended punishment in Assertive Discipline. Detention may take place under the teacher's direction, or students may spend their detention time in the principal's office. Sometimes there is a special room in the school set aside for detention. A detention room is a particularly effective punishment for children who have not completed their assignments during class time. Their detention time can be used to finish their work.

4. Being sent to the principal's office is often used as punishment. Larger schools commonly have vice principals who take primary responsibility for solving discipline problems. Principals and their assistants are often able to employ more drastic punishments than teachers can. They usually can administer detention, in-school suspension, suspension from school, transfer to another school, expulsion, and referral to other professionals.

5. With Assertive Discipline, parents may be called upon to help when their children are disruptive. Teachers can call students' homes or send notes when children act inappropriately. Conferences with parents can be held. Canter also recommends that teachers arrange with parents to provide punishments at home for infractions of school rules. For example, parents may lecture their children, take away their television privileges, require them to stay in their room, or keep them from various social activities. Just the fact that parents are involved is often a sufficient deterrent to misbehaving children.

6. One highly effective means of curtailing the misbehavior of students is to send them to another class. Students ordinarily do not like being sent away. Embarrassment is not the intention of this tactic. Instead, it is meant to help children understand that their inappropriate behavior will not be tolerated. Misbehaving students would be sent to another class for the purpose of doing the assigned work. Prior arrangements would obviously have to be made with the other teacher. Before carrying out this punishment, teachers should show the offending student the seat that would be assigned in the new classroom.

7. Some teachers who use Assertive Discipline make a tape recording of their disruptive students. The tape can then be played for the principal or parents. When parents have a hard time believing that their child could do the things of which teachers accuse them, a tape recording provides an exact record of what happened. It is essential that tape recordings be made with the full knowledge of target children. They should not be spied upon. Instead, recordings should be made to provide an accurate record other adults can use to help misbehaving students. A tape recording gives a more realistic and accurate picture of events as they take place. Often these events are hard to describe adequately or to explain in believable terms.

In short, if teachers really care about students, they must be prepared to use any necessary and appropriate means to help them eliminate their inappropriate behavior. Students will sense their determination and quickly conclude that they have no choice but to comply with teachers' expectations. Following through on promised punishments cannot be overemphasized in the proper application of Assertive Discipline principles.

STEP 4: IMPLEMENTING A SYSTEM OF POSITIVE CONSEQUENCES

What do teachers ordinarily do when their students act appropriately? Unfortunately, many teachers do nothing. The good behavior of students is frequently ignored while attention is given primarily to unacceptable behavior. Some teachers claim to spend so much time dealing with bad behavior that they have little time to devote to reinforcing good behavior. It is essential, however, for teachers to respond not only to children's bad behavior but also to their good behavior. Responding to good behavior as well as bad clearly establishes the types of behavior teachers will or will not accept. Children need to be provided with positive consequences so that they are more likely to repeat their good behavior. If only punishment is given as a consequence of students' behavior, the classroom will take on an oppressive feeling and tension will be created between teachers and their students. Praise and other kinds of rewards, on the other hand, will increase the positive regard students have for their teachers.

Canter proposes a less systematic reinforcement program than is recommended in the Behavior Modification approach to discipline. He does not include such tactics as token economies, in which students are told in advance of the specific positive behaviors and their accompanying rewards. Instead, in his system "catching children being good" is emphasized. He encourages teachers to respond to the good behavior of students (1) in a way with which they are comfortable, (2) with rewards children want and enjoy, (3) immediately after children behave appropriately, (4) as often as possible, and (5) after some advance planning.

Canter suggests that the following positive consequences be used to reward acceptable behavior by students:

1. *Personal attention by the teacher.*   Personal attention can involve not only praise but also spending time with students. Students may be invited to work with teachers on special projects or just stay after school to help. Perhaps, on occasion, small groups of students may accompany their teacher to get treats at a local fast food restaurant.

2. *Positive notes or telephone calls to parents.*   It is a refreshing experience for most parents, who hear reports from school only when their children are misbehaving, to receive good news. Teachers need to create methods to recognize all their students in positive ways. One teacher, who volunteers to teach all the difficult students in his school, makes a practice of calling the parents of his most difficult students without warning and giving them a variation of the following message: "This is Mr. Wong, Roberta's science teacher. Roberta has really been doing well in my class. In fact, she did something really wonderful today." The teacher then hangs up the phone. The call, of course, leaves the parents completely surprised. They no doubt have never received such a call. When the children arrive home, they are unable to explain the teacher's call because there has been no prior indication, either of misbehavior or of noteworthy accomplishments. By the time these students arrive in class the next day, they are completely baffled and much more subdued.

3. *Awards.*   Special awards for good behavior and academic performance can also have a positive influence on students. Plaques, trophies, certificates, and other awards may be given for excellence in whatever attributes you wish to encourage. These awards can be of your own design or copied from fellow teachers. Awards have a high degree of motivation for some students.

4. *Special privileges.*   Children can be rewarded for good behavior with attractive activities such as assisting the teacher, running errands, calling the roll, being the lab assistant, playing games, having an extra physical education period, being first in line, spending time in the reading corner, using the tape recorder, using the microscope, helping to correct papers, doing a special project, tutoring younger children, playing with the building blocks, spending a class period talking with friends, or using the word processor.

5. *Material rewards.*   There are many tangible objects and edibles that can be used as rewards: gift certificates, toys, marbles, books, dolls, models, coloring books, pencils, crayons, comic books, stickers, badges, ribbons, raisins, cookies, nuts, ice cream, and hamburgers.

6. *Home rewards.*   Teachers may collaborate with parents to provide a reward system at home. Students who complete their work may be given extra time to watch television or play video games. Other home rewards may include parties, movies, eating out, favorite home meals, ice cream treats, and even such things as radios, tape players, or use of the family car.

7. *Group rewards.*   Canter also advocates rewards for the whole class. One mechanism for rewarding the class is to drop marbles into a jar when the entire class works hard and remains on-task during the period. The benefit of using marbles is that they are easily noticed. Students are able to hear the marbles drop into the jar while they work, which encourages them to continue. Once the jar is filled, the class may have a party or some other special activity.

Canter emphasizes that positive rewards should not be used to replace limits and punishment. A balance is needed, he claims. Rewards should be used when possible, but there are times when it is necessary to punish students for misbehavior.

Preventing Discipline Problems

Assertive Discipline is designed primarily as a reactive method of discipline with a less well-defined preventive component. It is a preventive method only insofar as students try to achieve rewards or avoid punishments. Teachers using this approach generally observe whether students' behavior is good or bad and then supply rewards or punishments as appropriate. There is no assumption that misbehavior will be prevented if children become more responsible and self-governed. Proper discipline is achieved when teachers are assertive and control students in their classrooms. Force must be employed to get children to behave properly.

The establishment of firm rules gives Assertive Discipline a somewhat preventive orientation. When children know the rules and the associated punishments, these punishments act as deterrents. If the punishments are visible enough and applied consistently, many students will try to avoid them. However, some children will go to great lengths to avoid control. They may, for example, do things for which they know that they will be punished. Some even feel rewarded when they are punished because of the attention punishment brings. Canter believes that if a child finds a particular punishment rewarding, more severe punishments should be applied. However, with the increase in severity of punishment, negative feelings will also increase and it may be hard for children in these circumstances to feel comfortable in class again. They may not misbehave, but they may decide to drop out mentally.

Schoolwide Discipline

Assertive Discipline can be organized on a schoolwide basis. The first step is to create rules. These rules usually define unacceptable behavior on the school grounds, in the hallways, in the lunchroom, and even off the school grounds when children are traveling to and from school. Students may be permitted to play or congregate only in designated areas. Playground rules usually involve safety and courtesy. In the hallways, students ordinarily have to refrain from running, shoving, and throwing objects. Lunchroom rules usually govern queuing up, disposing of unused food, returning trays and utensils, and cleaning up, and they remind children to follow directions and not to throw food.

Punishment for violating schoolwide rules is similar to that implemented in individual classrooms. Children are given a slip for each rule violation. On the playground, for example, the following punishments might be applied: The first slip means the loss of playground privileges for three days. A student who receives a second pink slip loses playground privileges for a week and must help clean up the playground as well; the student's parents may also have to sign the slip. After a third slip is given, the student's parents are called in for a conference with the student and the principal. A fourth slip earns the student automatic expulsion.

Rule infractions in the lunchroom might be punished first with a warning. After being caught throwing food once, students might be given a slip that would have to be signed by parents and returned. The punishment for a second offense might be the loss of lunchroom privileges for a week, and a signature from the parents would again be required. A third slip might bring the loss of lunchroom privileges for two weeks and a conference between the student, parents, and the principal. If a student received a fourth slip, suspension from the lunchroom might be permanent.

The breaking of attendance rules, such as unexcused absences and tardy arrivals, can be handled in a similar manner. Students would ordinarily be detained after school for tardiness. Unexcused absences would receive more severe punishments. Punishments would become increasingly severe if students continued to violate attendance rules, and parents and school officials might be involved in cases of habitual infraction.

More serious rule violations may incur harsher punishment. Canter and Canter (1981) suggest three criteria for determining the seriousness of an offense:

1. A student willfully inflicts physical harm on another student.

2. A student willfully destroys property.

3. A student blatantly refuses to follow instructions.

Strengths and Weaknesses of Assertive Discipline

STRENGTHS

1. It is simple to use.

2. The personal desires of the teacher can be enforced.

3. It involves parents and administrators in the discipline process.

WEAKNESSES

1. Punishment may produce undesirable side effects.

2. The practice of warning students by putting their names on the board may entice some students to misbehave who otherwise would not.

3. Students may band together to give the teacher trouble.

4. Students angered by warnings and sanctions may go further in their rebellion than they ordinarily would.

5. Students may be embarrassed by having their names on the board.

6. This approach fails to promote self-direction in students.

7. It fails to deal with the underlying causes of discipline problems, such as emotional illness, divorce, poverty, racism, and so forth.

8. It advocates suspensions for extreme misbehavior when far too many children are out on suspension already. Suspensions are generally ineffective and often have negative long-range consequences. It would be better to use the services of Intervention Assistance Teams to help teachers deal with extreme discipline problems and thereby keep these children in school.

9. It condones meaningless writing as a punishment. Many educators feel that making students copy out sentences is an absurd action for teachers to take.

10. It advocates sending children to a different classroom as punishment, claiming that children will not find this relocation embarrassing. Some children would be embarrassed, whereas others might be reinforced by this action.

11. Although Canter recommends using positive reinforcement while emphasizing punishment, in actual practice positive reinforcement is ordinarily excluded.

12. Canter recommends strictly enforced rules in the cafeteria. Children frequently go to fast food restaurants for lunch without supervision and cause no problems. Perhaps schools could learn something from this fact.

SUMMARY

Assertive Discipline is a system in which punishment is consistently meted out for rule infractions. Rules are determined by the teacher or other school personnel and given to students to be obeyed. The severity of punishments is increased when students persist in misbehaving. When students continue to misbehave, teachers are able to enlist the help of parents and the principal. Conferences with the principal or parents are held in a effort to force unruly students to change their behavior. In addition to rules and punishments, teachers should use a program of rewards to encourage students to behave properly in school. The best discipline program is one in which both rewards and punishments are given in proper balance.

CENTRAL IDEAS

1. Canter believes that teachers have the right to
   a. establish classroom rules,
   b. insist that students follow rules, and
   c. receive help from parents and school administrators in disciplining their students.

2. Being assertive is the key to discipline. Teachers must create and enforce rules assertively to be successful in the classroom.

3. Assertive Discipline involves

   a. establishing rules,

   b. punishing students who violate rules, and

   c. rewarding students for good behavior.

4. What Canter calls consequences is the same as punishment in the view of other discipline theorists.

QUESTIONS AND ACTIVITIES

QUESTIONS TO CONSIDER

1. How is Canter's approach to discipline similar to and different from Behavior Modification? What do you believe the differences in the outcomes would be for each of these approaches?

2. What obstacles would you be likely to experience in implementing Assertive Discipline in the schools?

3. What do you believe are the strengths and weaknesses of Assertive Discipline?

CLASSROOM ACTIVITIES

1. Use role-playing to simulate the following classroom situations: The teacher applies the principles of Assertive Discipline in handling a student who

   a. refuses to be quiet in class and work on the assigned task.

   b. is habitually tardy.

   c. fights with other students.

   d. throws spit wads at other students.

2. Break the class into two groups and debate the relative merits of Assertive Discipline and Behavior Modification.

STUDENT APPLICATIONS

1. Think about the problems you may encounter in the school. Create a list of rules that you believe will be necessary to eliminate these problems. Prepare a list of punishments you would apply to deal with various infractions. Your list should allow for variations in punishment for increasingly serious violations.

2. Prepare a system of rewards you could use in your classroom. Include various categories such as edibles and special privileges.

3. Create a schoolwide discipline program for the type of school in which you plan to teach.

▼

REFERENCES

Canter, L. (1989). Assertive Discipline: More than names on the board and marbles in a jar. *Phi Delta Kappan, 71,* 57–61.

Canter, L., & Canter, M. (1976). *Assertive Discipline: A take-charge approach for today's educator.* Seal Beach, CA: Canter and Associates.

Canter, L., & Canter, M. (1981). *Assertive Discipline follow-up guidebook.* Los Angeles: Canter and Associates.

5

Logical Consequences: Rudolf Dreikurs

OBJECTIVES

This chapter is designed to help you
1. distinguish between different motives
2. use Dreikurs' discipline model to
   a. ascertain students' motives
   b. help students understand their motives
   c. help students exchange their mistaken goals for useful ones
   d. help students learn the consequences of their actions
3. understand how to deal with misbehavior designed to satisfy students' mistaken goals
4. apply Dreikurs' plan for preventing discipline problems

ASSUMPTIONS

1. Inappropriate behavior is motivated by a need to gain attention, exercise power, exact revenge, or display inadequacy.
2. If the motive for attention is satisfied, inappropriate behavior associated with other motives will not be manifested.
3. Inappropriate behavior can be terminated by helping students find legitimate ways to satisfy their needs.
4. Children can learn to understand their own motives and consequently eliminate misbehavior by having teachers help them explore *why* they behave as they do.
5. Students behave more appropriately in the classroom when they suffer the logical consequences of their behavior.
6. Presenting students with a choice between two alternative behaviors offers a sufficient basis on which they can learn to be responsible.

Introduction

Rudolf Dreikurs was a native of Vienna, Austria. After he received his degree in medicine from the University of Vienna, he became an associate of Alfred Adler, the famous psychiatrist. Dreikurs emigrated to the United States in 1937 and became the director of the Alfred Adler Institute in Chicago. Although his primary interest was child and family counseling, he became interested in classroom discipline and with various colleagues wrote several books on the subject. He died in 1972 at the age of 75.

▼ Max is a second-grader who for a couple of weeks was constantly out of his seat, leaning on his desk, and doing his work from a half-standing position. His teacher finally asked him whether he preferred to stand or sit while doing his work. Max said that he would prefer to stand. The teacher explained to him that he would no longer need a seat and that his chair could be used somewhere else in the school. Max's chair was immediately removed, and he had to stand up for the rest of the day. The following day, at the beginning of the period, Max was asked whether he preferred to stand or sit for the day. He said that he preferred to sit. His chair was replaced. Max no longer tried to do his schoolwork from a half-standing position.

▼ One day a group of junior high school students seemed particularly restless. Several students were talking rather belligerently and interrupted the teacher's lesson repeatedly. Finally, the exasperated teacher informed the students that she would be in the library reading and that when they were ready to have her teach, they could come get her. The teacher was fearful as she started reading her book, but in a few minutes two serious-faced youngsters came in and said, "We're ready now—if you will come and teach us." After this incident, whenever the class became unruly and the teacher appeared annoyed, someone would say, "Be careful, or we'll lose our teacher again."

These two examples illustrate the application of the Logical Consequences model and how children may be expected to respond. A key tenet of Logical Consequences is that children should be given a choice rather than forced to behave as directed. Dreikurs believed that although some degree of force could be applied a generation or two ago, present social conditions necessitate the use of more democratic procedures. In the past, large groups of people—poor people, women, people of color, laborers— could not openly rebel against authoritarian domination. The same, of course, was true of children. Although they may occasionally have defied their parents or teachers, they could be satisfactorily controlled if sufficient force was applied. Most rebellion could be adequately suppressed. In this day and age, however, people are far less likely to submit to the control of others. They consider themselves to be of value and worthy of respect and thus refuse to permit others to deprive them of liberty and dignity.

In addition to changes in the social scene, more enlightened views of personality development have emerged, giving rise to new ways of interpreting human experience and dealing with human beings more productively. Believing that behavior is driven by an individual's purposes is one critical aspect of these new assumptions about human personality and behavior (Dreikurs, 1960). Even behavior that appears destructive is purposeful. Each behavior has the goal of self-determination. We do not simply react to forces that confront us from the outside world. Our behavior is the result of our own biased interpretations of the world. We act not according to the reality that surrounds us but rather according to our own subjective appraisal of it. For example, when a teacher selects one child to be a classroom leader, other children may interpret this selection as a personal rejection.

Unfortunately, when situations are open to personal interpretation, all of us routinely make unavoidable mistakes in perception. When we choose how to behave, we almost never have all the facts we need to make adequate choices. Our choices, therefore, are very subjective; they lack the validity more unbiased information would provide. Few humans make a habit of investigating the conditions present in particular situations and analyzing the assumptions they make about them. Nevertheless, we tend to act on these assumptions and conditions as if they were true. Of course, as we mature, we are more able to evaluate possible consequences in advance and choose our course of action in a more knowledgeable way.

Human beings all have a need to belong and be accepted. The combination of our human need for acceptance and our biased human perceptions sometimes helps to create distortions in our relationships with others. Children, for example, may not realize that acceptance by others depends on an individual's contributing to the welfare of the group; instead, they may strike out against the very people who could best satisfy their needs. When children's misguided perceptions lead them to abuse others, they commonly feel the acute rejection such actions engender. When they sense rejection, they begin to withdraw and experience even greater deprivation.

Dreikurs believes that the disposition to view the world as unaccepting is in part related to the order of one's birth (Dreikurs & Grey, 1968). The only child is the sole object of parental attention. With the arrival of another sibling, however, the older child is always dethroned. Older children then attempt to regain lost status. They may or may not feel successful in this attempt. Older children are prone to maladjustment.

Second children are always in a position of having older, more capable rivals to overtake. If they are successful, or if they find a different but constructive direction, they usually make satisfactory adjustments. If these children gain the recognition they want, they may develop more daring and flexible personalities. However, if they fail to achieve the status they desire, they may turn to destructiveness as a way to gain recognition. Often second children are very competitive.

When a third sibling arrives, second children may feel squeezed out. They often find that their older siblings have assumed a position of greater responsibility and their younger ones play the role of the baby. Second children may not have the rights of older children nor the privileges of younger ones. They may then interpret life as unfair and feel that there is no place for them.

Youngest children, although they are often babied and spoiled, appear to have a somewhat easier time than the others. For one thing, they are never displaced. They remain the baby for the rest of their lives—even if they outdo their siblings—and consequently get a disproportionate amount of attention from parents. It is common for youngest children to get attention not only from parents but from older siblings as well. Older brothers and sisters serve as "substitute parents" and often must perform parenting duties assigned to them.

In large families, the effects of birth order also extend to groups of siblings. There may be a group of oldest children, a group of middle children, and a group of youngest children. Within these groups, there may be an oldest child, a middle child, and a youngest child. Knowing a student's place in the birth order helps teachers better understand the basis for development of the student's personality and lifestyle.

Motives for Behavior

Attaining recognition as a worthy, able individual is central to personality development. Dreikurs accepts the basic idea of Alfred Adler that all behavior—including misbehavior—is orderly and purposeful and directed toward achieving social recognition (Dreikurs, 1968). Unfortunately, our culture does not furnish sufficient means for children to achieve this recognition. In many children, the desire for attention goes unfulfilled. When children solicit recognition without success, they usually misbehave to gain it. All misbehavior is the result of a child's mistaken assumption about how to find a place and gain status. Parents and teachers need to be aware of what children do to be recognized and appreciated so that they can more fully accommodate them. They must also learn to avoid falling for the unconscious schemes children use to achieve their mistaken goals. Dreikurs has identified four such goals and the schemes used to achieve them:

1. gaining attention
2. exercising power
3. exacting revenge
4. displaying inadequacy

These motives have a hierarchial relationship to one another. Children first try to achieve recognition and status through strategies designed to gain them attention. If these strategies do not work, the children employ power. Power may be followed by revenge. Finally, children use inadequacy as an excuse when earlier strategies have proven unsuccessful.

GAINING ATTENTION

Attention is by far the most common goal for most young children. Children who seek excessive attention are often a nuisance in class. They distract their teachers by showing off, being disruptive, being lazy, asking special favors, needing extra help on assignments, asking irrelevant questions, throwing things around the room, crying, refusing to work unless the teacher is right there, or being overly eager to please. They seem to function appropriately only as long as they have their teachers' approval. Teachers often respond to these children by giving them too much attention—reminding them often, coaxing them, showing pity for them, or feeling annoyed at them.

Giving attention to attention-seeking children does not necessarily improve their behavior. When attention is given in response to children's misbehavior, the misbehavior increases. Although the search for attention is usually manifested in the form of misbehavior, even the cooperative behavior of very young children may stem from a desire for special attention. Often these children try to do better than others, and they are very sensitive to criticism and failure. As with other misguided children, these youngsters must be helped to realize that they do not need constant testimonials to affirm their worth. They also need to learn that greater satisfaction comes from cooperating in groups than from provoking group members to get attention.

Four different attention-seeking behavior patterns have been identified: active-constructive, passive-constructive, active-destructive, and passive-destructive (Dreikurs, Grunwald, & Pepper, 1982).

Active-Constructive Behavior.   Active-constructive children are very cooperative with adults and conform readily to their expectations. These children are highly success-oriented but usually have poor relationships with children their own age. They are very industrious and have an exaggerated conscientiousness. They tend to be perfectionists and are often spurred on by parents who are themselves overambitious and perfectionistic. Active-constructive children are very competitive and try at all costs to maintain their superiority over others; in doing so, they accept the role of the model child or the teacher's pet. Their goal is to receive praise and recognition, and they sometimes tattle on others who fall short of their high standards. The following example illustrates active-constructive behavior in an elementary school child:

> ▼   Jane looked up from her drawing assignment just long enough to observe her classmates. It required only a glance to see that they were far behind and that their drawings were of much poorer quality than her own. Smugly she busied herself again, humming as she worked. In a few minutes she raised her hand. "Look, Mr. Lowe," she said to her teacher, "I'm all done. Is there something else I can do?"
>
> Mr. Lowe replied, "Jane, you always finish your work so quickly. You have done an excellent job, as usual. Class, look at Jane's picture. Don't you like the way she has blended her colors?"

Passive-Constructive Behavior.   Passive-constructive children try to achieve their goals by charming others. In this way they manipulate adults into serving them, often by putting on a façade of helplessness. These children are never involved in destructive, disruptive behavior. To be so occupied would only diminish their power. They give an appearance of being interested in others, but in reality they are very self-centered. They are the vain, cute, flattering children who are always clinging to those upon whom they depend. The story of ten-year-old Robby illustrates this behavior:

> ▼   Robby entered the classroom wearing brand-new slacks and a sports jacket. "My, Robby," Mr. Wallace remarked delightedly, "what a sharp-looking outfit!" Robby beamed and took his seat, looking pleased. "Look at Robby's new clothes," continued Mr. Wallace. "Don't they go well together? Robby is always dressed so neatly. We could all use him as an example."

Active-Destructive Behavior.   Children who are impertinent, defiant, clownish, or bullying are classified as active-destructive. These children may be confused with those who seek primarily power or revenge. Power-oriented children want more than momentary attention; they want their own way all the time and keep pestering others until they get it. Active-destructive children, however, will stop provoking others when they receive the attention they desire. For example:

▼ "I won't do this dumb assignment," yelled Rose as she threw down her pencil in anger. Ms. Phippen looked at her momentarily and immediately turned her attention to the papers on her desk. "Ms. Phippen, you can take this assignment and choke on it for all I care." Ms. Phippen looked up again, smiled, and then returned to her work. Rose sat grumbling to herself for a while and started on the assignment.

Passive-Destructive Behavior.   Passive-destructive children are characterized as "lazy." Through their lack of positive action, these children force others to be overly concerned with them and to help them. They claim that what they are asked to do is too hard. Often they claim not to understand what is expected. Their behavior patterns include bashfulness, dependency, untidiness, lack of concentration, and self-indulgence. The story of Dwayne provides an illustration:

▼ Dwayne sat looking out the window as his classmates busied themselves with their math assignment. Ms. Clegg watched him for a moment and then suggested that he start his work.
"I can't do these problems," whined Dwayne.
"You're going to have to start them sometime," replied Ms. Clegg.
"I just need a little help to get me started," implored Dwayne.
Ms. Clegg went to Dwayne's desk and began helping him with his problems. With each problem, Dwayne claimed to have difficulty understanding. By the end of the period, Ms. Clegg had helped Dwayne finish all his work.

EXERCISING POWER

When children fail to gain all the attention they seek, they often engage in a power struggle with parents and teachers. Teachers should avoid putting pressure on these children in an attempt to make them behave properly because such pressure usually leads to a power contest. As teachers apply pressure, they are likely only to increase the frustration of these children, which in turn provokes even more irrational, power-seeking behavior in the children. Teachers almost never win in these power contests. Children win because society expects adults to behave in a responsible, moral way. The same behavior is not expected of children. They can argue, cry, contradict, throw temper tantrums, lie, and be stubborn and disobedient. Adults are expected to be composed, trusting, loving, honest, and helpful. These expectations for adults are often exploited by power-seeking children for their own purposes, as the following example illustrates:

▼ Ching sat in the back of the room talking with friends as his fifth grade teacher, Ms. Finch, tried to explain the meaning of the Bill of Rights to the rest of the class. She stopped a number of times in her lesson to remind Ching to be quiet, but after a minute or two he would continue talking. Eventually Ms. Finch became angry and demanded that Ching leave the room and stand out in the hall. He told her that he would not go. Ms. Finch then went to Ching's seat and demanded that he leave immediately. He looked back at her defiantly. She tried to pull him from his seat forcibly. He would not budge. Ms. Finch started screaming at Ching uncontrollably. Soon her voice cracked and her vision blurred with frustration. As she retreated from the room, visibly shaken, Ching sat with a look of contentment on his face.

Ms. Finch was handicapped by assuming that she had the responsibility to subdue defiant children. She felt an obligation to show misbehaving children who was boss and to make them follow orders. In addition, she became personally involved in the power struggle, and her fear of losing face and prestige as the teacher proved to be a stumbling block. She will continue to fail to resolve power conflicts as long as she fears humiliation. She must learn not to fight and not to give in. Instead, she must focus on the problem. She needs to realize that power-hungry children will always try to defeat those who try to control and suppress them. Unfortunately, their success in defeating adults who try to control them adds to their power. With the support of the whole class, they are able to wield considerable influence over teachers. This power can be reduced through discussions in which all class members are given an opportunity to comment about power-seeking behavior.

EXACTING REVENGE

When children's efforts at control are thwarted, they usually claim to have been dealt with unfairly. They believe that others have deliberately tried to hurt them, and they attempt to get even. Commonly they take out their revenge on anyone around them. They are convinced that nobody likes them and create proof of this dislike by provoking others to retaliate. These children lash out by tripping, hitting, kicking, or scratching others or by destroying their property. They may knock books and supplies on the floor or scribble on classmates' papers. They may also seek revenge against the teacher by marking the teacher's desk, ripping pages from books, insulting the teacher publicly, or deliberately breaking equipment. Revenge-seeking children are very difficult to help. Teachers must realize that they hurt others because they feel hurt. Causing them more pain will only provoke more revenge-seeking behavior. Instead, teachers must offer understanding and assistance. They need to ensure that other children do not retaliate when revengeful children behave improperly. In the following example, Mr. Bright plays into the hands of a revenge-seeking student:

▼ Carter was the only student absent in Mr. Bright's seventh grade music class that day. When Mr. Bright sat in the puddle of glue on his chair, he knew immediately who had put it there. He even caught a glimpse of Carter peering through an outside window in an effort to see what the teacher's reaction would be. Screaming at the top of his voice, Mr. Bright dashed to the window and threatened Carter with expulsion. He then stormed out of the room to report the incident to the principal.

DISPLAYING INADEQUACY

Children who fail to achieve a sense of self-worth through attention, power, or revenge often become so discouraged that they give up and seek to wrap themselves in a cloak of inadequacy. They are joined in this misguided quest by other children who at an early age conclude that they are not as capable as others and also give up. These children strive to be left alone and avoid the humiliation group participation inevitably brings. They attempt to retain what little self-esteem they have left by avoiding any kind of public display. They believe that others will leave them alone if they are believed to be inadequate. The purpose of this behavior in a student, like that of other behaviors, is to somehow affirm the student's significance. A display of inadequacy is a last-ditch effort to reach this ultimate goal of being accepted for what one is, even if one is inadequate.

Teaching Styles

The reaction of teachers to students' misguided goal-seeking behavior can be instrumental in either reducing or increasing the incidence of misbehavior in the classroom. Avoiding these discipline problems depends to some degree on teachers' personalities. Different teachers tend to react to their students in different ways, and their reactions produce different results. Dreikurs identifies three types of teachers: autocratic, permissive, and democratic (Charles, 1989).

AUTOCRATIC

Autocratic teachers force their will on their students. They take firm control and refuse to tolerate any deviation from the rules. They force rather than motivate students to work, and they punish those who refuse to conform. Autocratic teachers use no humor or warmth in their classes. Instead, they enforce their power and authority over their students. Students are not very receptive to the tactics of autocratic teachers. They usually react with hostility to the demands, commands, and reprimands of these teachers.

PERMISSIVE

Permissive teachers are also ineffective when working with students. They fail to realize how critical rules are in the classroom. In addition, they do not follow through on consequences. The need for students to develop self-discipline is unimportant to them. Instead, they allow their students to behave as they wish. The usual result is general chaos and a poor learning atmosphere. These teachers encourage the misguided goal-seeking of their students rather than help them to adopt a more responsible lifestyle.

DEMOCRATIC

In a democratic classroom, teachers provide firm guidance but do not promote rebellion. Students are allowed to participate in making decisions about what is studied as well as in formulating rules. Democratic teachers help students understand that making decisions is firmly tied to responsibility. Students are allowed freedom, but they are expected to assume responsibility for what they do. These teachers do not feel compelled to habitually correct the behavior of their students. Allowing students some leeway, they believe, is the best way to help them eventually learn to be self-governing. Democratic teachers have a way of establishing order and limits without usurping their students' right to autonomy. They are firm and yet kind, and they involve students in cooperative learning experiences. Children in their classrooms are free to explore, discover, and choose their own way as they increasingly assume personal responsibility. Children in a democratic classroom develop a sense of belonging to and having a stake in the class.

Helping Students Correct Their Misbehavior

The following steps, suggested by Dinkmeyer and Dinkmeyer (1976), are useful for helping students correct their misbehavior. Some of the steps can be applied to preventing discipline problems.

1. Teachers attempt to ascertain students' motives.
2. Students are helped to understand their motives.
3. Students are helped to exchange their mistaken goals for useful ones.
4. Students are encouraged to become committed to their new goal orientation.
5. Students are taught to apply logical consequences.
6. Group discussions regarding class rules and problems are held.

UNDERSTANDING STUDENTS' MISTAKEN GOALS

Before teachers can help children alter their mistaken goals and improve their behavior, it is imperative that they understand children's behavior from a psychological point of view. That is, teachers need to understand the private logic of their misbehaving students (Dreikurs, Grunwald, & Pepper, 1982). Private logic consists of what a person really believes and intends. Included are a person's long-range and short-range goals and the reasons and rationalizations created to justify related behavior. Individuals begin in childhood to explain to themselves, with varying degrees of insight, the appropriateness of their behavior. Even maladaptive behavior can thus be judged acceptable if it can be rationalized.

Children have limited conscious understanding of their goals or motives. However, when the purpose of their behavior is explained to them, they recognize its connection to their goals. Younger children will either willingly admit that they misbehave for the reasons suggested or betray themselves by exhibiting an obvious recognition reflex: a smile, an embarrassed laugh, or a twinkle in the eye. Older children are too sophisticated to admit the motives behind their contrary behavior. They recognize the fact that society looks upon such behavior as childish and therefore resist disclosing their motives. They put on deadpan expressions in an effort to hide their recognition, but they give themselves away with their body language. Their lips may twitch or their eyes may blink or bat more frequently; they may adjust their seating position, swing a leg, tap the desk with their fingers, or shuffle their feet.

To get children either to reveal their goals or to expose themselves through a recognition reflex, Dreikurs, Grunwald, and Pepper (1982) recommend that you ask the following questions:

1. "Do you know why you _____?" (Even if a child does not know the reason for the misbehavior, this question is raised in preparation for the next step.)

2. "I would like to tell you what I think." (Ask one or more of the following questions from the group that is related to the mistaken goal.)

Gaining Attention:
"Could it be that you want me to notice you more?"
"Could it be that you want me to do something special for you?"
"Could it be that you want to be special to the group?"

Exercising Power:
"Could it be that you want to be the boss?"
"Could it be that you want to show me that I can't stop you?"
"Could it be that you insist on doing what you want to do?"

Exacting Revenge:
"Could it be that you want to punish me?"
"Could it be that you want to get even with me?"
"Could it be that you want to show me how much you hated what I did?"

Displaying Inadequacy:
"Could it be that you want to be left alone because you believe that you can't do anything?"
"Could it be that you want to be left alone because you can't be on top?"
"Could it be that you want to be left alone because you want me to stop asking you to do something?"

One way of reaching a child who is particularly resistant to your questions is to use the "hidden reason" technique. This technique is applied when a child says or does something out of the ordinary. You try to guess what is on the child's mind. If a child answers "no" to your initial question, ask a follow-up question. Continue asking follow-up questions until the answer is "maybe" or "perhaps." This response will lead you to a correct guess. The following example shows the use of this technique:

Darryl has on several occasions refused to do as the teacher directed. Now, in yet another episode, Darryl has been told to start an assignment and has again refused to do it in class. But this time the teacher decides to look more closely into Darryl's behavior.

Teacher	Darryl, could it be that you want to make me feel guilty and sorry for something I did to you?
Darryl	Well, not exactly.
Teacher	Could it be that you want to show me how much smarter you are than I am?
Darryl	No.

Recognizing that Darryl appeared to be very popular with most of the other students in the class, the teacher decided to explore the possibility that Darryl's behavior reflected a desire to be the group leader.

Teacher	Darryl, do you have a lot of close friends in the class?
Darryl	Yes, I do.
Teacher	Do your friends try to be like you and do what you do?
Darryl	Yeah, sometimes.
Teacher	Could it be that you want me to give you control over what you and your friends do in class so that you can have control over them?
Darryl	Yeah, I guess that's right.

There are two additional methods teachers can use to discern their students' motives (Charles, 1989). The first method requires teachers to analyze how they feel when a student responds.

- If they feel *annoyed*, the student is probably seeking attention.
- If they feel *threatened*, power-seeking behavior is being expressed.
- When teachers feel *hurt*, the student probably wants revenge.
- A feeling of being *powerless* is an indication that the student is displaying inadequacy.

A second way teachers have of determining a student's motives is to observe the reactions of the student.

If the student:	*the student's goal is to:*
stops the behavior and then repeats it	gain attention.
confronts or ignores authority	exercise power.
becomes devious, violent, or hostile	exact revenge.
refuses to participate or cooperate	display inadequacy.

Determining a child's motives can be difficult and complex. However, if teachers use the recommended techniques, they will get a better idea of the nature of these mistaken goals. These mistaken goals must be revealed to children before teachers can successfully help them pursue more worthwhile goals.

HELPING STUDENTS CHANGE THEIR MISTAKEN GOALS

Once teachers understand children's mistaken goals, they can take more valid and decisive action. Until they know these motives they are more likely to do more harm than good. In fact, they may unwittingly reinforce bad behavior. Children's behavior can then become painful and intolerable. Dreikurs believes that it is essential to identify the mistaken goal correctly. Otherwise, the behaviors encouraged to satisfy an assumed motive will not be appropriate to the situation.

Dealing With Attention-Seeking Behavior.   Attention-seeking children seem unable to tolerate being ignored. They prefer the pain of humiliation or other forms of punishment to receiving no attention. If they fail to receive the attention they desire, they do things that cannot be ignored. When a small disturbance elicits no response, more provocative behavior can be expected. Teachers ordinarily pay attention to these behaviors by nagging or scolding the misbehaving students. However, they should avoid falling into the trap of reinforcing bad conduct. When students behave unacceptably, teachers must ignore them. If their misbehavior is consistently ignored, children will not learn to associate attention with inappropriate behavior. Sometimes teachers complain that ignoring bad behavior "does not work." They commonly reach this conclusion when in fact they are giving children attention through the use of various nonverbal cues. For example, students' bad behavior may be reinforced when their teachers stand and glare at them with hands on hips and say impatiently, "All right, class, we'll have to wait until everyone is ready to continue with the lesson." Ignoring misbehavior is also more effective when accompanied by reinforcement of good behavior. Teachers need to be on the lookout for occasions when their students are listening attentively or working on their lessons productively. When they do, attention should be drawn to the fact. Teachers may give them a pat on the back or tell them how much they appreciate their cooperation.

Dealing With Power-Seeking Behavior.   It is commonly believed that teachers must react decisively and with force if students try to usurp their authority. It is indeed very difficult for teachers to restrain themselves when children make a play for power. Teachers are usually unprepared to avoid power struggles with students who threaten their authority and prestige. Consequently, struggles for power are waged in most classrooms. Teachers fight back to avoid letting students get the best of them. After all, they believe, teachers must avoid losing face at all costs. Unfortunately, fighting with students—even though teachers may win the contest—breeds more hostility.

One way to avoid power struggles is to make it necessary for errant students to confront the whole class in the quest for power. Most students will realize the futility of this confrontation. For example, if a student constantly disrupts your teaching, stop the work of the entire class and wait for the disruptive behavior to cease before continuing the lesson.

Teachers must also make sure that they do not give in to the demands of power-seeking children. To children who are trying to provoke them, teachers may say, "I am sure you prefer to be the leader, but the class has decided to rotate the leadership among all members during field projects" or "I can see that this situation is a difficult one for you. However, the class has agreed not to be disruptive during discussions and demonstrations." To children who are refusing to do their work and saying that the teacher cannot make them, the teacher may respond, "You're right. I can't make you. You will have to decide whether or not you want to participate with the rest of the class on your project."

Teachers need to remember that they must not fight with students. They can often avoid power struggles simply by refusing to play the role of authoritarian. Students cannot meet their mistaken goal of power if there is no one with whom to fight. Children rebel in direct proportion to the autocratic level of their teachers' behavior. Autocratic teachers complain about the unruliness of their students, and the misbehaving students protest the controlling rigidity of their teachers. Each party sees the other as being in the wrong; both are unable to see their own part in the difficulty. If a child initiates a confrontation with an autocratic teacher and the teacher takes the bait by responding negatively, the student will usually become more resistant and disruptive. This reaction is illustrated in the following example:

▼ During a chemistry lesson, Daphne was listening to her portable stereo and beating on her desk in time to the music. Ms. Edwards told her to stop, but she just looked back at her teacher and continued drumming on the desk. Ms. Edwards then scolded Daphne and threatened to take away her stereo if she did not stop. Daphne just smiled back at her and continued to keep time with the music. Infuriated, Ms. Edwards demanded that Daphne wipe the silly grin off her face. Daphne's smile broadened, and she started to move her whole body in rhythm with the music as she continued banging on her desk. Ms. Edwards stormed over to Daphne's desk and in a rage snatched the earphones from her head, knocking the stereo to the floor. For an instant, shock registered on Daphne's face, but it quickly faded. In its place came an enormous grin as she started again to thump her hands against the wooden surface of the desk. Ms. Edwards' face was red with anger as she demanded that Daphne come with her to the principal's office. Daphne just continued drumming. Ms. Edwards grabbed Daphne's arm and tried to pull her from her seat, but Daphne grabbed the side of the desk and held on. The smile on her face was accompanied by a defiant laugh.

This example shows a teacher becoming increasingly demanding and controlling and a student becoming more resistant and defiant. The grin displayed by the student was a sure way to infuriate the teacher. It was the student's way of publicly belittling the teacher. The student was able to remain calm and under control, but the teacher was out of control. If the whole class witnessed this episode, they would likely side with the student, not with the teacher. Certainly the student's peers would provide reinforcement for the daring confrontation with the teacher.

Classmates also sided with the student in the following episode. The example is given as an illustration of a student making a play for power, although another student exhibiting the same behavior could simply be pulling a prank.

▼ As the students in Mr. Larsen's biology class slowly filed in, their attention was drawn to Gordon, who was standing near the display table in the front of the room on which Mr. Larsen had placed his prized stuffed fox. From his pocket Gordon took a cigarette. He put it to his lips, lit it, and placed it in the fox's mouth. Hurrying along, he took his place near the front of the room and pretended to read his book. Smoke from the cigarette curled up toward the ceiling as Mr. Larsen strode into the room. His attention was immediately drawn to the ludicrous sight of the smoking fox. Complete surprise registered on his face, and then rage as he demanded that the culprit who put the cigarette in the fox's mouth come forward and stand in front of him. Nobody moved. The entire class was immobilized with fright. Then an audible snickering was heard from the front of the class. Mr. Larsen demanded to know who thought a smoking fox was so funny. Gordon raised his hand. Mr. Larsen went straight to where Gordon sat, grabbed him by the arm, and spirited him out the classroom door. A few minutes later a red-faced Mr. Larsen appeared at the door and marched to the front of the room. He ordered the students to take out their texts and begin reading silently.

There was to be absolute quiet. It was so quiet for nearly five minutes that you could have heard a pin drop. Then Ruth, unable to contain herself any longer, giggled softly to herself. Miggs followed suit. Then Lois started in. Mr. Larsen looked up from his desk and glared at the class. Another snicker was heard from the back of the class. Mr. Larsen demanded to know who had snickered and promised to make an example of that student. No one responded. Then more laughing erupted. Mr. Larsen stood and moved toward the back of the room in an effort to detect the source of the noise. He had not gone two paces before Gordon appeared at the classroom door with a grin on his face. He defiantly walked to his seat, laughing loudly. The rest of the class joined his laughter and then began clapping. Mr. Larsen continued to move toward the back of the room and proceeded on out the door.

Both Mr. Larsen and Ms. Edwards were successfully drawn into a power contest with students. In each case, coercive control was increased in an effort to maintain order. However, both teachers failed. Instead, the students became more defiant. In the case of Mr. Larsen, the whole class turned against him. Had Mr. Larsen come into the room and burst into laughter when he first saw the smoking fox, Gordon's play for power would have been undermined, the class would have had a good laugh, and Mr. Larsen's reputation and status would have been preserved.

Sometimes students' desire for power can be redirected. They may be satisfied with taking a leadership role in the class instead of confronting their teachers. A child who seeks power by disrupting the class may, for example, be asked to be in charge of maintaining order during class activities. The student could be asked to report on which techniques helped in keeping order or to make recommendations for improving the atmosphere of the class.

Doing the unexpected is another way to deal with power-seeking students. When children misbehave, teachers usually have an immediate emotional reaction. Reactions ordinarily are predictable because most people tend to react in the same way in a given situation. Children commonly have ready-made responses to these standard reactions. Therefore, teachers can nip an impending power struggle in the bud by doing the exact opposite of what they feel like doing. Children are put off balance because the teacher's behavior is new and unanticipated.

Dealing With Revenge-Seeking Behavior.   The desire for revenge is often closely tied to the desire for power. It may sometimes be hard to differentiate between the two. Revenge is usually the motive in children who are convinced that they are right and can do whatever they please. They often try to hurt others and feel that those who try to stop them are their enemies. They feel the need to hurt others because they have been hurt themselves. Ordinarily their need for attention and acceptance has gone unfulfilled because others view them with contempt and refuse to associate closely with them, sometimes because they are different in some way or because they exhibit bizarre behavior in their attempts to gain the attention they so desperately desire. It is difficult to reason with these children. Convinced that they are hopelessly disliked by everyone, they distrust any effort to persuade them otherwise.

Children who pursue their desire for attention or power are sometimes unaware of the purpose behind their behavior. Those who feel hurt and disliked, however, are very much aware of their goals. They seem oblivious, though, to their own suspiciousness. They are also unaware of the hostility they provoke and the fact that their own behavior dictates how they are treated. They rarely accept the responsibility for the destructive relationships they have with teachers and classmates. It is always others who are wrong. These children are firmly convinced that they are right in what they believe and justified in retaliating against those who, they believe, are their enemies.

Helping revenge-seeking children is a very delicate matter. Teachers can enlist the help of other class members, but they should do so with care. Children often will side with teachers by shunning revengeful children. Unfortunately, teachers may be prone to accept such alliances because of their own sense of failure in dealing with these children. Instead, teachers need to encourage the class to be more positive. They could, for example, persuade more popular peers to take a special interest in outcast children. Such a program will take considerable effort, and teachers will have to give their helpers the support they need to stay with this task. Revenge-seeking children are likely, in the beginning, to be antagonistic in the face of friendliness and kindness. They will obviously retain a sense of distrust for a time. Even after trust seems to be developing, they may put everyone to the test by doing something outrageous. When they do, children whose help has been solicited should be encouraged to avoid rejecting their revengeful peers but at the same time not to accept their behavior. The following example illustrates this point:

> Tui disdainfully watched the other students successfully working on their experiments in the biology lab while at the same time feeling unsure of himself and the results he was obtaining on his own experiment. He was particularly incensed by the way certain students sought and obtained special help from Mr. Bingham. It wasn't fair that Mr. Bingham ignored the rest of the class when they asked for help and gave the teacher's pets all the help they wanted. A clever idea suddenly clicked in Tui's mind. He turned in his seat and looked toward the back of the room. A sinister grin spread across his face as he quietly slipped from his seat and made his way stealthily to a cage on the back counter. Throwing a quick glance in Mr. Bingham's direction, he noiselessly opened the cage and took out the huge bullfrog that was kept inside. He promptly put the enormous amphibian behind his back and walked unobtrusively toward a group of "*A* students" who were working together at a lab table. While they were looking down at their experiments, he set the frog on the table and quickly returned to his own seat and pretended to be immersed in his own experiment. The frog suddenly croaked and jumped right into the middle of the area where the group was working. To Tui, the pandemonium that ensued was beautiful to behold. All five let out a yell and jumped back from the table, knocking over stools and lab equipment and strewing papers everywhere. Three of them made such a mess that it took them nearly ten minutes to clean up after Mr. Bingham had captured the frog and returned it to the cage. The rest of the class was laughing uproariously, some doubled over with tears running down their cheeks. Mr. Bingham was seething and his face was bright red. As the students began to notice their teacher's rage, the room grew quiet. No one dared breathe. Mr. Bingham searched the room with penetrating eyes, looking for the guilty party. His gaze settled on Tui. He noted the satisfied look on Tui's face. "You," Mr. Bingham said with feigned control as he pointed at the door, "go to the principal's office immediately. I'll be following you."

This situation was obviously handled badly if Mr. Bingham sincerely wanted to help Tui overcome his vengefulness. Had Mr. Bingham quickly captured the frog, reassured the flustered students, and helped them to laugh at the situation, he would have not only taken the wind out of Tui's sails but also added to his credibility in the classroom. The momentary fright and embarrassment caused by the incident could not be ignored, of course, but revengeful behavior on the part of the teacher would not solve the problem either.

Dealing With Displays of Inadequacy.   If children have been sufficiently rebuffed in their efforts to gain attention, they may become so discouraged that they behave like blobs. When they do not achieve their goals of attention or power or revenge, they may just give up. These children wish to be left alone. They believe that their case is hopeless and want their teachers to believe it too. Many teachers do give up on these children.

Students who display inadequacy do so for one of the following reasons:

1. They are *overly ambitious.*   This is probably the most frequent cause of giving up. These children despair of not doing as well as they want to do. If they cannot be first, make the best grades, be the leader, be the star athlete, or the like, they refuse to put forth any effort. Children with debilitating overambition will not participate in an activity unless it provides them an opportunity to prove their superiority. These children must be helped to see how they defeat themselves. They must learn to continue trying even though others may outperform them.

2. They are *overcompetitive.*   Some children are convinced that they have no chance to do as well as others. They believe that they are not good enough to be successful, and comparisons with others usually serve only to confirm their belief. Unfortunately, parents and teachers sometimes try to motivate these children by making such comparisons: "When I had your sister in my English class, she was my best student." "Why don't you do as well on your tests as your brother?" These comparisons should be avoided for all children, but especially for those who are overcompetitive.

3. They are *oversensitive to pressure.*   Students who are oversensitive to pressure feel that they cannot do as well as others expect. They therefore refuse to live up to others' expectations. Two of the misfortunes of our present educational system are the emphasis on avoiding mistakes and the practice of trying to motivate children through criticism and competition. Teachers need to tell children that they are all right as they are and to remove pressure by being less critical. Children need to learn and grow in a less competitive environment. They must be given sufficient time to achieve at their own speed.

Teachers must learn never to give up on students who believe themselves to be inadequate. They must provide these students an abundance of support and encouragement. Encouragement is especially needed when students make mistakes. These students need to feel successful and accepted for what they are. Because of the competitive environment found in most schools, students who are more successful are likely to reject their less productive peers. One of the most important duties teachers can perform is to help other students accept those who feel inadequate.

Preventing Discipline Problems

It is obviously better to prevent discipline problems than to correct them after they occur. Unfortunately, many children have longstanding problems that need correction. These tenacious problems are often extremely difficult to solve. Misbehavior that has become a habit is very resistant to change. Children may be convinced that their way of behaving is the only one that can adequately satisfy their needs. Dreikurs suggests several procedures that can be used not only to deal with these problems but to prevent them as well.

ENCOURAGEMENT VERSUS PRAISE

Encouragement is a useful technique for preventing discipline problems because it corresponds so well to children's goals. Children seek approval, and encouragement provides a legitimate means of receiving it. Encouragement focuses on effort rather than achievement; it thus gives positive feedback to children who are trying hard but may be somewhat unsuccessful. Encouragement stimulates them to continue trying. When encouragement is properly given, students gain status and satisfaction more from learning than from relative achievements. Test scores, for instance, have less value than learning itself. Children who have been encouraged accept themselves as they are, even when they are less than perfect. Encouragement can also solidify their place in the group. They can feel that they are contributing members of the group and that the group accepts their efforts as valid. In this process, students become aware of their strengths without undue focus on their weaknesses. When children exhibit more realistic confidence in their abilities, they are less likely to cause discipline problems.

Praise needs to be differentiated from encouragement. Praise focuses on the level of accomplishment or achievement; encouragement highlights the value of learning. Praise is given for high achievement and is ordinarily reserved for those who are more successful according to some measure of performance. Praise fosters the idea that only test performance is worthy. Students who receive praise for their efforts do not work for self-satisfaction. Instead, they are governed by extrinsic rewards. Encouragement, on the other hand, stimulates cooperation rather than competition, effort and enjoyment rather than quality of performance, independence rather than dependence, and helpfulness rather than selfishness. The following examples show the difference between praise and encouragement:

Praise	*Encouragement*
Your art work is excellent.	You seem to really enjoy art.
You got the highest mark on your exam.	I can tell that you worked hard to prepare for your exam.

Teachers need to appreciate children who have diverse abilities, not just those who perform well on tests. Limiting what is acceptable or valued always restricts the number of students who feel encouraged to work for success in school. Teachers also must be careful not to add restrictions ("but"s or "however"s) when they offer compliments to their students. Avoid such compliments as "Your drawing is very elaborate, but you must remember to incorporate proper perspective."

LOGICAL CONSEQUENCES

Regardless of how encouraging teachers are, they are still likely to encounter misbehavior in students. While they are encouraging their students, teachers should be identifying logical consequences in advance and preparing to apply them as behavioral problems develop. Logical consequences need to be distinguished from natural consequences as well as from punishment. Natural consequences are those that occur without a teacher's intervention. For example, if children throw snowballs or rocks at one another, someone may get hit in the head and injured. Students who do not study for tests often get poor test scores. These consequences are not arranged; they happen naturally. Teachers do not need to threaten children with natural consequences. Children can discover them on their own.

Logical consequences are contrived and then applied as necessary to influence students' behavior (Dreikurs & Grey, 1968). They do not happen naturally, but they do have a reasonable connection to some action. For example, a student who breaks something may be expected to replace it.

Sometimes the use of logical consequences is confused with punishment. Punishment, however, does not have a logical connection to a particular behavior. Instead, it is arbitrarily administered and usually designed to be painful enough so that misbehaving students have no choice but to change their behavior. If students, for example, talk during lectures and discussions, the teacher may punish them by subtracting points from their grades. In reality, grades have little to do with talking during instruction. A logical consequence may be to have students leave class until they indicate that they will no longer talk during instruction. Students may be punished by being kicked out of class for a week for talking disruptively. This action is punitive because the length of time students are excluded is arbitrary. For such an action to be a logical consequence, students would have to be kept out of class just until they were able to make a plan to improve their behavior.

Punishment promotes revenge and causes students to feel that they have a right to retaliate (Dreikurs & Cassel, 1972). Students do not associate punishment with their own behavior but rather with the person providing it. Because children's main objective is to feel acceptable and accepted, they will not meekly endure punishment. They will feel humiliated and try to punish the teacher for how they feel. They believe that it is their right to do so. Employing logical consequences helps them understand that it is their unacceptable behavior that brings unpleasant results, not the arbitrariness of teachers.

To be effective, consequences have to be applied consistently. If a teacher applies them a few times and then discontinues their use, students will soon take advantage of the teacher's inconsistency. They will gamble that the teacher will be in a good mood or that they will have good luck. Applying consequences consistently in school helps students become acquainted with the reality of the society in which they live.

Logical consequences must be explained, understood, and agreed upon by students. Students more readily accept consequences they have helped determine. Teachers should avoid applying consequences that have not been agreed to by students. When consequences are administered at the time of misbehavior without prior discussion, they have an effect similar to that of punishment. Consequences promote good behavior. Punishment fails to teach correct behavior and often encourages more inappropriate behavior.

Dreikurs, Grunwald, and Pepper (1982) suggest the following examples of logical consequences:

1. If a student pushes someone on the stairway, the teacher may let the student decide whether to avoid pushing in the future or go back to the class and wait until everyone else has cleared the stairway before going down.
2. If a student hands in an incomplete or dirty paper, the teacher may read the paper only if the student submits a complete, clean copy.
3. If students write on the walls, they can either clean them or pay the janitor to clean them.
4. Students who mark their desks can be required to sand and refinish the desks or pay for having them refinished.
5. Students who fight during recess may be barred from recess until they provide the teacher with a plan outlining how they propose to avoid fighting.
6. If students disturb others, they may be isolated from the group until they agree to disturb the class no longer.
7. If students are late for class, they may be directed either to come on time or to wait at the door until they receive a signal that their late arrival will no longer disturb the class.

DISCUSSIONS IN THE CLASSROOM

Classroom discussions are helpful in preventing discipline problems. Group influence can have a positive impact on the behavior of almost all children. Group discussions, which are imperative in a democratic setting, have several purposes. First, they provide an excellent atmosphere in which students can better learn interpersonal skills and effective communication. Second, they can be used to create common goals and procedures so that class members know their roles and how to perform them; children learn to accept responsibility and understand the consequences they may expect. Third, students can learn more about themselves and others as they take part in discussions. This knowledge provides them with a basis for cooperating with one another and working successfully together.

Teachers must provide expert leadership in group discussions. They should make sure that students are free to express themselves in the group without feeling intimidated. More dominant students should not be allowed to monopolize. Everyone's rights must be respected (Dinkmeyer & Dreikurs, 1963). Teachers should promote active, voluntary participation. Teachers must avoid taking too dominant a role, although they do need to ensure that these discussions are productive, implementing a minimal amount of manipulation if necessary.

Group discussions can serve the class as a forum for determining class values and expectations as well as a means of enforcing them. If some students fail to follow group directives, the unacceptable behavior they exhibit can be brought up for group discussion. Bringing up the names of offending students should be avoided. Only the types of misbehavior need be discussed. The teacher must provide the necessary leadership to ensure that a group discussion does not degenerate into a free-for-all.

Group discussions should promote an inner freedom for both students and teachers. All must feel free to choose and take responsibility for their choices. The mutual respect that is thus generated will encourage the free exchange of ideas and a greater tolerance for one another. Proper classroom order can be expected as a result. Dreikurs believes that children should gradually develop more self-management skill. This development must take place in an atmosphere of social reality. Children must learn the rules we live by in society, become accustomed to them, and adopt them as their own. These same rules should be applied in the classroom. All students must accept responsibility for themselves and their behavior and learn to respect themselves and others. They should realize their strategic role in helping others in the group and develop a sense of group responsibility.

Strengths and Weaknesses of the Logical Consequences Model

STRENGTHS

1. It promotes a degree of autonomy for students.
2. It incorporates a preventive approach to discipline.
3. It helps students understand why they behave as they do.
4. It helps students learn correct behavior.
5. It promotes mutual respect between teachers and students.
6. It relies on logical consequences instead of arbitrary punishment and systematic reinforcement.
7. It helps teachers focus on causes for behavior before they take action.

WEAKNESSES

1. Teachers have trouble determining the actual motives of their students.
2. Students may not admit their real motives, either because they believe that their motives are unacceptable or because they do not know what they are.
3. Teachers may find it difficult to respond to students in a noncontrolling way.
4. Teachers may have a problem dealing with the complexity of engaging in a dialogue with their students.

SUMMARY

Democratic principles are central to Dreikurs' approach to discipline. Teachers who are democratic will be more successful in helping children become more responsibly self-governed. These principles can also be used more effectively to deal with students who have mistaken goals. Teachers' effectiveness can be improved when they realize that the behavior of all students is an outgrowth of a desire to be accepted on a social level. Misbehavior results when children pursue the mistaken goals of gaining attention, exercising power, exacting revenge, and displaying inadequacy. Children's disposition to seek these mistaken goals is often related to their family experiences as well as to their treatment in school.

A summary of Dreikurs' recommendations for good discipline can be found in his list of *don'ts* and *dos* (Dreikurs, Grunwald, & Pepper, 1982):

*A List of **Don'ts***

1. Do not be preoccupied with your own prestige and authority.
2. Refrain from nagging and scolding, which may reinforce misbehaving children's quest for attention.
3. Do not ask children to promise anything. They will use a promise to get out of an uncomfortable situation with no intention of fulfilling it.
4. Avoid giving rewards for good behavior. Doing so will only condition children to expect rewards.
5. Refrain from finding fault with children.
6. Do not hold your students and yourself to different standards.
7. Do not use threats.
8. Do not be vindictive.

*A List of **Dos***

1. Always try first to understand the purpose of children's misbehavior.
2. Give clear-cut directions for actions expected of children.
3. Focus on children's present, not their past, behavior.
4. When children misbehave in class, give them a choice either to remain where they are without disturbing others or to leave the room.
5. Build on the positive and avoid the negative.
6. Build trust between yourself and children.
7. Discuss children's behavior problems only when neither you nor they are emotionally charged.
8. Use logical consequences instead of punishment.
9. Treat children with consistency.
10. Use cooperative planning to establish goals and solutions to problems.

11. Let children assume increasingly greater responsibility for their own behavior and learning as they are able to do so.

12. Use the whole class to create and enforce rules.

13. Be kind but firm with children.

14. Show that you accept children but not their misbehavior.

15. Help children become more responsibly independent.

16. Make sure that students understand the limits.

CENTRAL IDEAS

1. According to Dreikurs, students misbehave because their needs are not met.

2. The needs to gain attention, exercise power, exact revenge, and display inadequacy form a hierarchy: If one need (attention, for example) is unmet, the next need in the hierarchy (power) becomes predominant.

3. To avoid having to deal with a variety of misbehavior, teachers should make sure that their students' need for attention and acceptance is met.

4. Discipline problems can be prevented through the use of class discussions and the application of logical consequences.

QUESTIONS AND ACTIVITIES

QUESTIONS TO CONSIDER

1. What evidence is there that the purpose of misbehavior is to achieve social acceptance?

2. What motives besides the ones Dreikurs accepts do you think explain misbehavior?

3. How does your own experience corroborate or contradict the conclusions Dreikurs reaches regarding the influence of birth order on behavior?

4. To what extent have social conditions changed sufficiently to require more democratic methods of working with children?

CLASSROOM ACTIVITIES

1. View the audio-visual materials associated with Logical Consequences that are listed in Appendix A.

2. Compare Canter's Assertive Discipline and Dreikurs' Logical Consequences.

3. Divide the class into groups of four or five members. One member of the group is given a list of behaviors and associated motives. This person describes each behavior to the other group members. They try to determine the motive behind the behavior by asking questions of the group member holding the list. For example:

Behavior	Motive
A student digs into the desk with a knife.	Revenge
A student fights with other students.	Attention
A student is late for class.	Power
A student cuts into the lunch line.	Attention
A student uses foul language in class.	Power
A student talks boisterously.	Attention

STUDENT APPLICATIONS

1. With two classmates, use role-playing to discover how a teacher can apply logical consequences to help a misbehaving student in the following situations. One person plays the role of the teacher; another plays the role of the student. The person playing the student should be told only what the misbehavior was. That person then decides on one of the mistaken motives without revealing it to the person playing the teacher. The third person is to observe and help the two other participants analyze the situation.

   a. Bill makes paper airplanes and flies them around the classroom.

   b. Shon trips other students as they walk up the aisle.

   c. Steve rips pages out of textbooks.

   d. Lynette spends time talking instead of working quietly at her desk.

2. With a group of classmates, use role-playing to simulate a class discussion in which learning goals as well as classroom rules are determined.

▼

REFERENCES

Charles, C. M. (1989). *Building classroom discipline: From models to practice* (3rd ed.). New York: Longman.

Dinkmeyer, D., & Dinkmeyer, D., Jr. (1976). Logical consequences: A key to the reduction of disciplinary problems. *Phi Delta Kappan, 57,* 664–666.

Dinkmeyer, D., & Dreikurs, R. (1963). *Encouraging children to learn.* New York: Hawthorne Books.

Dreikurs, R. (1960). *Fundamentals of Adlerian psychology.* Chicago: Alfred Adler Institute.

Dreikurs, R. (1968). *Psychology in the classroom: A manual for teachers* (2nd ed.). New York: Harper and Row.

Dreikurs, R., & Cassel, P. (1972). *Discipline without tears*. New York: Hawthorne Books.

Dreikurs, R., & Grey, L. (1968). *A new approach to discipline: Logical consequences*. New York: Hawthorne Books.

Dreikurs, R., Grunwald, B. B., & Pepper, F. C. (1982). *Maintaining sanity in the classroom: Classroom management techniques* (2nd ed.). New York: Harper and Row.

6

Transactional Analysis: Eric Berne and Thomas Harris

OBJECTIVES

This chapter is designed to help you

1. understand how human ego-states develop and how they influence behavior
2. consider the evidence that our entire life's experience is recorded in the brain in the form of sounds, sights, other sensations, and feelings
3. determine which ego-state students are in when they make various statements
4. know the four life positions and how each is achieved
5. analyze verbal transactions and determine whether the transactions are compatible
6. learn how to remain in the Adult ego-state in transactions with students
7. understand the games students play that create problems in the classroom and how to react to them

ASSUMPTIONS

1. Behavior is an outgrowth of information stored in the subconscious mind that has been learned by interacting with others.
2. Most of our experiences in life are recorded unaltered in our subconscious minds.
3. Behavior designed to control others is nearly automatic and comes from the Parent ego-state.
4. Exuberance and self-centeredness come from the Child ego-state.
5. Children can learn to be more responsible by learning how to let their Adult ego-state monitor both their Child and Parent and alter the automatic behaviors that would ordinarily occur.

Introduction

Eric Berne, a psychiatrist from California, is credited with originating Transactional Analysis, a method of dealing with behavioral disorders. In creating this new approach to psychiatry, Berne relied heavily on the research of Dr. Wilder Penfield. Penfield found that stimulating various parts of the brain with a mild electrical impulse evoked images of past life experiences in the minds of patients. He concluded that all our life experiences are faithfully recorded in the subconscious mind and later influence how we behave.

Thomas Harris, as Director of Education at DeWitt State Hospital in Auburn, California, spent ten years studying with Berne. *I'm OK—You're OK*, Harris' book about the principles of Transactional Analysis, spent more than a year on the *New York Times* bestseller list. The popularity of this book contributed to a widespread interest in Transactional Analysis, interest that led to its eventual use in the schools to manage students' behavior.

Where do behavior patterns come from? They are based on behaviors that have been observed and/or enacted during previous life experiences and faithfully recorded by the brain for future use. As children go through life, they accumulate experiences with other children as well as adults. Much of what they learn comes from interactions with parents and siblings. These interactions and the feelings associated with them are filed away in the brain for later use in similar situations.

Behavior and the Brain

This conception of the brain as an information storage system is supported by the work of neurosurgeon Wilder Penfield. During the course of brain surgery used to treat patients with focal epilepsy, Penfield conducted experiments in which he touched the temporal cortex of a patient's brain with a weak electric current transmitted through a galvanic probe (Penfield, 1952). The experiments were conducted under local anesthesia, and consequently the patients were fully conscious. Penfield found that by touching the brain with an electrode, he could produce what were clearly recollections of the patient's past. He concluded that all experiences of which we are consciously aware are "recorded" in detail in the brain and that they can be "played back" later with the clarity of the original recording. In Penfield's experiments, patients not only recalled various events but also experienced again the emotions and feelings that were associated with them. Penfield also concluded that each time he touched the brain with the electrode, a single recollection was evoked. Memories were not mixed nor generalizations created. Instead, a single memory was elicited. The following example, reported in Penfield's work and related by Harris (1967), illustrates the results of some of these experiments:

When the probe was placed in a specific location of the right temporal lobe of a patient, the individual reported that there was a piano playing somewhere. A second touch of the probe brought the response, "Someone's speaking to another." A name was mentioned. When the probe was touched to the brain a third time, the patient said, "Yes, *Oh Marie, Oh Marie!*—Someone is singing it." When the same area was stimulated a fourth time, the patient heard the same song and explained that it was the theme song of a certain radio program.

When a different place on the brain of a second patient was stimulated, the individual stated, "Something brings back a memory. I can see the Seven-Up Bottling Company . . . Harrison Bakery." When this patient was told that he was being stimulated but in fact was not, he reported no evoked memories.

In a third case, the superior surface of the right temporal lobe was stimulated within the fissure of Sylvius. The patient reported to be hearing a specific popular song being played as though by an orchestra. Repeated stimulation brought the same report. While the electrode was kept in place, the patient hummed along with the orchestra she was hearing.

Sometimes a single stimulation produced just an image. One patient, for example, saw a man walking a dog along a road near his home in the country. At other times the person reported just hearing a voice. On one occasion a patient whose brain was stimulated heard a voice she could not understand. When the probe was placed at approximately the same place again, she heard a voice distinctly calling, "Jimmie, Jimmie." Jimmie was the nickname of the young man she had recently married.

Penfield also concluded that the response of patients to the probe was involuntary. In one instance, a patient had a familiar experience appear in his consciousness on which he did not necessarily want to focus his attention. A song he had heard on a previous occasion went through his mind. He found himself becoming part of that occasion, which unfolded just as it had originally. He was experiencing a second time what he had experienced before. He had the sense of being both the actor and the audience, both subjectively experiencing the feelings he had experienced before and objectively watching himself re-experiencing them.

One of the most significant discoveries of Penfield was that feelings associated with past events are also faithfully stored in the brain, recorded in great detail. Apparently the events in our lives are inextricably connected with feelings. One cannot be elicited without the other. When an image or experience was evoked by the probe, the individual experienced anew the original feelings associated with the image or experience. Thus, a memory evoked by the probe is not like a photograph, phonograph record, or videotape. Instead, it is an exact reproduction of what the individual felt and understood as well as saw and heard.

To evoke an exact reproduction of previous experiences does not necessarily require one's brain to be probed. These experiences can also be stimulated by signals from the environment. For example, a forty-year-old woman was walking down the street one morning and, as she passed a music store, heard some music that created in her an overwhelming melancholy. She felt herself gripped by a feeling of sadness she could not understand. The intensity of it was almost unbearable. There was nothing in her conscious mind that could explain how she felt. Several days later she reported that she had continued to hum the tune over and over till suddenly, in a flash of recollection, she saw her mother sitting at the piano and heard her playing this song. The mother had died when the woman was just five years old, and the song had somehow been associated with her death. The woman now had the experience of reliving the same feelings she had at that time.

Good feelings can also be evoked. Most of us have had smells or sounds arouse pleasurable feelings that can be traced back to enjoyable childhood experiences. The smells associated with joyful trips to the old swimming hole during the heat of summer can bring back the same feelings one had as a youth during those special times. In people of a certain age, the smell of bread baking can often elicit feelings of love and contentment associated with coming home from school and eating their mother's fresh baked bread.

The work of Penfield is cited as evidence that all our experiences are permanently recorded in our brains, to be called forth as needed by stimuli in the environment. The responses stimulated by these recorded messages are not intentional. Instead, they appear automatically and are ordinarily carried through faithfully unless the person makes a conscious effort to modify them.

The Three Ego-States

An ego-state is "a consistent pattern of feeling and experience directly related to a corresponding consistent pattern of behavior" (Berne, 1966). An individual's ego-states are developed from life experiences and retained both consciously and unconsciously in the brain. Many behaviors appear as if from nowhere, without any conscious thought. Even so, they are well articulated and purposeful and appear to have been carefully formulated. Displaying these behavior patterns is somewhat like automatically turning on a tape machine: Information recorded long ago is simply played back. But words and feelings too are expressed as they were once learned, and they require little or no conscious effort to produce. According to the principles of Transactional Analysis, all people have three ego-states that form the basis of their behavior: the Parent, the Child, and the Adult.

THE PARENT

The Parent ego-state is a huge collection of recordings of unquestioned or imposed external events experienced by the person during the first five years of life. This recorded information includes the pronouncements made by real parents or parent substitutes. Everything these individuals are observed to do is also recorded in the Parent ego-state of the child.

Because these experiences are recorded during the early years of life, they are unedited. Young children have no way of knowing how to modify what they experience. Therefore, if parents are malicious or hostile toward their children or toward one another, their conduct is recorded as it occurred without the benefit of interpretation. Young children will also record the terror they feel as they observe the very people upon whom they depend for sustenance and love battle with one another or abuse them. There is no way for children to deal with extenuating circumstances. For example, abusive parents may have personal problems unrelated to their children; if the children understood these problems as an adult might, they could better interpret their parents' behavior. But young children have no such capacity.

The Parent ego-state is the repository of all the admonitions, rules, and laws issued by parents and other adults during the course of children's early life. In addition to spoken words, such things as tone of voice, facial expressions, and physical contact are also recorded. Included in this set of experiences are the many thousands of *nos* and *don'ts* with which children are ordinarily bombarded as they attempt to express their native curiosity and understand their world.

The Parent ego-state also contains the smiles, hugs, pride, and delight of parents, grandparents, teachers, and other important adults—and the contexts in which the approval was given. These positive experiences are important components of children's growing-up years. Their sense of well-being depends on receiving them in abundance.

As children grow, they make a mental record of the complicated, well-intentioned platitudes and precepts to which they are subjected—pronouncements of which they have only a vague understanding:

Remember to wear your coat when it's cold.

Don't go out at night alone.

Associate only with people of your own kind.

Never tell lies.

Pay your bills.

Clean up your plate.

Eat your dessert last.

Do unto others as you would have them do unto you.

Do unto others *before* they do unto you.

The idle mind is the devil's workshop.

You will be judged by the company you keep.

You have to dress the part.

You can never trust a cop.

Haste makes waste.

These admonitions can be judged by adults as good or bad when interpreted with a reasonable ethical standard. Children, however, record them as *truth*. After all, they come from their source of security, the people on whom they depend for survival. Once these bits of advice are recorded, they are available for immediate replay, and they exert a powerful influence all though a person's life. They determine whether our behavior will be permissive or coercive. We tend to internalize them rigidly and depend on them as patterns for dealing with other people in most situations. The internal Parent ego-state serves the same purpose as our physical parents served in protecting us as young children. It continues to issue warnings and admonitions to protect us from harm.

Sometimes messages received from parents are inconsistent. One parent or parent substitute may contradict another. When faced with such contradiction, children suppress the Parent so that it has less influence on their behavior. There may also be data stored in the Parent that are no longer valid but are heeded anyway. For example, a child was once told by her mother never to put her hat on a table nor her coat on a bed. She followed this admonition throughout her life and insisted that her own children follow the same practice. Finally, when her mother was very old, she asked why she was told never to put a hat on a table nor a coat on a bed. Because, her mother replied, some of the neighborhood children years ago were infested with lice (Harris, 1967).

THE CHILD

While the Parent is being recorded, the ego-state of Child is being recorded simultaneously. This recording consists of the responses children make to what they see and hear. Because children have little or no understanding of the meaning of language during their early years, most of their reactions are feelings. During this time, children are faced with numerous uncompromising demands with which they must comply, regardless of how they feel or what they want to do. To receive parents' approval, children must satisfy expectations. This conflict between the desires of children and the demands of parents creates a good deal of frustration for children. On the basis of these feelings, children often conclude that they are "not OK." Even children of "good" parents carry a burden of not being "OK." So it is not hard to imagine how much heavier an emotional load abused children have to bear.

Like the Parent, the ego-state of Child also strongly influences people's reactions as they engage in transactions (give-and-take verbal exchanges) with others. Many situations similar to those experienced in childhood have the power to arouse the same feelings. The original frustration, rejection, or abandonment can surface again as individuals relive earlier experiences. They may respond by becoming withdrawn. They may throw tantrums. They may lose control emotionally, letting anger dominate reason.

Fortunately, there is a more positive side to the Child ego-state. The Child also contains such positive traits as creativity and curiosity. The Child is filled with the happy first discoveries of life: the first taste of homemade ice cream, the first puppy, the way a cereal bowl bounces across the floor when thrown from a high chair, the feel of a kitten's fur against your face, the warm water in your first bath. The delightful feelings these experiences create are also recorded. These "OK" feelings may also be relived in day-to-day transactions. Unfortunately, in many of us the "not OK" feelings predominate. For this reason, Harris (1967) concludes that most of us have a "not OK" Child inside us.

THE ADULT

Until the age of about ten months, children are bound by their own ineptness. They respond mainly to external demands and stimulations. After this time, however, they are able to move around and more successfully manipulate their surroundings. Eventually they learn that they are able to do things that arise from their own awareness and original thought. When this realization occurs, the Adult ego-state starts to emerge. The Adult grows as children find out for themselves the difference between the "taught concepts" of the Parent and the "felt concepts" of the Child. The outgrowth of this process is the development of "thought concepts."

The Adult during these early years is fragile and subject to injury and distortion, which may occur when there are too many commands coming from the Parent or too many fears emanating from the Child. Without such interference, children would be able to tell the difference between life as it was taught and demonstrated to them, life as they felt it or wished it or fantasized it, and life as they figured it out for themselves. If it is not excessively distorted, the Adult can examine rules from the Parent to determine their trustworthiness and current applicability and then accept or reject them. The Adult can also examine the Child to ascertain whether feelings stored there are acceptable in present circumstances or are just responses to obsolete dictates of the Parent. This examination does not automatically erase the data stored in either the Parent or the Child ego-state. Instead, it provides a way to restrict their influence. For example, a young child may initially experience fear of snakes or anger at not being allowed to play with them. A later awareness that most snakes are not dangerous or that parental caution may have been warranted will not erase that fear or anger. However, in the Adult ego-state, the child can choose just to turn it off.

The day-to-day task of the Adult is to monitor both Parent and Child and ensure that the behavior each may promote is valid and useful under present conditions. It tests the rules and information of the Parent to determine whether they can be wisely used. It also determines when the feelings of the Child can be appropriately expressed.

▼ Betty Jane had left Ms. Tobler's cooking class every day that week without cleaning up her work station. She would pretend to be cleaning, and then when the bell rang she would dash out the door before Ms. Tobler could stop her. Ms. Tobler decided that she would make a point of standing by the door on Monday to intercept Betty Jane. When Monday's class ended, Betty Jane saw Ms. Tobler by the door and quickly cleaned up her area and left with the rest of the class. Ms. Tobler, who had been watching her, decided to let her go. On Tuesday, Ms. Tobler again stood by the door, and again Betty Jane cleaned up her area. Ms. Tobler decided that Betty Jane had changed her ways. However, on Wednesday, while Ms. Tobler busied herself answering the questions of other class members, Betty Jane again left a mess and slipped out of the room unobserved. Ms. Tobler made up her mind to somehow confront Betty Jane and so on the following day pretended not to be paying attention as the students began to leave at the end of the period. She watched Betty Jane out of the corner of her eye and could see that Betty Jane was also scrutinizing her. Ms. Tobler deliberately turned her back for a few moments and then walked toward the door. Betty Jane was on her way through the door when Ms. Tobler stopped her and brought her back to her work station. The area was covered with cookie crumbs and drips of batter from the day's baking lesson. Ms. Tobler asked, "Betty Jane, what do you need to do now to make sure that your work station is as it should be when you leave class?"

In dealing with Betty Jane, Ms. Tobler acted correctly in terms of Transactional Analysis theory. She responded primarily from the Adult ego-state, approaching the situation rationally and helping Betty Jane to think through the problem herself.

Had Ms. Tobler responded from her Parent ego-state, she might have scolded Betty Jane: "I'm sick and tired of your sneaking out of class without cleaning up your work station, Betty Jane. When are you going to learn to keep your area neat and tidy like the other students?" or "Look at the mess you have left here. You are the messiest student I have ever had in class."

Had Ms. Tobler responded from her Child ego-state, she would probably have complained petulantly: "Betty Jane, how come you always leave this mess for me to clean up?" or "Betty Jane, you make me so mad. I'm not going to let you do any more cooking for the rest of the week!"

It is easy to see that responses expressed from the Parent or Child ego-states are not helpful. Students will usually fail to improve their behavior when approached in this way. Yet it is a very common way for teachers to interact with their students. Greater success can be achieved when teachers understand the nature of the transactions they make with students and how their own behavior patterns can determine the way their students respond. If teachers learn to respond from the Adult ego-state, fewer discipline problems will occur.

The Four Life Positions

If the Adult is not unduly subdued by abuse, it will help to make appropriate modifications in both the Parent and the Child. For example, the Adult will help the Child learn to express feelings safely that may otherwise be communicated in socially unacceptable ways. When these adjustments are successfully made, children are able to make fruitful transitions from the control-bound existence they have experienced as children to autonomous self-regulated living as adults. This transition is critical to becoming a fully functioning person. Failure to make this transition creates problems that are resistant to correction. The individual then may become locked into a behavior pattern that prohibits good personal and social adjustment. Discipline problems may be the result.

Harris (1967) identifies four possible outgrowths of this transition process, which he calls life positions:

- I'm Not OK—You're OK
- I'm Not OK—You're Not OK
- I'm OK—You're Not OK
- I'm OK—You're OK

I'M NOT OK—YOU'RE OK

I'm Not OK—You're OK is the universal life position of early childhood. Because children are much smaller than adults as well as much more inept, they naturally perceive that they are Not OK. If they are helped through stroking (the process of positive approval) to feel good about themselves and gradually appreciate the genuine contributions they are able to make, they will eventually feel OK about themselves. If they are unsuccessful, Not OK feelings will persist and hinder their life adjustment. Children's perception of themselves is not based on their own assessment. They depend on others to provide this information. Children lack the mental acuity and experience to form an accurate picture of themselves. Sensing this lack, they constantly question adults about their performance in various situations in an effort to assess their own worth. Because of their inherent insecurity, they require a lot of stroking and recognition. Without assurance from adults, children usually conclude that they are unacceptable and unable.

The emphasis on social recognition as the source of positive personal development is a major difference between Transactional Analysis and the work of Sigmund Freud. Freud believed that sex is the basis of human struggles in life. Adler and others believed that feelings of inferiority are more critical adjustment factors. Although both Freud's Psychoanalytic Theory and Transactional Analysis focus on the subconscious life of human beings, there is another important difference between the theories. Freud believed that experiences stored in the subconscious mind have unalterable effects upon human behavior. It thus becomes necessary to bring these subconscious experiences to consciousness, where they can be understood. Once understood, they no longer have debilitating influences. Adler, Berne, Harris, and others who promote Transactional Analysis believe that behavior is driven by unconscious experiences. However, through conscious thought, these behaviors can be altered before they are expressed. Unlike Freud, Adler and his associates believe that behavior can be controlled and directed.

I'M NOT OK—YOU'RE NOT OK

Sometimes children who have experienced only a limited amount of stroking during the first year of their lives later receive none. Life, which in the first year had some comforts, now has nothing to offer them. If this lack of approval continues throughout the second year, children conclude not only that I'm Not OK but also that You're Not OK. The Adult ego-state stops developing and the child, seeing no hope, gives up. Such individuals commonly end up in mental institutions in a state of extreme withdrawal, hoping to achieve the kind of stroking they received as infants.

Once this life position has been established, all experiences in life are selectively interpreted to support it. These people are very hard to help because when they conclude that their parents are Not OK, they apply the same conclusion to all other people and reject stroking even though it may be genuinely given.

I'M OK—YOU'RE NOT OK

If children are brutalized long enough by parents whom they initially felt to be OK, they will move to the life position of I'm OK—You're Not OK. This position is decided in the second or third year of life and is resistant to change. These children are able to achieve an OK feeling through self-stroking. They are apparently able to realize that their parents will not provide stroking for them. In addition, they realize that despite their own inabilities as young children, they are better than their abusive parents. They survive in the face of extreme rejection and physical pain. This experience promotes hatred and a determination to strike back. This hostility is what sustains them. Because their treatment has been so bad, they lack the capacity for introspection; they cannot see their own role in what happens to them. They become persons devoid of moral conscience, who believe that whatever wrong they do is the fault of others. They are, therefore, extremely unwilling to change, because those who try to help them are seen to be the same as their parents. Essentially there are no OK people in their lives. These children are likely to develop criminal psychopathologies.

I'M OK—YOU'RE OK

The fourth life position, I'm OK—You're OK, is dramatically different from the other three positions. Children who reach this life position are able to deal realistically with life and achieve a greater sense of fulfillment. The first three positions are based on feelings. The fourth position is founded on thought, faith, and the ability to act without the certainty of outcomes. These children are fortunate to have had repeated exposure to situations in which they could prove, to themselves, their own worth and the worth of others.

Analyzing Transactions

It is a fundamental premise of Transactional Analysis (TA) that all individuals need to feel adequate. Both the acceptable and unacceptable behavior of children is designed to ascertain how others feel about them. From the reactions to their behavior, they decide how to think about themselves. Teachers, therefore, need to have an affirming attitude even toward students who display excessive misbehavior. They should apply stroking techniques: They must give attention and affection. They must learn to appeal to children's Adult ego-state by approaching them with their own Adult. And they must affirm the positive aspects of children's Parent and Child. Stroking promotes rational thought, which supports the Adult, affirms the positive aspects of restraint coming from the Parent, and facilitates the creativity that is characteristic of the Child.

RECOGNIZING EGO-STATES

Using Transactional Analysis effectively in the classroom to eliminate learning disruptions depends on how well teachers understand the principles of TA as well as how perceptive they are in determining their own internal state. It also depends on how skilled they are in discovering the internal states of their students and how adeptly they interact with them. How can you tell which internal state a student is operating from? Part of the answer is revealed in the verbal information that is transmitted—that is, what the student says. The rest comes from nonverbal cues. Nonverbal cues include facial expressions, gestures, and voice inflections. Evidence that the Parent is in control may be hands on hips, arms folded across the chest, tongue-clucking, sighing, pointing the index finger, head-wagging, a furrowed brow, pursed lips, a tapping foot, or a look of disgust. Confirmation that the Child is in charge may be tears, temper tantrums, complaining, pouting, the quivering lip, shrugging shoulders, giggling, squirming, laughter, or downcast eyes. The Adult ego-state is manifested as smiles of approval and looks that ask for more information.

Both verbal information and nonverbal cues should be considered in making an assessment of which ego-state is active. Taken together, they shed light on one another. Often verbal information has more than one possible meaning. For example, the question

"Where are my shoes?" coming from the Adult is just a request for information. There would be no innuendo in the voice. However, these same words spoken by the Parent could suggest that the person to whom the question is directed has stolen the shoes.

The verbal expressions of the Parent usually demand, command, and reprimand. They are designed to control and direct. They also contain criticisms and labels. The following examples show a Parent talking:

1. Pick up those books now!
2. Go back to your seat. You don't have my permission to sharpen your pencil!
3. I can't see why you continue to act like that.
4. You never remember to turn in your homework.
5. You are just like your brother/sister when it comes to cleaning up your messes in the lab.
6. How can anyone be so lazy?
7. You are just being ridiculous.
8. When are you going to stop blowing your nose in class?
9. You ought to be ashamed of yourself, the way you carry on.
10. You're always getting into trouble.

The verbal clues expressed by the Child usually take the form of uncontrolled emotion. They may be expressions of great exhilaration or declarations of uninhibited disgust; they may lack either concern or resistance. The Child may make such statements as:

1. I ain't gonna pick up my tools.
2. Why can't I go to lunch? Everyone else is.
3. Who cares about your old rules?
4. I want my ice cream now!
5. When I grow up, I'm going to be a millionaire.
6. I want the biggest one.
7. Give me that piece of cake. Yours is bigger than mine.
8. My dad can whip your dad.
9. My bike is better than yours.
10. I guess so.

One can tell that the Adult is in control by listening for the following kinds of questions and statements:

1. How much time will it take you to finish the job?
2. How does the job you did today compare with the one you did last week?
3. I think I understand what you mean.
4. When will you present your plan to your chemistry teacher?
5. I think that what you have in mind will be possible.

6. What do you think the consequences will be for failing to do your homework?

7. When do you plan to start on your experiment?

8. On what do you plan to base your decision?

9. In my opinion, you would be better off looking at more of the possible consequences before you make up your mind.

10. I have no idea what will happen if you don't show up for class.

AVOIDING INCOMPATIBLE TRANSACTIONS

When teachers are armed with clues to understanding ego-states, they can more effectively analyze transactions and help students improve their behavior. They can also more insightfully monitor their own transactions and alter how they respond to their students. Some transactions are incompatible—that is, they take place between individuals in different ego-states. These are the transactions about which teachers must be most concerned because they produce the most trouble. A student may, for instance, say to the teacher, "How am I going to finish this assignment by tomorrow?" The teacher could respond, "How much have you got left to do?" or "How can I help you finish your assignment on time?" These are Adult-to-Adult responses. The teacher could say, however, "Why don't you try working for a change?" In this case, the teacher's Parent would be making the response. Incompatible transactions (sometimes called ulterior transactions or crossed transactions) create conflict and impede students' work; they also erode student-teacher relationships.

Sometimes crossed transactions occur when one person receives the words of another and reads negative intent into them. For example, a student may ask, "When is this assignment due?" The teacher might respond sarcastically, "Why? Do you plan to turn it in late?" Another student could ask, "Should we bring our textbooks to class tomorrow even though we are having a test?" The teacher might reply, "Why? Do you plan to use it to cheat on the test?"

Let's analyze a lengthier transaction. Suppose that a student is visiting quietly with other students nearby. Assume that the class has been given time to work on a written assignment. Other members of the class are busy writing.

Teacher	Garn, you couldn't be done with your assignment already. Don't you have something more to do?
Garn	Yeah, too bad, but I do.
Teacher	Well, you had better get started on it. You have to turn it in at the end of the class. Why are you are still sitting there when you have time to work? A lot of the work you have turned in lately isn't very good. Maybe if you'd spend time on it, you could make it look more decent.
Garn	Well, it's about as good as this class. How can we be expected to do an assignment like this when everything is so vague in here?
Teacher	You have been told repeatedly that you can't learn the content of this course unless you listen and take notes. You spend all your time talking with other students. It's no wonder you don't know what to do.

Garn	Yeah, well, this course is a waste of time. When are we ever going to use this stuff? I get bored to death in here.
Teacher	If you ever plan to go to college, you'd better sit up and listen. They won't put up with this kind of behavior in college.
Garn	Who says I'm going to college, anyway?

This episode illustrates how crossed transactions promote conflict. The teacher is acting out of her Parent, whereas the student is responding from his Child. When the teacher tries to get Garn to work, she assumes that he is lazy rather than just in need of help. She believes that she has to order him to work rather than ascertain why he is not working. Even when he claims that he cannot do the assignment because he is confused, she blames him for his predicament instead of providing the help he needs. Although what she claims might be true, confronting Garn in this manner will not help solve the problem. It would have been better to make an Adult response: "Garn, I see you haven't started your writing assignment yet. Is there some part of it you don't understand? I'd be happy to help you if you'd like." With this approach, the teacher avoids reading anything into the situation. Rather, she determines whether valid problems exist that need to be corrected. Instead of being helpful, however, the teacher scolds and judges Garn. He in turn displays an "I don't care" attitude. In reality, he has little choice. He cannot appear to be interested in the class when the teacher is so critical of his performance. It is inconceivable for Garn to try as hard as he can and yet fail to receive approval. It is safer for him to confront the teacher. In this way he can prove to himself that she is the cause of his poor performance. He probably believes that he could be successful if it were not for the teacher. The teacher fosters this belief when she interacts with him out of her Parent ego-state.

Now let's look at this same situation as it would be played out if the teacher handled it from the Adult ego-state:

Teacher	Garn, I see you haven't started your writing assignment yet. Is there some part of it you don't understand?
Garn	I don't understand any part of it. This class is so confusing. Why can't things be explained so I can understand them?
Teacher	Let's look at page 254 in your textbook. See that diagram of the Krebs Cycle? Now look at the accompanying page. There you have an explanation of the chemical reactions that take place.
Garn	Oh, now I see. I never noticed this before.
Teacher	Have you been reading the textbook much during the year, Garn?
Garn	No, not much. I don't seem to get anything from it.
Teacher	When do you usually try to read your textbook?
Garn	I do it during class mostly.
Teacher	Are there things that happen in class that disturb your reading?
Garn	Well, some of the other kids talk to me while I'm trying to read.
Teacher	Where would you like to sit so this won't happen any more?
Garn	I guess I could take a seat up by your desk.

In this example, the teacher stays in the Adult ego-state. She does not try to correct Garn directly. Instead, by asking questions that both give Garn information and allow him to see his alternatives so that he can make responsible choices, she tries to get him to think through his problems and change his behavior himself. When the teacher stays in the Adult, students are encouraged to respond in their Adult. In this example, the student initially makes Child statements. When the teacher avoids making Parent responses, which the student's statements tend to encourage, the student is eventually drawn into using his Adult as well.

Even though it is advisable for teachers to act in the Adult and encourage children to do the same, there are times when Parent-to-Parent or Child-to-Child interactions are appropriate. These transactions do not create conflict and may be productive. For example, a student who has just won first prize in a contest may exclaim, "Wow, look what I did!" This is a Child statement. The teacher may respond from the Child and say, "Look at you! You took first place!" These Child-oriented interactions provide students with a healthy outlet for this part of their personality.

The Parent can also be constructive. Suppose that a student suddenly proclaims, "I'm not going to be able to finish this project here at school. I guess I will have to take it home and finish it over the weekend." The teacher could reply, "Yes, that's right. You'll need quite a lot more time to do this project right." Both of these statements have a Parent orientation, but they do not contradict one another. No conflict is produced. And the result is positive for the student as well as the teacher.

Staying in the Adult Ego-State

Because the Adult develops later than either the Parent or the Child, it seems to be in the process of catching up throughout life. In addition, Parent and Child occupy the "primary circuits" in the brain and tend to respond automatically (Harris, 1967); a conscious effort must be made to enter the Adult ego-state. It is therefore helpful when trying to stay in the Adult to become sensitive to Parent and Child signals. Child signals usually are accompanied by aroused feelings, feelings ordinarily associated with being Not OK. Just being aware that the Not OK Child is asserting itself is helpful. When you can attribute anger to your Child and know that your Adult can alter the course of this anger, you are better able to modify childish expressions. It is possible to detach yourself mentally from the Child and analyze it, quickly dousing the fire that might otherwise flare up and burn uncontrollably.

Parent signals can be monitored in a similar way. It is helpful to decide in advance how the Adult plans to deal with the tendencies of the Parent that automatically appear. For example, the Adult may interrogate the Parent, asking it a series of hard questions. The biting, irrational orientation of the Parent can be subdued if it is forced to respond to questions such as:

- Where did this idea come from?
- Is it true?
- What evidence is there?
- What can happen if this response is made?

- Does this response really apply to this situation?
- Is this action appropriate in this situation?

Managing the Parent in this way short-circuits its automatic expression. The strength of both Parent and Child lies in their unconscious manifestation. They require no thought. They have been recorded in the past and stored in the subconscious mind, ready to be expressed when appropriate environmental stimuli appear. But if these automatic behaviors are scrutinized, consciously and rationally, their expression can be modified or eliminated.

Teaching Transactional Analysis to Children

Obviously, if teachers intend to use the principles of Transactional Analysis, they must understand them and know how to apply them successfully in their own lives. In the classroom, teachers must not only use TA principles while interacting with students but also teach their students to use TA in regulating their verbal transactions with others. Children too need to understand TA and know how to apply it with their teachers as well as fellow students. Concepts that could be taught to students include:

1. the three ego-states (Child, Parent, and Adult)
2. what it means to be trapped in the Parent or the Child
3. the four life positions
4. the basic need of human beings to feel capable and accepted
5. how to treat others so that they feel accepted and capable (stroking)
6. how to analyze transactions
7. how to increase the power of the Adult and more reasonably regulate the influence of Parent and Child in transactions with others

Games Students Play

If teachers are to improve their transactions with students and help students cultivate better relationships, they should be aware that students play certain behavioral games. Games involve an ongoing series of complementary, ulterior transactions that progress toward a well-defined, predictable outcome (Berne, 1964). Students play these games for a reason—ordinarily to cover up Not OK feelings or to excuse themselves for not improving their behavior. But the people who play these games are essentially innocent in the sense that they are not fully aware of what they are doing. The subconscious behavior patterns of the Child and the Parent form the basis for most of the games, and the feeling of being Not OK provides the motivation.

Games are usually played for the benefit of the person who initiates them and at the expense of someone else. At other times, both parties benefit from the game and need one another to successfully play. Game players want to stimulate others to play so that they can receive their payoff: a solution to their problems, some stroking, or an excuse for themselves.

To keep students from playing these games, a teacher must first analyze the games and discover what the students' motives are. What are students hoping to gain from the game? Are they in need of stroking? From whom do they want stroking? It is also useful to determine the ego-state from which the students are operating and the ego-states of the teachers to whom they are appealing.

Once the game is understood, the teacher must refuse to play it. In making this refusal, the teacher suppresses the automatic reactions of Child and Parent and responds from the Adult ego-state exclusively. Games are played by the Child and Parent components of our personalities. When Adult responses are made, students will more readily see these games for what they are and avoid using them in the future.

Children should not be left without support when their games have been analyzed and exposed. The need behind their game-playing is still unfulfilled. Students require stroking at this point. In fact, children require a lot of affirmation. They need to feel accepted and acceptable. When these needs are more fully realized, students will be far less active game players.

Finally, students need to be socially successful without playing games. They need alternative ways of responding that do not involve manipulating others. They need to learn to solve their own problems without creating games to excuse their own perceived ineptness. Students need encouragement from their teachers while they are learning to make these new responses. A good deal more stroking will be necessary.

The following list, drawn up by Ernst (1972), describes some of the games students and teachers play in school:

Uproar.   The primary goal of Uproar is to stimulate the teacher's Parent. Students try to provoke negative reactions by creating various distractions: talking out, turning around in their seats, rattling papers, dropping books on the floor, coming in late, drumming on the desk, clicking their pens, snapping their fingers, kicking their neighbors, or trying to sidetrack the lecture. When students succeed in getting the teacher to rebuke them, they claim that they are being picked on unfairly. This perceived persecution justifies continued provocations.

Clown.   Students who play the game of Clown entertain the whole class and are admired by their peers for their daring. It is difficult even for the teacher not to like them; their antics may appear playful and even enjoyable. However, when their games get out of hand, teachers who feel that they are losing control of the class may rebuke them. Most of the time clowns perform for the benefit of their peers, often making teachers the butt of their jokes and trying to avoid being discovered by them.

Stupid.   Students who play Stupid also need an audience. They try to appear dumb, affecting mannerisms that make them appear dim-witted. They become quite skilled in this portrayal, pretending not to know how to do assignments correctly and asking questions no one else would ask. They may also try to appear clumsy or inept. Their object is to get their peers to call them stupid—that is, to give them attention, even if the attention is insulting.

Chip on the Shoulder.   In Chip on the Shoulder, students who are asked to perform in some way fear that they may appear stupid to their peers, so they choose to be belligerent rather than run this risk. Their behavior is often interpreted as hostile. If they can create discord, they can easily avoid the possible failure they associate with a teacher's demands. They produce a smoke screen to cover their Not OK feelings.

Make Me.   Children who refuse to complete assignments may be playing the game of Make Me. These students refuse to budge unless extreme force is used. They try to provoke a clash of wills, daring the teacher: "Just try and make me do it." They may flatly state that they will not cooperate or just sit with a look of defiance on their faces.

Schlemiel.   Students playing Schlemiel, the physical equivalent of Stupid, give the appearance of being klutzes. They deliberately bump into others, knock things over, or drop things. They often make a mess of others' belongings and then lamely apologize, "It was an accident" or "I was only trying to help." They are always quite willing to help clean up the mess they make, but they usually succeed only in making matters worse.

Let's Find Out.   What can you do in school to create a little excitement? Discovering the answer to this question is the purpose of Let's Find Out ("Let's find out what would happen if . . ."). Students who play this game are always thinking up little pranks they can pull to stir things up. Usually the participants try to pull their pranks without getting caught. They may, for example, throw a firecracker into the principal's office after planning how to escape undetected. They may also steal or vandalize school property.

Cops and Robbers.   Cops and Robbers requires more confrontation than Let's Find Out. Students who play this game try to see how far they can go without suffering any consequences. They may, for example, violate the school's no-smoking rule or dress code in front of their teachers, daring them to enforce these rules. They play "robbers" and try to entice their teachers to play "cops." Most teachers willingly play the "cop" game of Now I've Got You when students so blatantly flout authority.

I Want Out.   Some students complain that they cannot stand school and want to get out as soon as they can. They often are heard exclaiming how much they hate school. In reality, they would prefer to remain in school. But they match their actions to their words, and their games often get them expelled. As they leave the school they usually explain to others how happy they are to be leaving and how much more exciting and desirable a life they can now live. After they are expelled, however, they are often found back in school wandering the hallways and attending some classes. Commonly when these students are on the brink of suspension, they beg school authorities to give them just one more chance. If they fail in this quest, they may spend some of their suspension at school rather than at home or on the streets.

Sweetheart.   Sweetheart is a game played by "sugar-coating" a hurt intended for someone else. This game ordinarily starts with innocent-sounding comments. These remarks, however, are cutting and are intended as insults. Such comments come from the Child ego-state:

"I'm only telling you this because I'm your friend."

"It is really nice that they make some things in larger sizes now, don't you think?"

"I really admire the way you don't mind being around those people."

"I don't care what the others say about you, I like you."

Why Don't You . . . ? —Yes, But. . . .   This game is played to excuse oneself and evade responsibility. It consists of creating an extensive list of excuses in an effort to explain away any suggestion that problems could have been solved by taking some appropriate action. For example:

Teacher	Where is your homework assignment, Peggy? It was due yesterday.
Peggy	I didn't have time to do it. I had to work the last two nights.
Teacher	The assignment was given two weeks ago. You have had plenty of time to do it.
Peggy	When I don't work I have to tend my little brother. While I'm with him I can't do any homework.
Teacher	Why don't you tell your parents that you need more time to do your schoolwork?
Peggy	They would just tell me to finish my assignments at school before I come home.
Teacher	Why don't you do that?
Peggy	You can't study at school; there's too much noise.

Late Paper Game.   Jay failed to turn in his paper for his English class. Ms. Catanni reminded him that it had been due the week before. Jay said, "Gee, Ms. Catanni, I'm really sorry I didn't get my paper to you. I'll bring it tomorrow." Jay did not come to school for three days. When he finally did come to his English class, Ms. Catanni reminded him that he needed to turn it as soon as possible. Jay responded, "I hope I can finish it by Friday. My uncle died last week and the whole family has really been broken up about it." Ms. Catanni said, "Take your time, Jay. I know these things sometimes take a long time to get over." Jay has succeeded in getting the paper deadline put off indefinitely. His teacher believes that he has a legitimate excuse, but he is just playing games. Sometimes students even get their peers or siblings to falsely verify their excuses.

Buddy.   Teachers also initiate games. Buddy is one such game, sometimes started when teachers have an overwhelming need to be liked by their students. Teachers who play this game try to be pals with their students. They talk to selected students about their private lives and encourage these students to do the same. Commonly they try to befriend the most popular students, giving them special privileges not available to others, accepting late assignments from them, and including them in choice activities. Other students usually view such teachers as wimps and their student friends as brown-nosers.

Dealing With Students' Games

What should teachers do when students play games with them? First, they should determine the purpose of the game. Usually these games are played to bolster students when they are feeling Not OK. Often people who are Not OK want to avoid appearing inept and approach others with chips on their shoulders. Sometimes, because they are insecure about what they can do, they deliberately try to appear dumb in the hope that others will not expect much of them. Sometimes they create a smoke screen to draw attention away from their performance, which they feel is woefully inadequate. The underlying problem, having Not OK feelings, is fairly common.

Second, teachers should avoid playing the game. To do so, they must remain in the Adult themselves. It does no good to scold, as the Parent would. This reaction is precisely what many games are designed to provoke. Students are more able to forgive their own feelings of ineptness while they are being abused by the teacher's Parent. Teachers, therefore, must resist the temptation to play the game from their Parent ego-state. Instead, they must formulate questions that will help students accept themselves as they are and understand that games are unnecessary.

Third, teachers should provide stroking. Statements of affection, touching, and smiling help students feel accepted. Stroking communicates that they are genuinely liked and are therefore worthy. Without stroking, the question of students' personal worth is left unanswered. This is the reason why children try to involve their teachers in games: They need verification of their self-worth (Berne, 1964).

Preventing Discipline Problems

No explicit distinction is made in the literature between procedures for preventing and procedures for correcting discipline problems using Transactional Analysis. However, if teachers help their students apply Transactional Analysis principles, they will foster prevention. Prevention, then, is a matter of teaching Transactional Analysis to students and encouraging its application. This instruction and encouragement amounts to a passive prevention program rather than a vigorously active one.

Schoolwide Discipline

Transactional Analysis focuses on data transmitted between students and their teachers. Theorists do not describe a schoolwide program. However, administrators could conceivably be trained in Transactional Analysis so that in their own relationships with students they could support the work of teachers. Students referred to the principal for disciplinary action, for example, would be given the same kind of treatment as individual teachers would provide.

Strengths and Weaknesses of Transactional Analysis

STRENGTHS

1. It is derived from a well-documented examination of how information is stored in the subconscious mind.
2. It promotes self-analysis and self-correction.
3. It has applications beyond the classroom in students' personal lives.
4. It helps children avoid destructive roles often played in interpersonal relationships.
5. It helps children understand their own messages and those of others.
6. It provides a framework for communication and understanding.

WEAKNESSES

1. Overcoming the automatic behaviors coming from the Parent and Child ego-states may be difficult.
2. It cannot be applied as readily to discipline problems other than those involving verbal exchanges.
3. It may encourage students to "psychoanalyze" one another.
4. Students may not have the language, cognitive skill, or reasoning necessary to employ this technique.
5. Making necessary distinctions between Parent, Child, and Adult may be difficult.

SUMMARY

Relationships between students and teachers depend on transactions—that is, everyday verbal exchanges with one another. These transactions, in turn, depend on the ego-state from which each person is operating and the compatibility of the transactions. There are three ego-states: (1) the Child, which is the emotionally reactive or exuberant inclinations of individuals, (2) the Parent, which is the component of a person's behavior that controls and directs, and (3) the Adult, which is the rational aspect of human personality. Incompatible, or crossed, transactions occur when the ego-states of interacting human beings conflict with one another.

Conflict is often produced when children play behavioral games with their teachers. Such games are designed to help compensate for their feelings of being Not OK. Children assume that they are Not OK when they fail to gain a sense of acceptance, which occurs when they do not receive the stroking they need. When children are abused, their Not OK feelings may become solidly established. If the abuse is extreme, they may instead come to believe that they are OK and that everyone else is Not OK. These individuals have extreme social difficulties and often end up in correctional institutions.

Teachers need to practice staying in the Adult ego-state when they interact with their students. They need to avoid playing behavioral games with their students and must remember to supply the necessary stroking. Finally, students also can benefit from understanding Transactional Analysis and learning how to respond to others from their Adult.

CENTRAL IDEAS

1. In human beings there are three collections of behaviors or ego-states, which have different functions:
   a. The Parent controls and directs.
   b. The Child is compulsive and expressive.
   c. The Adult applies conscious judgment and thought to behavior.
2. All of our experience is recorded in our brains in a subconscious state. This repository of experience is composed of feelings as well as basic sensory impressions. These stored, subconscious experiences are the genesis of much of our everyday behavior. Our behavior is therefore sometimes manifested without careful thought or a conscious decision on our part.
3. If children receive proper stroking, they will move from the life position of I'm Not OK—You're OK to that of I'm OK—You're OK. Children who fail to receive this assurance remain as they are. When children are abused, they may shift to the position of I'm Not OK—You're Not OK. If abuse is severe, they may move to the I'm OK—You're Not OK life position and end up with an antisocial or even criminal orientation to life.
4. Teachers need to remain in the Adult ego-state and teach their students to do the same.
5. Students play games such as Uproar, Clown, Stupid, Make Me, Schlemiel, and I Want Out to satisfy their needs. Because these games can adversely affect classroom discipline, teachers must stop them by
   a. determining the purpose of the games,
   b. refusing to play the games, and
   c. providing stroking for students.

QUESTIONS AND ACTIVITIES

QUESTIONS TO CONSIDER

1. What are the major differences between the ideas of Freud and those of Harris and Berne?

2. To what extent does the work of brain surgeons support the basic ideas behind Transactional Analysis?

3. How successful are teachers likely to be in teaching their students about Transactional Analysis?

CLASSROOM ACTIVITIES

Use role-playing to study the use of Transactional Analysis in various school situations. Have one member of the class play a student with a behavior problem. Discuss the actions taken along with possible alternatives.

STUDENT APPLICATIONS

With one or two classmates, use role-playing to act out discipline situations in which students have made the following initial statements. Apply the principles of Transactional Analysis. Include follow-up interactions.

a. To a teacher: "I hate this work. I can't understand how we can be expected to learn this junk."

b. To another student: "You're just going to have to turn it in to the teacher the way it is and suffer the consequences. I'm not going to help you finish it."

c. To a teacher: "You always have your pets."

d. To a teacher: "I'm not going to do those problems. You can't make me."

e. To another student: "Give me that book. You're too stupid to read it."

REFERENCES

Berne, E. (1964). *Games people play*. New York: Ballantine Books.

Berne, E. (1966). *Principles of group treatment*. New York: Oxford University Press.

Ernst, K. (1972). *Games students play*. Millbrae, CA: Celestial Arts.

Harris, T. A. (1967). *I'm OK—You're OK*. New York: Avon Books.

Penfield, W. (1952). Memory mechanisms. *A.M.A. Archives of Neurology and Psychiatry, 67*, 178–198.

7

Reality Therapy/Control Theory: William Glasser

OBJECTIVES

This chapter is designed to help you
1. follow the steps of Reality Therapy to correct students' unacceptable behavior
2. understand the difference between Reality Therapy and Control Theory
3. recognize human needs and know how to help students satisfy their own needs without depriving others of the opportunity to satisfy theirs
4. understand the difference between boss-management and lead-management
5. implement a preventive discipline program that incorporates Glasser's concept of a quality school

ASSUMPTIONS

1. Human beings are basically self-regulating and can thus learn to manage their own behavior.
2. Children learn to be responsible by examining a full range of consequences for their behavior and making value judgments about their behavior and its consequences.
3. Avoiding an exploration of motives will help children accept responsibility for their behavior and not make excuses.
4. Human behavior consists of an effort on the part of each individual to satisfy needs for love, power, freedom, and fun.
5. Each person has a unique way of satisfying needs.
6. Children cannot be forced to change what they believe about how to best satisfy their needs.

Introduction

William Glasser is a prominent psychiatrist who gained national attention with the publication of *Reality Therapy: A New Approach to Psychiatry* (1965). His rejection of classical psychotherapy in favor of a more behavioral approach has been acclaimed by many as an enlightened move away from the beleaguered field of Freudian psychology. Instead of looking for the antecedents of inappropriate behavior in the subconscious mind, Glasser helped his patients find solutions to their behavioral problems in the present.

Through his work with juvenile offenders, Glasser became interested in helping teachers deal with school discipline problems. He now conducts workshops across the country for teachers and others in the helping professions.

▼ Ricardo was still upset. He had been sitting in the time-out room for two days, chafing because Ms. Danielson had told him that she would allow him back in class only if he made a plan that would guarantee no more disruptions. He had been routinely talking out in class and throwing spit wads. Ricardo was a high school junior, popular among his peers and respected as one of their leaders. He had won his leadership status, in part, by boldly confronting teachers when they tried to correct his bad behavior. Right now he wanted desperately to be back in class with his friends, but he did not want to comply with Ms. Danielson's demands. He felt that he would lose face with his friends as well as forfeit some of the power he had acquired. In the past, because he demonstrated high achievement as a student and because his father served on the school board, teachers had usually backed down eventually. This time, however, Ms. Danielson was really holding out. He decided that it was just a matter of time until she caved in and let him come back to class.

As Ricardo sat pondering, Mr. Boden, the time-out supervisor, sat down next to him and asked to see his plan. Ricardo had only a blank sheet of paper to show. Mr. Boden asked, "Do you plan to go back to class?"

Ricardo replied, "Of course I do. I don't know why I have to sit here, though. This isn't doing anyone any good."

"If you really do want to go back to class, you'd better start on your plan," advised Mr. Boden.

Ricardo sat and considered the situation. What could he do, he wondered, that would help him save face with his friends and still satisfy Ms. Danielson?

Mr. Boden broke the silence. "What is the only way you will be able to get back to class?" he asked.

"I guess I'll have to write a plan," admitted Ricardo.

"When do you plan to start?" prompted Mr. Boden.

"I guess I should start now," volunteered Ricardo.

"I'll check back with you in fifteen minutes to see how you are coming along," said Mr. Boden.

Reality Therapy

The case of Ricardo illustrates what happens to students whose unacceptable behavior is excessive. In this case, although Ricardo had been involved in creating classroom rules, he had chosen to violate them repeatedly. He therefore had to prepare a plan outside class that would solve the problem. Prior to his removal from class, Ms. Danielson may have taken Ricardo aside on one or more occasions and gone through the steps in Glasser's Reality Therapy to get him to change his unacceptable behavior. In Ricardo's case, these efforts failed, so he was assigned to the time-out room until he prepared a plan for readmittance to class.

Over the years there has been an evolution in Glasser's views on dealing with discipline problems in the school. Glasser's initial background and training was in Freudian psychoanalysis. He eventually rejected these ideas in favor of an approach oriented more toward responsibility, an approach that made different assumptions about human needs and motives. Whereas psychotherapists assume that basic needs are psychosexual in nature, Glasser believes that human needs are defined more in terms of successful social relationships. Psychotherapists might attempt to uncover the source of poor psychological adjustment among various repressed, subconscious experiences; Glasser instead tries to help people live successfully in the conscious world. He does not accept the psychoanalytical axiom that the source of present behavioral and psychological difficulties consists of unconscious mental conflicts. To him, traumatic events experienced earlier in life do not unconsciously direct behavior. Rather, he believes that social and psychological problems are an outgrowth of bad decisions made about social relationships. His approach is to help people identify behaviors that are inconsistent with accepted social norms, accept them as irresponsible, and replace them with more socially desirable ones. He believes that good psychological health depends on loving and being loved and feeling worthwhile to ourselves and others. According to Glasser, being responsible is essential in successful relationships with others. Individuals must learn that their own needs can be satisfied only in a reciprocal way. The gratification of personal needs depends on how successfully each person can satisfy the needs of associates (Glasser, 1965).

CORRECTING UNACCEPTABLE BEHAVIORS

Children who fail to satisfy their needs create problems in school. They tend to be lonely, angry, frustrated, and openly rebellious. The teacher's role is to help them learn a way to behave that better satisfies their needs. Teachers must help students take responsibility for acknowledging their own behavior and for changing it as necessary. There are a number of things teachers can do to help unruly students act more responsibly. Interviews with students in which the following steps are followed can be useful (Glasser, 1969):

1. Help students identify their inappropriate behavior. Do not accept excuses. Do not invite excuses by asking students *why* they behave as they do.

2. Have students identify various consequences if their inappropriate behavior continues.

3. Have students make value judgments about their behavior and its consequences.

4. Help students create plans to eliminate inappropriate behavior.

5. Help students stick to their plans or suffer the consequences if they fail to do so.

Identifying Inappropriate Behavior.   People find it difficult to admit doing something wrong. Commonly they deny bad behavior by shifting blame or claiming that they could not help what they did. However, to improve behavior, students must first admit their misbehavior. The teacher helps by getting students to identify the behavior considered inappropriate. No attempt is made to judge the behavior as good or bad.

Consider the case of Gordon, an elementary school student whose teacher is trying to help him identify his role in fighting with other students:

Teacher	Gordon, what was it you did to Owen out on the playground during the morning recess?
Gordon	I didn't do anything.
Teacher	What did you do to Owen just as he was starting to use the swing?
Gordon	I hit him, but he hit me first. He never shares the swing with any of the rest of us.
Teacher	So what did you do to him?
Gordon	I hit him.
Teacher	Who else have you been fighting with this past week?
Gordon	Nobody.
Teacher	Who were you shoving yesterday by the drinking fountain?
Gordon	Sarah.
Teacher	And who did you throw sand at on the playground during the afternoon recess?
Gordon	Ruth.

Gordon tries to excuse his behavior by explaining that Owen started the fight. He also justifies himself by telling his teacher that Owen never shares. To claim that another person started a conflict or problem is the usual way in which youngsters shift the blame for misbehavior. Misbehaving children can then claim that the bad behavior of others justifies their own. When students attempt to excuse their behavior in this way, teachers need considerable skill to avoid ridiculing them or giving support to their excuses. One way teachers can avoid these pitfalls is to bypass the students' remarks by asking them to state their own role in the difficulty. In this way, conflict about "who started it" can be avoided. Trying to resolve a "who started it" conflict usually interferes with helping students take responsibility for their inappropriate behavior.

Making students describe their behavior is better than having their teachers do it. It is unlikely that students will "own" their behavior if teachers identify it for them.

Questions, therefore, must be asked that direct students to state what they have done to cause problems. They will, of course, resist admitting fault. They will even lie to avoid accepting blame. If students do tell a lie about their role in a problem situation, just ignore it. Ignoring lies is unnatural for most adults, who feel that not challenging the lies of children will somehow corrupt them or encourage them to lie even more. However, children often would rather have parents and teachers focus on lying than admit the inappropriate behavior in question. When interrogated about lying, children often create a diversion by accusing parents and teachers of not trusting them. Discussions about trust usually weaken teacher-student relationships and fail to help children act more responsibly. Fortunately, once children get used to being more responsible for their own behavior by having to admit it, they are less likely to lie.

Notice in the dialogue that Gordon is given clues about the specific way in which he is expected to respond to the teacher. For example, Gordon is asked what he did to Owen at morning recess just as Owen was about to use the swing. These clues are designed to make it difficult for Gordon to claim that he does not know what the teacher is talking about. Children often say that they do not know what is meant by teachers' questions. Clues help avoid this problem. They also define the domain in which students are expected to respond. Without these clues, students can direct attention to many different areas and get the conversation off track. Notice also that Gordon is required to identify several instances of fighting. This pattern helps establish that there is a serious problem that needs solving. There is no reason to have a meeting if the student has misbehaved only once. It is only when misbehavior persists that it must be corrected.

Identifying Consequences.   The next step in Reality Therapy is to help students identify whatever adverse consequences are associated with their inappropriate behavior. Gordon identifies such consequences for fighting:

Teacher	You have indicated that you have been involved in fighting with several class members. What can be the result of this?
Gordon	I can get into trouble.
Teacher	What kind of trouble?
Gordon	Maybe I'll get sent to the principal's office.
Teacher	Yes, perhaps. What action do you think the principal might take in a case such as yours?
Gordon	I don't know.
Teacher	What might happen to your privilege of being in school?
Gordon	I guess the principal might kick me out.
Teacher	Yes, I suppose you might not be allowed to remain in school. In your fight with Jon, you were back by the aquaria and the science equipment. What could have happened to those items during a fight?
Gordon	They could have been broken.
Teacher	If you broke them, who would have to pay for them?

Gordon	I would, I guess.
Teacher	Yes, I agree. When you fight with others, what could happen to you or the other person physically?
Gordon	I guess somebody could get hurt.

In this dialogue, several points need to be emphasized. Notice how the teacher responds when Gordon says that he could be kicked out of school for fighting. Gordon's suggestion indicates his belief that school administrators act arbitrarily. He tries to claim no responsibility. The teacher clarifies the situation—by fighting, Gordon could forfeit his participation in school—to help him understand that being excluded is a consequence of decisions he makes, not some arbitrary punishment imposed by the principal.

Notice also that Gordon is helped to understand the consequences he will undoubtedly experience if he breaks school equipment. Note that Gordon is specified in the teacher's question as the cause of the breakage. The teacher might have asked instead, "What is likely to happen if school equipment gets broken during a fight?" Had this been the question, Gordon might have said that the school would have to replace it, implying that he had no responsibility himself. The way questions are formed, therefore, is important in helping students accept responsibility for their behavior.

Finally, notice that the teacher's questions contain clues about what responses are expected. These clues help students learn what their teachers wish to discuss with them. They limit the kinds of responses that may be made and allow teachers to deal more directly with problems without getting sidetracked. For example, the question "What might happen to your privilege of being in school?" confines the topic to staying in school. Focus is kept on the problem and away from other topics that might come up if questions were more general. The teacher could have asked, "What do principals do when students fight?" There are a number of ways to respond to this question. Gordon might say that the principal would call his parents, give him a spanking, or put him in detention. These punishments may have little to do with what might actually happen.

Making Value Judgments.   After the consequences have been identified, students are asked to decide (1) whether or not they want the consequences to occur and (2) whether or not they judge their behavior to be inappropriate. The teacher in our example asks Gordon questions that help him make such value judgments:

Teacher	Gordon, you have said that you could possibly get yourself expelled from school by fighting. In addition, you have indicated that school property could be broken, in which case you would have to pay for it. And what is most important, you have said that someone could get hurt, perhaps even seriously. Do you want that to happen?
Gordon	No.
Teacher	What do you think about fighting, then?
Gordon	I guess I need to stop.

In this step, it is wise to have students make a statement about all the consequences collectively. Eliciting such a statement increases the likelihood that students will answer in a responsible manner. If consequences are presented one at a time, students may deny that some of them are significant problems. Another useful tactic is to embellish the students' responses with helpful additions. In the example, the teacher raises the stakes: *"And what is most important*, you have said that someone could get hurt, *perhaps even seriously."* The teacher has added the idea that getting hurt is a more serious problem than the other consequences. It is wise not to discuss this statement with students, however. Such discussions are usually counterproductive. The same is true of discussions involving the seriousness of injuries received during a fight. Actually, death sometimes is the result of mindless scuffling and brawling. Severe injury is always a possibility. However, children are more likely to think of outcomes in terms of their intentions than what could actually happen. They may not truly believe that debilitating or life-threatening injuries could occur if they did not plan to inflict them. They will claim that you are just overreacting. In addition, such discussions may degenerate into disputes about who is at fault or how the seriousness of an injury is defined.

Creating a Plan.   When students no longer accept their behavior as appropriate and wish to avoid the consequences associated with it, a plan can be devised to overcome the problem. Students must make value judgments about their behavior because, in the process of making a plan, they may resist changing behavior with which they have found some satisfaction in the past. If they put up resistance, you just have to ask them what they have already said about changing their behavior. Then help them formulate a specific strategy for eliminating the behavior. Gordon shows some initial hesitation in developing his plan:

Teacher	Now that you have identified the consequences of fighting, you are ready to devise a plan for eliminating it. What do you think you could do to avoid fighting in the future?
Gordon	*(after a long pause)* I don't know. I can't think of what I could do. Perhaps you could try to keep Dee and some of the others from picking on me.
Teacher	What did you already say you felt about fighting?
Gordon	I said I thought I should stop.
Teacher	I have noticed that some of your fights take place in the hall just outside the classroom. What could you do immediately as you come to class to get involved more productively and be less likely to fight?
Gordon	I could come into class, take my seat, and start to work.
Teacher	What specifically could you do, say tomorrow, when you come to class?
Gordon	I have a book I'd like to bring.
Teacher	Do you think that would work?
Gordon	Yes.
Teacher	Why don't you try it for a week and then let me know how you think you are doing.

Gordon is initially resistant and perhaps unable to think of how to avoid fighting. This way of thinking is new for most students, so their inability to make plans for avoiding difficulties is understandable. At first, teachers will probably have to provide clues that suggest possible plans. It is also necessary to have students be specific. When Gordon proposed what he thought was a good plan—he would come into class, take his seat, and start to work—it was still necessary for him to specifically identify what he would read. To follow through, the teacher should make sure that Gordon does in fact bring his book to class the next day.

Sometimes students are much less cooperative than Gordon appears to be. In such cases, a positive relationship still must be maintained. Teachers commonly react to students' rash behavior. When students are obnoxious, teachers are tempted to treat them harshly to show them that they cannot get away with such behavior. Such reactions must be avoided. Maintaining a positive relationship with students is critical. To illustrate, assume that when Gordon is asked to identify his fighting behavior, he responds in the following way:

Teacher   What did you do to Owen out on the swing at morning recess?

Gordon   I didn't do anything! I'm always getting blamed! Why can't you leave me alone? Nobody ever blames Owen! He's the one who started it!

Teacher   But what did you do to him?

Gordon   (silence)

Teacher   You probably need to think about what I asked. I need to work on a project at my desk. When you feel you would like to talk about the episode on the playground today, let me know. *(The teacher leaves Gordon to think about the problem and to cool down.)*

In this situation, little will be accomplished by maintaining contact with Gordon and trying to force him to respond. He will only become more hostile. It also does little good to sit and expect him to respond. It is better to move away and indicate a willingness to talk when he is ready. Students must realize that their problems cannot be resolved until they are willing to talk and that the teacher can wait as long as necessary. Sometimes the teacher must wait quite a while. However, the necessary time should be provided. If teachers try to force students to respond, they may become hostile and more inclined to shift the blame. Also, students know that if they wait long enough, they can usually avoid accepting responsibility for misbehavior. Teachers must be willing to wait longer than their students.

TIME-OUT

Sometimes students make a commitment not to misbehave and are unruly anyway. These students should be cycled again through the steps of Reality Therapy. They may also be required to suffer the consequences they have already identified. If students refuse to cooperate with reasonable classroom expectations, or if they violate rules they have previously agreed to accept, they may be candidates for isolation from the class. When students are a threat to the instructional program, it is appropriate to exclude them. These isolation (time-out) procedures are not intended to be punitive. Students are not assigned some arbitrary period of time-out as punishment. They are expected to stay in isolation only as long as it takes to produce a workable plan for returning to the classroom. If there is a schoolwide program for Reality Therapy, there will be a designated time-out room, monitored by a staff member. If teachers use Reality Therapy on their own, they can create a time-out area within the classroom by partitioning off a corner of the room. Assignment to the time-out area may be necessary when students habitually refuse to abide by class rules.

During time-out, students are directed to create a written plan that they believe will solve their discipline problems. The purpose of requiring a written plan is to help students achieve a greater sense of commitment. The plan becomes a statement of intentions, a contract between students and their teachers. If problems persist, students can be referred to other professionals as necessary.

Control Theory

In 1984, Glasser wrote *Control Theory*, which on the surface may appear to be a radical departure from his initial work in Reality Therapy. Although there are some significant additions to his earlier ideas, Control Theory is compatible with Reality Therapy. Actually, it is better to view Control Theory as an extension of Reality Therapy. Glasser's intention is for teachers to use Reality Therapy as the vehicle for teaching students the principles of Control Theory (Glasser, 1989). The major difference between Reality Therapy and Control Theory has to do with the central role of need gratification.

BASIC HUMAN NEEDS

The focus of Reality Therapy is on helping students become more responsible in a behavioral sense. When students behave more responsibly, their needs for social acceptance can be satisfied and their status among their peers enhanced. As a result, their sense of personal worth increases.

Control Theory has an expanded list of human needs, which are more central to its basic application. Glasser suggests that children be taught about these needs as well as ways of more legitimately satisfying them (Glasser, 1984). The list of needs associated with Control Theory includes:

- love
- control
- freedom
- fun

Love.   The need for love is similar to the need for social acceptance in Reality Therapy. As human beings, we need to love and be loved. We need to belong. We need to be accepted by others as significant and important. We need to believe that we are accepted by others for what we are and that this acceptance is unconditional. Children usually try to satisfy their need for love and acceptance through behavior designed to get attention. Children are constantly trying to get the attention of parents and others as a sign of love and acceptance. If others give approval, the children are satisfied.

Unfortunately, children often want more attention than teachers and parents can provide. When their efforts fail, children commonly resort to more drastic measures. These measures are the source of much misbehavior. Although it is difficult in a class of thirty or more students to see that each one gets sufficient love and attention, the need remains and must somehow be met.

Children who are lonely and ignored often behave outrageously in their quest to belong and be accepted. Even suicide may be considered when this need is not met. For these children, death is more desirable than living with the pain of loneliness. Sometimes love given on a conditional basis creates similar reactions. Love is conditional when acceptance depends on a child's conforming to expectations. Teachers as well as parents often communicate to a child that their love is conditional ("I'm happy when you make good grades"). Children need to be told, over and over, that they are loved—not because of what they do, not in spite of what they do, but just for who they are.

Control.   All of us need sufficient power to regulate our lives as we desire. Unfortunately, teachers usually deny children the opportunity to satisfy this need. Children are considered too immature to make responsible choices. Therefore, when children assert themselves, teachers ordinarily increase their own control. This increase in control only encourages greater rebellion. It is ironic that rebellion is promoted by excessive control and that control is the usual means by which teachers and school administrators attempt to quell rebelliousness. When teachers stimulate rebellion in this way and then punish children who act out, they usually reinforce bad behavior in the process. It would be far better to provide students a way to satisfy their need for control in legitimate ways.

Students need not only to have reasonable power and control over their lives but also to use power properly to satisfy other needs, such as love. For example, if children exercise power in abusive ways, they will not obtain the love and acceptance they desire. They must achieve an appropriate balance in satisfying these potentially contradictory needs. Children and adults often mistakenly think that they can force others to love them, which of course they cannot. In fact, love can occur only when needs for control are moderated. Children must understand how this relationship between love and power works to avoid having their need for love thwarted.

The need to control cannot simply be renounced. It is a legitimate need. However, the way in which control is exercised must usually be modified. People ordinarily use control to manipulate the environment or another person so as to satisfy their needs in a desired way. This use of control is appropriate so long as others can satisfy their needs as well. When we manage our needs and curb their gratification, we are able to create predictability in our lives. We can regulate important happenings and outcomes, defend ourselves against the arbitrariness of others, and avoid involvement in unpleasant situations. In a world where power is often abused, self-regulation is desirable and satisfying.

Children's efforts to obtain control are often awkward and lacking in consideration for others. So teachers may react negatively to students' efforts to manage themselves. They assume that students are irresponsible and immature. However, children's irresponsible behavior is often just a reaction to control by teachers. For example, a teacher may suggest that students be courteous and take turns with other children using the swings on the playground. Children may react angrily to such a suggestion, however, because they want to decide for themselves when to swing. They feel that the teacher's controlling behavior threatens their ability to maintain personal power, which is essential to them. Even if they are aware that their exercise of power often irritates or alienates others, some children are unable to modify their need for control sufficiently to avoid causing these reactions. Confronted with disapproval from others, such children may overreact and become even more controlling when teachers suggest that they take turns.

Freedom.   Children need not only to be in control of their own lives but also to be free from control by others. However, satisfying this need can also create conflict. Teachers usually interpret children's efforts to obtain freedom as affronts to their authority. In addition, they may doubt the ability of children to use freedom responsibly. Thus, opportunities for free expression are withheld pending evidence of maturity. Freedom, however, is a necessary component of learning to be responsible. It therefore cannot be used as a reward for becoming responsible. Wise teachers provide an increasing level of freedom as students show an inclination and ability to use it wisely. One way of providing freedom is to teach children decision-making skills. Even young children can learn to make valid decisions about various issues that concern them. For example, students can help make decisions about class rules and topics to be studied.

It is important to realize that providing freedom is no guarantee that it will be used responsibly. Unrestrained freedom can cause chaos. However, if too much control is exercised, rebellion occurs. Teachers therefore need to provide freedom gradually as children become more able to govern themselves. They must offer children several choices and at the same time teach them about the consequences of those choices. Choosing between various possibilities may be new to some children. They may not realize the nature of the consequences they can expect from specific choices. Some consequences can best be learned by experience; some can be learned only by experience. Children must learn that freedom exists only when consequences are carefully taken into account—that ignoring consequences will likely deprive them of the freedom they desire. For example, students who fail to take the consequences of drug abuse into account may find themselves deprived of the opportunity to complete an education, restricted by ill health or injury, or perhaps incarcerated.

Fun.   Children are driven by the need for fun, far more than parents and teachers are usually willing to accommodate. Even adults have a greater need for fun than they usually admit. Glasser believes that fun is as basic as any other need (Glasser, 1984). People of all ages desire it. In addition, he believes that a relationship exists between learning and our genetic need for fun. Learning, he says, is a lifelong pursuit, and fun is inherently a part of it. It is ironic that the academic part of schooling, however, is usually devoid of fun. Most students do not take pleasure in what they are currently learning. How can we expect them to do well in school if they do not enjoy much of what they do? In fact, students are told, often by teachers, that learning is not supposed to be fun. Rather, it is hard work. This admonition implies that work is not fun either. If tasks are not fun, they become a forced drudgery. When we have fun, we are able to work for long hours and look forward to doing it.

Children's need for fun is evident in their common query to one another: "Was it fun?" Fun is obviously important to them; it is a gauge against which to measure many different experiences and activities. Adults often ask the same question. They seek fun just as children do. One has only to look at the multibillion-dollar industries that supply us with an ever-increasing number of opportunities for "fun." But adults, forgetting that fun is a human need, often misapply the term "fun" exclusively to forms of entertainment. Many experiences can provide pleasure or enjoyment. But if they do not also provide a real sense of satisfaction, then, according to Glasser's usage, they are not fun.

BALANCING NEEDS

Balancing needs is an important part of Control Theory. As the following story illustrates, needs must be balanced, because overemphasis of one need may make satisfying other needs more difficult.

One day three eleven-year-olds were trying to decide how they would spend their day. Each suggestion proposed by one was swiftly rejected by the others. It was obvious that what mattered most was not to participate in a particular activity but to have one's suggestions accepted. One of the three suggested that they go to the union building at the university. The second favored playing video games at the arcade in the mall. The third had just picked up a new game and wanted the others to come over and play it.

"I want to go to the Wilkinson Center," said Chris. "I'm getting tired of sitting around playing games all the time. I want to do something more creative."

"Well, I think we should go to the mall," responded Alma. "We went to the Wilkinson Center last week. Besides, you can't do anything creative there."

"I've been wanting to play my new game," interrupted Bailey. "I got it especially so we could play it today. If we don't do it, then I shouldn't have got it in the first place."

This conversation went on for several minutes with each child trying to take the lead and persuade the others to follow. Finally, Chris and Alma decided that they would go to the Wilkinson Center and stop by the mall on the way back. Bailey was unbending, complaining to the others that they never did what anybody else wanted, and stomped angrily home to find someone else to play with.

A week later the same three children were having a similar discussion. This time Bailey wanted to go to the Wilkinson Center, Chris wanted to hang out at the mall, and Alma wanted to stay home and have the other two come over to play. They argued awhile, and then Alma and Bailey went off to the Wilkinson Center while Chris was left behind fuming.

This story of conflict between friends is a common scenario. Each child is hoping to maintain friendship and not give up control. Sometimes friendship wins out and sometimes control does. Control is hard to forfeit, even when temporary loss of friendship is the result. Glasser advocates teaching children to balance their needs by having them forgo some control in favor of developing friendships. Each child needs to feel accepted and loved. These needs can be met if friendships are cultivated. It is therefore unwise to be so controlling that potential friends are alienated.

The needs for freedom and control must also be balanced. Conflicts between freedom and control can be a problem when children want freedom but are unwilling to grant the same privilege to their peers. They want to be the ones who always get to tell the others what to do and yet never accept suggestions from them. This self-centeredness usually thwarts the playmates' need for fun and causes them to reject one another.

UNFULFILLED NEEDS AND MISBEHAVIOR

Unfulfilled needs promote misbehavior in many forms. Teachers can avoid these problems by discerning children's needs and by helping them satisfy their needs legitimately. Needs should be recognized and satisfied before patterns of inappropriate behavior develop.

For example, children's sense of well-being may depend on getting attention from teachers; they may perpetually seek approval as a sign that others accept them. In a class of thirty or more students, teachers cannot satisfy everyone's needs on demand. So some students resort to misbehavior, which is a sure way of getting the teacher's attention. It would be better for the teacher to anticipate students' needs for attention and satisfy them in advance rather than wait and react negatively when students misbehave. For instance, teachers could call attention to students by having them share their hobbies with the rest of the class or by giving them responsibilities in class that provide status.

It is not uncommon to claim that certain children require too much attention because they are used to getting it, even when in fact they come from an attention-deprived background. It is normal for children to want attention from adults. The problem is not so much a desire for too much attention as a result of receiving too little. Children may misbehave to make up for this deficiency.

Another common cause of misbehavior is the failure to satisfy students' legitimate needs for freedom and control. Teachers commonly believe that they must exercise control over their students. Students, on the other hand, desire more freedom. Children do in fact need more freedom than what is offered in most school situations. When teachers are too controlling, students may become rebellious. When students rebel, teachers may become more coercive. Rebellion by students is accepted as evidence that they are not responsible enough to use freedom wisely. Even when children simply get out of hand in an overexuberant effort to have fun, teachers often react negatively and conclude that the children are unable to govern themselves wisely. But when teachers apply more control to quell students' misbehavior, they can usually anticipate even more misbehavior.

THE PICTURES IN OUR HEADS

Glasser believes that each of us has a unique way of determining how our basic needs can best be satisfied, which he describes as a set of pictures we have in our heads. These pictures are stored in our minds as long as they continue to satisfy us. When we no longer consider them worthwhile, we remove them and replace them with more satisfying pictures (Glasser, 1984). Sometimes the pictures we have do not correspond to the real world, and irrational behavior is often the result. Teachers and students, for example, are likely to have vastly different pictures of how each wants to be satisfied by the other. Children may have a picture of teachers who let them out early for recess, who always explain complex concepts in an understandable way, who pay special attention to them, who lecture in an entertaining way, who give easy tests, who never give homework or pop quizzes, or who provide treats and lots of parties. Teachers may visualize students who sit quietly in their seats, who promptly turn in all work, who study hard, who pay attention, who become deeply involved in class discussions, or who write excellent papers. Obviously, these pictures are somewhat incompatible. And, unfortunately, both the teacher and the student find it difficult to adopt the other's pictures. To complicate matters for teachers, different students have different pictures of what is most satisfying to them. Consequently, meeting all students' needs is difficult if not almost impossible.

Glasser emphasizes that we do not picture ourselves doing badly. We all have a view of being successful and happy. We may at times choose to do self-destructive things, but we do not intend to destroy ourselves. Our pictures make sense to us; otherwise, we would not have them (Glasser, 1984). Students may, for example, take drugs despite repeated warnings about the hazards of doing so. Teachers who issue the warnings undoubtedly believe that these students are determined to destroy themselves, and they cannot understand why they would choose to do so. The students, on the other hand, may picture drugs as the only way to escape the misery they confront in life.

CONFLICTS IN SATISFYING NEEDS FOR CONTROL

According to Glasser, we always have control over what we do, even when we behave destructively. We react to the environment but are not directly controlled by it. For example, if we are hurrying to take someone to the hospital and are confronted by a powerful external stimulus such as a red light, we will not simply respond to the light and stop. Instead, we will make a decision based on other factors as well. Most of us in this case would check the traffic and go on through the light. Therefore, even those who appear to be controlled are not being controlled in a strict sense. They will continue to follow others' directions only as long as they find it satisfying to do so.

Part of this satisfaction, says Glasser, must include a sense of personal control. To illustrate, Glasser points out that even animals seek to maintain control. Piglets who are trained to respond to a stimulus of food by climbing up a ladder and going down a slide will *not* continue to perform indefinitely. They can be depended on to repeat these actions for only a few weeks (Glasser, 1984). Humans undoubtedly are even less susceptible to the control of others. We like to control but despise being controlled, which causes problems in our relationships with others. Although we are in a continual struggle for control to ensure that our needs are satisfied, we cannot in the process deprive our friends of the opportunity to satisfy their needs. Otherwise, our need for love and acceptance may be put in jeopardy.

If control can be successfully negotiated with our close associates, we can anticipate relative harmony. But the need to control is potent. When others interfere with our need to maintain control at a level we desire, we react in various ways. Small children usually cry or throw tantrums. Later, when these methods prove ineffective, children may resort to a manifestation of depression or even threats of suicide to gain control. These drastic steps usually have the desired effect, at least for a while, but they also create a level of misery beyond what the children anticipated and from which they find it extremely difficult to remove themselves. Once depression is established, its associated feelings become automatic, and the individuals who experience it may be convinced that they have nothing to do with its occurrence.

All our needs require satisfaction and play a very significant role in how we behave. Teachers must realize that students cannot deny their needs. Instead, they are dedicated to fulfilling them. Unfortunately, none of the needs Glasser describes is sufficiently satisfied in school, at least for many students. Because their needs are not adequately met, these students drop out in one way or another. Many of them create discipline problems. Glasser contends that a radical restructuring of the schools is necessary before students' needs can be met and that discipline problems will continue until conditions change. Glasser believes that students do what is most satisfying under the circumstances. We can safely assume that if students are more satisfied doing something other than their schoolwork, they will spend whatever time they can doing it. Sometimes they doodle or daydream or just look out the window. More often they try to enhance their relationships with their peers and carry on various social interactions during times when their teachers expect them to study.

The Quality School

The Quality School is Glasser's latest effort to improve the schools. In this work, he emphasizes that schools must provide students a better way to satisfy their needs, which involves a complete change in the nature of school management. Glasser has taken his school management model from the work of W. Edwards Deming, whose ideas about management have had such a profound effect on the economic growth of Japan since the end of World War II. In presenting his plan for the schools, Glasser criticizes current school managers for accepting low-quality work. He claims that no one, students included, will expend the effort necessary to learn unless they believe that "there is quality in what they are asked to do" (Glasser, 1990). Glasser contends that a manager cannot make people do quality work. In fact, no one can make anyone do anything. However, if students are allowed to do quality work, they will perform without coercion.

Glasser explains that the main complaint of students is not that school is too hard. They say that they could do the work if they wanted to. Instead, they claim that schoolwork is boring and fails to satisfy their basic needs. He points out that many proposals for school reform are too coercive, such as the recommendations contained in *A Nation at Risk* (National Commission on Excellence in Education, 1983): a longer school day and year, stiffer graduation requirements, and more homework. These recommendations fail to address the problem that doing *more* of what is currently offered would achieve nothing except to put more pressure on children to accomplish what they have already rejected as unsatisfying (Glasser, 1990).

BOSS-MANAGEMENT VERSUS LEAD-MANAGEMENT

Glasser believes that what school officials say are student discipline problems are in reality school management problems. School administrators fall into the trap of thinking that discipline problems, not unsatisfying education, cause low achievement levels. The real problem is that students struggle to resist the low-quality, standardized, fragmented curriculum that is being forced upon them through coercive administrative practices. When students who fail to become involved register their disinterest, some educators apply more coercion, which only serves to alienate them further. Glasser (1990) calls this approach boss-management and describes some of its characteristics:

1. The administrator or teacher (boss) establishes the task and standards for students. Students must simply adjust to the job as the boss defines it.

2. The boss usually tells, rather than shows, students how to do the work and rarely asks how it can be done better.

3. The boss is the exclusive evaluator. Students are considered unable or biased. Bosses tend to settle for just enough quality work to get by.

4. When students resist, the boss uses coercion, usually in the form of punishment, to obtain compliance. In the process, teachers and administrators create an adversarial relationship between themselves and students.

Glasser recommends a change from boss-management to lead-management:

1. The lead-manager encourages students to discuss the quality of the work they want to perform and the time constraints they wish to put on themselves.

2. The lead-manager constantly tries to fit the learning task to the skills of students.

3. The lead-manager provides students with models of how they should perform and allows them to evaluate their own work, acting on the assumption that students know not only what high-quality work is but also when they are producing it.

4. The lead-manager is a facilitator, establishing a nonadversarial classroom atmosphere without coercion.

A productive work atmosphere develops because the leader authentically does everything possible to provide students not only the best tools with which to learn but also the autonomy to govern themselves in the process. This autonomy helps students to satisfy the ever-present need to be in control as much as they possibly can.

THE QUALITY SCHOOL PROGRAM

Glasser (1990) has made a number of suggestions intended to help educators understand the specific attributes of quality schools:

1. School experiences should satisfy the basic needs of love and acceptance, control, freedom, and fun. The traditional practice of rewards and punishments must therefore be abandoned. Punishment often promotes misbehavior. Rewards satisfy needs, but students may still resent the power of teachers to give or withhold them. The competition established in a reward system automatically produces losers and winners instead of a high level of learning for all students. Teachers should not attempt to give rewards as an inducement for students to do what they find no satisfaction in doing. Giving students rewards only conditions them to the rewards and fails to promote excellence.

2. Learning teams should be organized as a basic instructional strategy. Students will satisfy more of their needs in a cooperative learning environment than in a traditional competitive one.

3. Teachers should allow for considerable variation in how students satisfy their needs. Each of us has a personal picture of how best to satisfy our needs. We are generally unable to adopt the view of someone else. Students need to include high-quality school experiences as a significant part of the picture they have of themselves and their world.

4. If teachers want to become a positive part of students' pictures of how to best satisfy their needs (the quality world of students), they must encourage students to express themselves and then listen carefully to what they say.

5. Teachers are ultimately in charge of what goes on in the classroom. However, they must avoid making their power an issue as they manage a class.

6. Teachers should make it clear to students that the higher the quality of their work, the more they will be in charge of it. Because high-quality work leads to greater independence and success in life generally, the message is conveyed that students are more in charge of their lives when they increase the quality of the work they do in school.

7. There is little lecturing in a quality classroom. Students are involved in discussions and in work done in groups or independently.

8. Students should be helped to understand the importance of delayed gratification. It often pays to endure some immediate short-term pain in order to increase the chance of obtaining some later, long-term pleasure.

9. If students are asked whether it takes hard work to get a good education, they will answer "Yes." If they are asked whether they are smart enough to get a good education, almost all will answer "Yes." However, if they are asked whether they are working hard in school, most will answer "No." Students will work harder to obtain a quality education when they are taught what it consists of and how it can be obtained.

10. If teachers treat their students coercively, students will waste time, size up their teachers, and try to outwit them.

11. When students are coerced, they usually refuse to accept ownership of the work they are asked to do. They will not accept the responsibility of evaluating their own work and improving it. Students need to set their own standards for quality, not just do well according to the teacher's standards.

12. In a quality school, there are no bad grades. All permanent low grades are eliminated. A low grade would be considered temporary, a problem to be solved by students and teachers working together. Hopefully, students would conclude that it is worthwhile to expend more effort to achieve a higher level of quality. High grades would be retained in a quality school because, if they are fairly earned, their coercive power is not destructive.

13. The lowest grade would be a *B*. The level of quality expected for the grade of *B* would be about as it is now. Students could also earn *A*s and *A*+s.

14. Quality schools would not concern themselves with outside measures of productivity such as state-mandated achievement tests. Students would be involved in advanced placement programs.

15. Mandatory homework, which is ordinarily intended to increase students' productivity, in practice severely reduces it. The emphasis on compulsory homework should be drastically reduced and the importance of classwork stressed.

16. Classroom rules should be few and simple. If there are too many rules and teachers assume the role of enforcing them, an adversarial relationship develops between teachers and their students. Students should be involved in the formulation of rules. Teachers will probably need to help them understand that if they are courteous with one another, they are unlikely to need many rules.

17. Teachers should avoid accepting the role of the punishing authoritarian. Consequences for breaking rules should be discussed with students, and students should accept the consequences when they break rules. Those who break rules should be asked to suggest ways to prevent rules from being broken in the future.

18. Teachers should show an interest in students' personal lives and reveal selected information about their own lives that will help students appreciate them as human beings.

19. Teachers should ask students for help and advice when a need actually exists and the students can give valid assistance. Such requests help to break down barriers between teacher and student and create a friendlier atmosphere in the classroom.

20. Teachers should avoid calling students' homes when the students experience difficulties in school. When students' families are notified of problems at school, students correctly perceive the school to be the cause of problems at home. In addition, some students will misbehave in school with the intention of getting an ambivalent parent involved, even when negative attention from that parent is expected.

21. In disciplining children who have broken the rules, teachers may find the following sequence of questions helpful: (1) What were you doing when the problem started? (2) Was it against the rules? (3) Can we work it out so that it does not happen again? (4) If this situation comes up in the future, what could you do and what could I do so that we do not have this problem again?

Correction Strategies

Although much of Glasser's Control Theory appears to have a prevention orientation, applying the principles he suggests can also help to correct discipline problems. When students' rebelliousness is extreme, teachers and administrators may have to work with them on a one-to-one basis using Reality Therapy. The following steps are helpful in this process:

1. Establish a quality school program with a lead-management orientation. The coercion-punishment model should be replaced.

2. Provide the target students with school experiences that are meaningful to them and that satisfy their basic needs of love and acceptance, control, freedom, and fun. Help them believe that they can achieve a high level of quality.

3. Help students identify their inappropriate behavior and its consequences.

4. Encourage students to make a value judgment about their inappropriate behavior and its unacceptable consequences.

5. Have students make a plan that has a real possibility of helping them be more autonomously productive in school.

6. Periodically meet with students and give them the opportunity to evaluate their school experience and make changes as necessary.

It is unlikely that students' disruptive behavior patterns will change in an immediate and dramatic way, particularly if the students have been significantly abused by the current boss-management system. The help of teachers and administrators is vital if such students are to gain confidence in the school and its programs.

Preventing Discipline Problems

Preventing discipline problems, in Glasser's view, depends to a large extent on establishing principles and procedures associated with a quality school and supplanting the coercive boss-management system with lead-management. Glasser's methods of discipline always include a significant prevention component. In *Schools Without Failure*, he recommends three types of classroom meetings designed to prevent discipline problems: social-problem-solving meetings, open-ended meetings, and educational diagnosis meetings (Glasser, 1969).

The purpose of social-problem-solving meetings is to encourage students to solve discipline problems as a class. Class expectations are established in these sessions, and the types of behavior the class finds unacceptable are discussed. Consequences for violating class expectations are determined in these sessions, and necessary, periodic changes are negotiated. Open-ended meetings serve as meaningful supplements to the regular curriculum. Glasser believes that one reason children misbehave in school is that they find the curriculum irrelevant. Discussions in open-ended meetings permit them to raise whatever questions they have that pertain directly to their classroom situation. Educational diagnosis meetings, on the other hand, are intended to enable students to evaluate their educational experiences. In these meetings, students can determine how effectively they learn and ascertain what gaps exist in their educational experiences.

One educational strategy Glasser advocates to promote more meaningful learning and reduce discipline problems is cooperative learning, also known as the learning team model. He believes that this kind of learning provides students a better way to satisfy their basic needs. Glasser recommends that students work on long-term projects with other students to go deeper into a subject and become more involved in the experience of learning. For this purpose, he suggests that teachers organize teams of from two to five students who have reached different levels of achievement. He lists several benefits to be gained from cooperative team learning (Glasser, 1986):

1. Working in teams provides students a sense of belonging, which helps motivate them to work harder and achieve more.

2. The more advanced students find it fulfilling to help less able team members because they want the power and friendship that go with a high-performing team.

3. Less able students also have their needs fulfilled. In the group, they are able to accomplish something, whereas they did very little before. Their contribution to the team is appreciated more than their previous individual efforts were.

4. By working in teams, students gain a greater sense of independence from the teacher and discover themselves able to make valuable contributions to the class.

5. Learning teams serve as a structure within which students can obtain a deeper understanding of school subjects. Unless students understand the subjects they study more deeply, they will be unable to make the vital connection between knowledge and power that must underlie any attempt to improve today's schools.

6. Teams provide a framework within which students can better evaluate themselves. More than just grades may be considered as evidence that students are learning.

Schoolwide Discipline

In a quality school, there would be no boss-management on the part of principals, counselors, or teachers. Traditionally, the school principal exercises veto power over students' decisions. To provide lead-management, principals need to give students greater autonomy, particularly as they demonstrate greater maturity. When children sense that opportunities for self-government are the result of responsible decisions and behavior, they will increasingly demonstrate trustworthy conduct. Principals need to anticipate that students will become more responsible when given more freedom instead of assuming that they will dream up devious, antisocial activities.

Within the classroom, each individual class would have the responsibility for determining rules. Outside the classroom, the student council would serve as a genuine governing body, and students would take an authentic role in determining school rules and procedures. The student council would have the duty to make sure that students behaved appropriately in such places as the lunchroom, halls, and school grounds.

Student councils should be organized in the elementary and junior high schools as well as in high schools. If such councils were consistently implemented, students would be more adept at self-government by the time they reached high school age. In the elementary school, participation in student council might be restricted to the older children, but children in the earlier grades could be taught how to take an active role later in school government.

Not only do students need opportunities to create their own rules, but they must also learn how to police themselves. There is always the possibility that students will want to deal punitively with those who break the rules. In a quality school, however, punishment in the traditional sense is unacceptable. Children should learn to apply appropriate consequences for breaking rules rather than seek retribution.

No standardized achievement tests would be administered. These tests are designed to separate students into categories based on a normal distribution curve. All students would be expected to achieve at a high level. There would be no need to give tests designed only to make comparisons among them or between them and group norms.

Strengths and Weaknesses of Reality Therapy/Control Theory

STRENGTHS

1. Reality Therapy and Control Theory promote a high degree of autonomy and responsibility for students.
2. They help students see a wide range of possible consequences for their behavior.
3. They allow students to determine solutions to their own discipline problems.
4. They help students understand their needs and how to satisfy these needs legitimately.
5. They help teachers avoid promoting rebellion.
6. They delineate clearly what a teacher needs to do for every misbehaving student.
7. Problem behaviors can be handled in classroom meetings involving the entire class, which helps all students understand the various discipline problems and what to do about them.

WEAKNESSES

1. It is difficult for teachers to help students satisfy their need for control without feeling threatened themselves.
2. It is difficult to react properly when communicating with students about their inappropriate behavior.
3. It is difficult to avoid giving responses that encourage students to make excuses for their bad behavior.
4. It is difficult to help students experience the true sense of autonomy implied by Control Theory if outside influences dictate what is taught in school and how children should be disciplined.
5. Classroom meetings may consume more time than is desirable.
6. It may be difficult to help students who do not want to be in school to make plans to improve their behavior.
7. Students may not have the necessary skill to make plans that will help improve their behavior.

SUMMARY

Glasser's ideas about discipline have evolved over the years. In his initial work, he recommended that students be allowed to suggest ways to make school more meaningful and to formulate appropriate rules for classroom use. Students who misbehaved were to be corrected through the use of Reality Therapy, which involves four basic steps: (1) helping students recognize and describe their behavior, (2) asking them to identify the consequences of their actions, (3) having them make value judgments about both the consequences of the behavior and the unwanted behavior itself, and (4) helping them formulate plans that they believe will help eliminate their problems. If these efforts fail, students can be given time-out until they come up with a more workable plan.

In his work on Reality Therapy, Glasser identifies successful social relationships as essential components of a happy, ordered life. In Control Theory, Glasser stresses the importance of a student's need for love and acceptance, and he expands his list of basic human needs to include control, freedom, and fun. Reality Therapy focuses on correcting students when they misbehave; Control Theory places a greater emphasis on helping children achieve their needs responsibly. Glasser claims that when children's needs are met, they find little cause to create trouble. The task of the teacher is to help them satisfy their needs legitimately and to help them learn to balance their needs. Balance is essential because full realization of various needs sometimes creates conflicts. Conflicts can also occur when the fulfillment of needs depends on others who are also trying to satisfy their own needs.

Glasser has recently begun advocating a change in the pattern of leadership used in schools, from boss-management to lead-management. He believes that such a change will create a more conducive atmosphere in which students can better satisfy their needs, and he urges the use of lead-management in the development of quality schools.

CENTRAL IDEAS

1. In Reality Therapy, teachers help students
    a. identify their inappropriate behavior,
    b. identify the consequences of that behavior,
    c. make judgments about their misbehavior and its consequences, and
    d. create and stick to a plan to eliminate problem behavior.
2. When Glasser created Reality Therapy, he identified successful social relationships as basic needs for humans. With the development of Control Theory, the needs of love, control, freedom, and fun were added.
3. Applying Control Theory involves helping students satisfy their needs in a legitimate way and abandon antisocial means of satisfaction.
4. A balance must be achieved between competing needs within an individual and between a person's own needs and the needs of others.
5. Low achievement levels may be more the result of an unsatisfying education than the result of discipline problems.

6. A quality school satisfies children's needs, aids cooperative learning, allows for variation, provides for autonomy, has expectations for high-quality work, avoids coercion, promotes students' ownership of their work, increases students' productivity, involves students in classroom decisions, and is relevant to students' personal lives.

QUESTIONS AND ACTIVITIES

QUESTIONS TO CONSIDER

1. How have Glasser's ideas about school discipline evolved?
2. What changes would have to be made in most schools to implement Glasser's ideas and principles?
3. What evidence is there that Glasser's ideas about human needs are correct?

CLASSROOM ACTIVITIES

1. Create an outline of a comprehensive discipline program that is consistent with Glasser's ideas. Include provisions for:
   a. the curriculum
   b. class organization
   c. activities that will satisfy students' needs for love and acceptance, control, freedom, and fun
   d. formulating classroom rules
   e. schoolwide discipline
   f. grading procedures
   g. adopting the characteristics of a quality school
2. Break into two groups and debate the relative merits of Glasser's approach to discipline and another approach.
3. View the audio-visual materials associated with Reality Therapy that are listed in Appendix A.

STUDENT APPLICATIONS

1. With two classmates, use role-playing to study how a teacher would use Reality Therapy to help a misbehaving student in the following situations. One person plays the role of the teacher. Another person plays the role of a student who has made a habit of disrupting the class. The third person observes and helps the other two participants analyze the situation.

    a. Jane is habitually tardy for class.

    b. Marjika never turns her homework in on time. Some assignments are never turned in.

    c. Randy has a long history of throwing spit wads in class.

    d. Ruth chatters incessantly during quiet study time as well as during lectures and discussions.

    e. Glen has carved his artwork into his desk.

    f. When Claron takes the hall pass to go to the restroom, she is usually gone for more than half an hour.

    g. Norm frequently uses profanity in class.

2. Use role-playing with several classmates to examine the process of establishing classroom rules and procedures. Define class learning objectives and requirements as well as expectations about students' behavior.

REFERENCES

Glasser, N. (1989). *Control therapy in the practice of reality therapy: Case studies*. New York: Harper and Row.

Glasser, W. (1965). *Reality therapy: A new approach to psychiatry*. New York: Harper and Row.

Glasser, W. (1969). *Schools without failure*. New York: Harper and Row.

Glasser, W. (1984). *Control theory: A new explanation of how we control our lives*. New York: Harper and Row.

Glasser, W. (1986). *Control theory in the classroom*. New York: Harper and Row.

Glasser, W. (1990). *The quality school*. New York: Harper and Row.

National Commission on Excellence in Education. (1983). *A nation at risk*. Washington, DC: U.S. Department of Education.

8

The Ginott Model: Haim Ginott

OBJECTIVES

This chapter is designed to help you
1. communicate in ways that build students' self-esteem and show acceptance for their feelings
2. encourage students' autonomy
3. express productive praise instead of destructive praise
4. understand the detrimental effects of punishment
5. apply Ginott's model of discipline

ASSUMPTIONS

1. Students' behavior can be improved if teachers interact with them more effectively, treating them with understanding, kindness, and respect.
2. Positive communication by teachers bolsters the self-concept of students, which in turn produces better classroom discipline.
3. Students can learn to be autonomous and responsible.
4. Accepting and clarifying students' feelings will improve their classroom behavior.
5. The improper use of praise encourages dependency.
6. Punishment encourages misconduct.
7. Insulting students causes them to rebel.
8. Promoting cooperation increases good discipline.

Introduction

Haim Ginott was born in Tel Aviv in 1922. He was trained in psychology at Columbia University and spent his professional career at New York University and at Adelphi University. He served as a consultant for UNESCO and as the resident psychologist on television's *The Today Show*. His weekly syndicated newspaper column, "Between Us," dealt with the subject of interpersonal communication.

Ginott focuses on helping teachers to build up rather than tear down the self-concepts of children. He describes how teachers attack children's character and points out alternative ways for teachers and students to interact. He has devised methods to help teachers deal with potential conflicts in the classroom and make their experiences with children positive and uplifting.

The discipline model of Haim Ginott consists primarily of communication methods to be used by teachers to help maintain a secure, humanitarian, and productive classroom environment. The basis of many of his recommendations can be seen in the practices endorsed by various other discipline theorists. In particular, he incorporates the work of Kounin (Ginott, 1971). Ginott places emphasis on what teachers should say and do and what they should avoid saying and doing as they work with students. Instead of outlining a theory for general application, Ginott supplies many examples of good and bad teaching practice. These recommended practices are organized around basic themes: practicing congruent communication, fostering independence in students, avoiding the perils of praise, renouncing the use of punishment.

Practicing Congruent Communication

Perhaps the most important concept advanced by Ginott is the need for teachers to practice congruent communication as they interact with children. By "congruent communication" he means communication that conveys acceptance instead of rejection and avoids blaming and shaming. Teachers must avoid the inclination to insult and intimidate their students and instead show increased sensitivity to their needs and desires. They must learn to motivate learning, encourage autonomy, bolster self-esteem, engender self-confidence, allay anxiety, diminish fear, decrease frustration, defuse rage, and de-escalate conflict.

DELIVERING SANE MESSAGES

Teachers have frightening power in the classroom. They can make a child's life either miserable or joyous. They can be tools of torture or instruments of inspiration. They can humiliate or humor, hurt or heal. They are in a position to either escalate or de-escalate crises in the classroom and either humanize or dehumanize the children there (Ginott, 1973). One of the greatest powers a teacher wields is the spoken word. Much of what teachers say "drives children crazy." This talk includes blaming, shaming, preaching, moralizing, ordering, bossing, admonishing, accusing, ridiculing, belittling, threatening, and bribing. These forms of speech brutalize children and have devastating, long-range consequences.

To "drive children sane," teachers must learn to change speech patterns from the everyday mode to an enlightened form that helps children to trust their perceptions, own their feelings, and believe in their worth. One way teachers can improve their speech when children misbehave is to always address the situation rather than attack the children's character and personality. The following situations and the teachers' spoken reactions illustrate this point:

1. A child forgets to bring gym clothes to physical education class.

    Teacher A   You are so irresponsible. You always are forgetting things. When are you going to learn to do what is right?

    Teacher B   You need to bring your suit tomorrow. It is impossible for you to participate in P.E. when you don't have the proper clothing.

2. A child fails to turn in some homework on time.

    Teacher A   When are you going to learn that I want your homework turned in on the day it is due? You're always forgetting things. What will you ever amount to when you can't remember anything?

    Teacher B   You didn't turn in your homework today. Remember to turn it in tomorrow so you can get proper credit.

3. The teacher believes that a student is cheating on a test.

    Teacher A   I've caught you now. You were looking on your neighbor's paper. I'm going to make an example of you, you cheater. You get a zero for the test.

    Teacher B   You need to keep your eyes on your own paper. That way you can always claim you have done your own work.

EXPRESSING ANGER APPROPRIATELY

Anger is inevitable, given the fatigue, frustration, and conflict inherent in most classrooms. Teachers cannot be expected to be saints when it comes to expressing anger. Such restraint is simply impossible. Teachers should never deny their feelings. They should always express them genuinely. However, they do need to learn how to express their anger appropriately. Anger must be expressed without insult. Even when students are exasperating, they should not be angrily abused by teachers. When situations that promote anger arise, teachers should simply describe what they observe and state how they feel about it using "I messages." Teachers may thereby convey feelings of anger in a more appropriate way: "You have thrown paper all over the floor. I am angry." "I am furious. You have endangered the lives of other students by ignoring safety rules in the lab."

"I am annoyed," "I am appalled," and "I am furious" are much better expressions than "You are stupid," "Look what you have done," "You're a real pest," or "Who do you think you are?" Teachers should always be authentic. Their words must fit their feelings. They should not hide their annoyance nor pretend to be patient. It is hypocritical to act nice when you feel nasty. Enlightened teachers are not afraid of anger, because they express it without doing damage to their students. They attack problems rather than persons (Ginott, 1972).

AVOIDING THE USE OF LABELS, CRITICISM, AND SARCASM

▼ Noretta sat playing with her pencil while her classmates busied themselves with the assignment. Ms. Wilde watched for as long as she could stand it and then blurted out, "Noretta, why don't you do your work like the other children? You are just lazy. Your brother was the same way when he was in this class. Do you have some kind of a heredity problem in your family?"

Labeling is disabling. There is no place for it in education. Unfortunately, labeling is far too common. Students are called clowns, jerks, fools, imbeciles, or worse. Some are labeled irresponsible and unreliable; others are told that they are incorrigible or a disgrace to the school and to their families. Labels not only deeply hurt but may also become a self-fulfilling prophecy. Not uncommonly, children who are called names feel compelled to exemplify the label. It is difficult enough for them to develop a healthy self-concept when conditions are good. When they are labeled, seeds of doubt are sown in their minds that are difficult to eradicate. These designations for students become their destinies.

Teachers should also avoid criticizing students. Critical teachers often say uncomplimentary things about students' work. English teachers may, for example, tell students that their work is pretentious or verbose. Instead, they should give students suggestions about how to make their writing less wordy and vain. Students may be told to use single words such as *because* instead of *for the reason that* or *while* in place of *during the time that*. They also might be told to begin a particular sentence with "views differ" rather than "it is apparent that there are different views." This approach provides help for students instead of criticism. The students are able to use the teacher's advice to improve their work instead of just reacting negatively to the criticism.

Ginott calls a teacher's acid tongue a health hazard. Caustic comments deflate self-esteem and block learning. When children are hurt by such assertions, they become preoccupied with revenge fantasies (Ginott, 1971). Sarcastic statements are made by some teachers as a matter of routine. Some students may take them as a joke, particularly when the sarcasm is directed at someone else. However, no one thinks that being the object of biting sarcasm is a laughing matter, particularly when the comments are made publicly. What students—or teachers, for that matter—appreciate hearing the following ridicule being heaped on them?

1. "You don't need a calculator. You need a tutor. None of your problems has a correct answer."

2. "You're not relying on your own judgment again, are you? Don't you remember what happened the last time you did that?"

3. "Do you think you can get your brains in gear again? They've been in neutral for the past half hour."

ACKNOWLEDGING STUDENTS' FEELINGS

Sometimes teachers try to assure their students that they have nothing to fear. When children are told that they have nothing to fear, their fear increases. They then have not only the original fear but also the fear of being afraid and of being unable to hide how frightened they are. Children's fear is real and should be openly acknowledged. A student who fears a test is better off being told by the teacher that "tests are sometimes scary." This message helps students recognize that others are suffering in the same way as they are. Other false assurances—"You have nothing to be angry about," "It's not such a big problem," "This is an easy problem to solve"—should also be avoided, because they imply that what the child feels is invalid.

Teachers should show students that their feelings are honored and their opinions are accepted. No attempt should be made to argue with what students claim to feel. When students' feelings are recognized as valid, their character remains intact and their delicate self-image is protected from abuse.

USING BREVITY

Students close their minds to overtalkative teachers. Teachers have a reputation for overstating the obvious and then spending an inordinate amount of time dwelling on it. They can be particularly long-winded when they are maintaining classroom discipline.

Many of their long tirades are laced with absurdities: "Did you find your pencil? I'd like to see what you did with it. I'll bet you threw it at someone in the hallway. What did happen to it? What color was it? Where was the last place you used it? How can you possibly do your work without it? I'll let you borrow a pencil for today. Make sure you bring your own pencil tomorrow. I don't want to hear you lost another pencil. You're supposed to make sure you have a pencil in class every day."

Not one of these statements is helpful. The teacher could simply have handed the student a pencil with a reminder to bring one the next day, thus avoiding the deadly diatribe. These lengthy confrontations not only adversely affect the target student but also have pernicious effects on the whole class. Teachers need economical ways to deal with minor mishaps. Missing books, broken pencils, lost paper, forgotten assignments, and a host of other incidental problems should not take up valuable time and blunt the potential excitement of learning.

Fostering Independence in Students

Teachers need to show interest in students' success and communicate acceptance to them. Furthermore, they need to help students achieve greater independence. Teachers are mistaken when they think that children regard them as their friends. Children are more likely to consider them enemies than friends. This reality is one of the tragedies of teacher-student relationships. Teachers sometimes ask why children are not more friendly and less destructive in the classroom. After all, aren't teachers trying to help students? "The answer is: They are dependent on us, and dependency breeds hostility" (Ginott, 1973). Improving student-teacher relationships does not involve doing more for students but rather helping them achieve greater independence.

ENCOURAGING STUDENTS' AUTONOMY

Children resent infringements on their autonomy. Far less enmity is encountered when students are given a full measure of autonomy. Children need to make as many choices as they are qualified to make as soon as they are able to make them. Otherwise, dependency will increase, and dependency breeds hostility. Teachers first have to accept students' autonomy as necessary and then find ways to implement it in the classroom. Teachers can begin to encourage autonomy simply by giving children choices about small things. They might be allowed to decide whether they wanted to do ten or fifteen math problems, for example. Subsequently, more difficult problems could be confronted. Students could decide which among several projects they wished to complete. Later, they might be required to determine their own projects.

Teachers must avoid issuing commands and ordering students around. Bossing students creates resentment. Once students are resentful, they resist learning. Instead of coercing students, teachers need to merely describe the situation to them. Armed with this information, children can decide for themselves what to do. They can draw their own conclusions instead of bowing to adult commands. The result is less defiance, reduced resistance, and more collaboration. For example, instead of using force, teachers can deflect students' demands by granting their fantasies. Suppose that a group of students surround your desk while you are busy and ask a lot of questions until you feel annoyed. You could tell them not to bother you and take their seats. A better alternative would be to say, "I *wish* I had the time to listen to you and respond to your questions. Perhaps a little later on I can accommodate you." The fanciful statement "I wish" provides a noncoercive way to inform students that they should take their seats and not bother you at that time.

Too often teachers use long, drawn-out directions in which each step is a command: "Put away your lab books. Now take out your textbooks. Also get your notebooks out. Don't forget your pencils. Turn to page 196 in your textbooks. Do all the questions. When you are done, put your papers in the basket here at my desk." Greater cooperation could be anticipated if the teacher said, "We are now going to start answering the questions on page 196 in your science text." This phrasing would encourage autonomy and promote cooperation. Because the students would be expected to demonstrate greater responsibility, their self-image would also improve. Encouraging autonomy breaks down students' dependency and helps avoid hostility. When teachers make their students too dependent, they often become excessively lethargic and indecisive and even resentful. Students who have many opportunities to behave independently are more likely to become actively involved in learning and to live by the appropriate behavior standards.

HELPING STUDENTS DEAL WITH THEIR FEELINGS

Students find it confusing when they are told by teachers how they should feel and realize that they do not feel that way. Instead of telling students how they should feel when they appear distraught, teachers need to help young people learn to sort out their feelings so that they can avoid confusion and unwarranted reactions. Teachers should first listen to the problem, rephrase it in a clarifying way, and ask students to examine their options before making a decision. In this way, children discover that they can effectively solve their own problems.

Ginott recommends that teachers withhold their opinions and merely act as sounding boards for students who have problems and are upset. Some statements should just be reflected back to the students. Teachers should obviously not argue with how students feel. Children's perceptions are much different from those of adults, and teachers must respond to them without expecting students to somehow understand adult perspectives. Children routinely exaggerate the truth and become overemotional in the face of even simple problems.

A child may, for example, run to the teacher exclaiming, "Maria shoved me on purpose! I could have fallen off the slide and gotten hurt. Everyone kept yelling at me to hurry, and then she shoved me. Everybody laughed at me, too. I hate recess! Maria should be kept in class during recess." It could be concluded from this emotional outburst that the complaining student slowed the playground activity down intolerably. The teacher could respond by invalidating the student's feelings and, in effect, blaming the student: "You shouldn't get all worked up. If you would hurry along when you got up on the slide, you wouldn't have any trouble." Such a response does nothing to help the child define and then manage those feelings of outrage. It would be better to paraphrase the student's statements: "You seem upset. You feel that the other students don't like you and laugh at you. You also feel that there needs to be some kind of regulation on the playground."

Paraphrasing communicates to students that you understand how they feel, and it helps them to see their emotions from a different perspective. You do not need to accept what they say as true. In fact, you should be careful not to support statements that are false. However, you can accept the expression of feelings and help children understand that you reject neither them nor their feelings.

After you have showed students that you accept their feelings and have helped to clarify them, you should also offer help. An offer of help assures students that they can solve problems and that you stand ready to support them.

Avoiding the Perils of Praise

Praise is generally accepted as an excellent way to help children improve their behavior. It is given by most adults automatically. The form in which it is given is commonly believed to be unimportant. Ginott, however, believes that praise can be either destructive or productive depending on how it is used. Evaluative praise, he says, is destructive. Statements such as "Good boy, Darryl," "Hey, great job," and "Good work, Angela," invite dependency, evoke defensiveness, and create anxiety. Praise of this kind fails to promote self-reliance, self-direction, and self-control. These qualities, he says, require that students be free from outside judgment and rely instead on personal motivation and evaluation. Children who are given excessive evaluative praise feel compelled to satisfy the desires of others and soon respond more to these external stimuli than to their own internal standards. Their sense of well-being eventually becomes connected to receiving praise.

To praise appropriately, teachers need to tell students what they have accomplished and let them draw their own conclusions about its value. For example, instead of telling Doug, a student lab assistant, that he did a wonderful job of setting up the lab and helping other students, the teacher might say, "You have arranged things so that students can work successfully and find all the materials they need to do their experiments. It was a difficult job, but I appreciate the fact you have finished it and everything is in order." This approach allows Doug to determine for himself what is praiseworthy about his work.

Teachers can also offer interpretations rather than evaluations. Rachel, for instance, had just finished her painting of trees in autumn. Mr. Craner looked at her work and declared, "Rachel, you apparently feel the same way about fall I do. Look how you have painted a huge pile of leaves with children playing in them. That is what I remember about my own experiences every fall." It is easy to predict Rachel's response. She announced to her friends, "Look at my painting. Mr. Craner really likes it. I have shown what fall leaves are really all about." Rachel created her own assessment without depending on her teacher. Her dependency on the teacher's praise is avoided.

Sometimes praise that focuses on students' desirable attributes backfires. Praising students for their academic performance is a poor practice. Students who are publicly praised for getting the highest score on a test and told how "smart" they are may react negatively. They may suffer embarrassment and experience a sense of loathing as they anticipate the taunts from peers this kind of praise may bring. But it is not only the student being praised who is adversely affected. When some students are praised for high marks and told that they are good because they have performed so well, other students may well draw the conclusion they are bad students because they have not achieved as much. School achievement does not determine students' worth. Students are not better than others because they know more or worse because their achievement scores are low. Praising academic performance, however, validates this association of worth with achievement. Students who are unsuccessful in school already have a heavy burden to carry. Praising their more successful peers adds to their despair.

Sometimes children see evaluative praise for what it is and rebel. A teacher may, for example, praise a class for their good behavior only to have them react negatively later. The dismayed teacher may find this reaction hard to believe. After all, praise had just been given for good behavior. When students realize that they are being manipulated through the teacher's praise, they may react to it. Humans dislike being manipulated. The power of teachers to praise is also the power to condescend. When they dispense praise, teachers have an appearance of superiority over their students. Although teachers are older and more experienced, they should not emphasize their position. Ginott underscores this point by turning the situation around. If we met Picasso, he says, we would not say to him, "This painting is well done. Keep up the good work." Instead, we might say, "Thank you for enriching my life with your paintings." Children need statements of appreciation instead of praise that compares them with others or condescends.

Praise can be beneficial to students when it is correctly given. When it describes the teachers' positive feelings about the work of students, it will have a good effect. Teachers might say how much they like working with a group of students or how good they feel about the high quality of the class members' work. These statements are devoid of value judgments about students' personalities and lack elements of manipulation. Students will react positively to affirmation of this kind but respond negatively to evaluative praise.

Disciplining Students

Many classroom situations routinely irritate teachers and inhibit learning. Ginott indicates that teachers commonly respond to their students with a host of negative reactions: issuing threats, losing their temper, being rude, overreacting, punishing everyone in the class for the misbehavior of one student, and making arbitrary rules. Many teachers try to curtail the passing of notes by embarrassing the participants. Students who talk loudly may be given a lengthy lecture. When students drop objects, they are likely to suffer insults. Daydreaming students may be subjected to their teachers' cruel taunts. Students who fight may be called names and ultimately expelled. None of these actions is helpful, and all of them should be avoided.

According to Ginott, the most critical aspect to discipline is finding effective alternatives to punishment. Punishment is the universal way most discipline problems are handled. Its appropriateness is rarely questioned. The purpose of punishment is to provide children with a convincing deterrent to unacceptable actions. However, Ginott says that punishment is more likely to enrage students and make them uneducable. They become hostile, full of rancor and vengeance. So preoccupied are they with the desire for revenge that their minds have little time or inclination for study. The very purpose of being in school is thereby subverted. Children are very susceptible to a teacher's abuse. They come to school with distorted self-images and require very few negative experiences to convince them that they are unworthy. Good discipline requires teachers to act with kindness and patience over a period of time. Good discipline, says Ginott, "is a series of little victories in which a teacher, through small decencies, reaches a child's heart" (Ginott, 1971).

Discipline requires a lot of self-control on the part of the teacher. There should be no insults, name-calling, loss of temper, rudeness, cruelty, threats, lectures, or overreactions. Teachers cannot afford to create scenes. They must exhibit compassion and love even when children defy them. Children often misbehave to get their teachers to react. Their negative reactions confirm what students predict, that adults are insensitive and uncaring. Teachers must resist falling into the trap of substantiating such predictions. They must choose their words and actions themselves; they must not be triggered and compelled by students.

Teachers who discipline with punishment eventually succumb to increasing levels of brutality. Punishment promotes increased misbehavior, which in turn encourages more severe punishments. Sometimes the masochistic needs of a few students stimulate them to goad their teachers into degrading or punishing them. When these students openly defy teachers, they are in effect rewarded with verbal and physical abuse.

Punishment does not deter misconduct, even in students who ordinarily try to avoid the sting of teachers' punitive actions. It simply makes these students more cautious. They become more adroit in concealing the evidence of their misdeeds, more skillful in escaping detection. When they are caught and punished, they become more careful, not more trustworthy and responsible. As one student who was late for school decided when he claimed to have overslept and was punished nonetheless, "I'll just have to make up a more convincing story." Children do not think of how they are going to improve their behavior while they are being punished. They do not, while suffering the inflicted pain, vow to become more generous, loving, and responsible. No! They seethe inside and plan their revenge.

Some teachers naively ask, "Don't children have to be taught to be responsible and have respect for others by being punished when they act irresponsibly?" The answer is an emphatic *no*. These virtues cannot be enforced by punishment. Responsibility and respect cannot be forced into children any more than loyalty, honesty, charity, or mercy can. Children learn these characteristics by watching the behavior of others and emulating it. This principle is illustrated by the all too common ordeal of parents whose children are in trouble with the law. More than once these parents have said, shaking their heads, "I can't understand where I went wrong. I always taught them what was right. Whenever they did wrong, I whipped them so they'd know to do right." These children who find themselves in trouble or in jail generally reveal no more insight than do the parents who beat them. They are unlikely to make any connections between punishment and rebellion. They typically have no better advice for dealing with other children's misbehavior than to say, "Don't let what happened to me happen to them. Beat them till they see the light. Make sure they do what is right." Even those who believe that they have been indulged too much characteristically offer the same kind of advice: "If only my parents had made me do what was right, I wouldn't be in trouble. They should have punished me when I started to go wrong."

Few teachers believe that threats of punishment do any good. Usually they admit that threats are actually harmful. This admission does not deter some teachers from resorting to warnings and threats many times each day. When students misbehave, teachers may out of desperation make threats that students know will never be carried out. In the process, teachers usually assault students with rebukes as well as blame and shame. In reality, threats act as an invitation to misbehave. Some students see the threat as a challenge and want to see how far they can go before it is enforced. Others receive encouragement from their peers to test teachers' threats. Nothing is more rewarding to these students than to publicly force their teachers to back down from a threat they have no power to carry out.

Preventing Discipline Problems

Ginott does not propose an explicit plan for preventing discipline problems. Instead, he emphasizes the need for teachers to be loving, warm, and patient. This approach, he says, will prevent many discipline problems. Many more problems will be avoided when teachers begin applying Ginott's procedures for dealing with day-to-day discipline situations and when they implement his recommendations for using congruent language, motivating students appropriately, and avoiding the perils of praise.

Schoolwide Discipline

Ginott's work contains no specific suggestions regarding schoolwide discipline. If teachers applied his recommendations, a schoolwide discipline program might be unnecessary. There is nothing that could be done on a schoolwide basis that could not be handled better by individual teachers in their individual classes. Ginott emphasizes one-on-one contact between students and teachers and depends on teachers to respond to students in sensitive ways and provide positive experiences for them. He also advocates more involvement of students in decisions that affect them. Students who have more autonomy are much less likely to behave unacceptably.

Strengths and Weaknesses of the Ginott Model

STRENGTHS

1. It focuses on the development of self-concept, which is a key to avoiding discipline problems.
2. It helps teachers avoid promoting rebellion.
3. It encourages positive relationships between teachers and their students.
4. It emphasizes students' autonomy.
5. It provides a means of preventing many different discipline problems.

WEAKNESSES

1. It is composed of a long list of *dos* and *don'ts* rather than a comprehensive set of principles to apply.
2. It has no specific steps for dealing with discipline problems.

SUMMARY

Ginott believes in establishing a positive learning environment for children in school. In the classroom, teachers must use congruent communication; they must show concern for students' feelings and realize that students are greatly affected by what teachers say. Teachers must, therefore, avoid attacking students' character and address the situation instead, specifying what is going on and what needs to be changed. Students' rebellion and distrust of adults can be reduced if teachers avoid both bossing students and slapping uncomplimentary labels on them. In working with students, teachers should treat them as they themselves would like to be treated. Teachers should provide choices for, request cooperation from, and offer help to students who are experiencing frustration.

CENTRAL IDEAS

1. Congruent communication conveys acceptance instead of rejection and helps teachers avoid blaming and shaming students.
2. Sane messages point to the students' misbehavior, not to their character and personality.
3. When students need correction, brief messages will produce better results than lengthy harangues.
4. Giving students autonomy will decrease enmity between students and teachers.
5. Teachers can better deal with students' feelings by acting as sounding boards than by trying to control the expression of their emotions.
6. Praising students' academic performance in an evaluative way or in a way that emphasizes their subordinate position will probably cause them to rebel.
7. Punishment persuades students to rebel and make excuses.

QUESTIONS AND ACTIVITIES

QUESTIONS TO CONSIDER

1. What are the significant differences between Ginott's discipline approach and those of Glasser, Dreikurs, and Harris?
2. What problems are teachers likely to experience using Ginott's discipline approach?

CLASSROOM ACTIVITIES

1. Create a list of discipline problems and, without benefit of discussion, have students write down how they would respond to each of the situations using Ginott's recommendations. Discuss and compare these responses, and draw conclusions about which responses would be most positive.
2. On small slips of paper write statements that might be made by students or descriptions of discipline situations. Fold the slips of paper and mix them together.

Have members of the class draw a slip of paper and make a verbal response to what is written on it. Have other members of the class critique the responses.

STUDENT APPLICATIONS

You are the teacher of a rather active class. For each of the following situations, provide a response that is consistent with Ginott's recommendations. Compare your responses with those of other students and decide which response is most appropriate.

1. Joyce screams out in class, "I hate this class! I hate you too! Your assignments are so unfair."
2. Hal throws torn-up pieces of paper all over the floor.
3. Walter trips Thayne as he tries to walk up the aisle.
4. You see Georgia looking on Don's paper during an examination.
5. Francine habitually fails to turn her homework in on time. When she does, it is incomplete.
6. You observe Miggs passing a note to Lois.
7. Ramona grabs Arlene's hair and shakes her head savagely.
8. Betty Jane takes Darold's research paper and rips it up.
9. Camille is sitting in the back of the room softly crying to herself.
10. Ann picks up her books and walks to the door five minutes before the bell rings.
11. DeVerl has cut deep marks in his desk with his knife.
12. Jerry has taken Norma's shoe and dropped it out the window.
13. Delbert accuses Rose Marie of sleeping around.
14. Thedora has moved from her seat in the front of the room and has taken a seat next to Dee. They are sitting holding hands instead of working on the assignment.
15. Nyles pokes Darlis with his pencil. Darlis calls Nyles every profane word that comes to mind.

REFERENCES

Ginott, H. (1971). *Teacher and child*. New York: Macmillan.

Ginott, H. (1972). I am angry! I am appalled! I am furious! *Today's Education, 61*, 23–24.

Ginott, H. (1973). Driving children sane. *Today's Education, 62*, 20–25.

9

The Kounin Model: Jacob Kounin

OBJECTIVES

This chapter is designed to help you

1. define the ripple effect and explain how it is influenced by the clarity, firmness, and roughness of desists
2. explain how identifying the proper student and using the proper timing in correcting students' misbehavior contributes to withitness in the classroom
3. indicate what teachers must do to ensure overlapping in the classroom
4. understand how movement management (avoiding jerkiness and slowdowns), group focus, and techniques for preventing boredom can be used in maintaining good classroom discipline

ASSUMPTIONS

1. Negative or positive moves by teachers toward students radiate out and influence students around them.
2. Students need to be controlled by their teachers.
3. Control can be improved by increasing the clarity and firmness of the desist.
4. Teachers can improve the control they have by displaying withitness.
5. When target students have been appropriately identified and when teachers' moves are properly timed, greater control of students' behavior is possible.
6. Effective control depends on well-executed overlapping.
7. Avoiding jerky transitions can improve discipline in the classroom.
8. Stopping instruction to deal with discipline problems only adds to the problems.

Introduction

Jacob Kounin was born in Cleveland, Ohio, in 1912. He was educated at Iowa State University and spent his professional life at Wayne State University. As a college professor, he noticed a phenomenon he later termed "the ripple effect" when he reprimanded one of his students for reading a school newspaper during one of his lectures. This insight led him to a two-decade study of the effects of teachers' interventions in the classroom. Kounin wondered what differences there were between teachers who managed their classes well and those who did not. He made hundreds of videotapes of teachers in the classroom, which he analyzed in detail. From this work he identified several important techniques good teachers routinely use in their teaching. His research was published in *Discipline and Group Management in Classrooms* (Kounin, 1970a). Kounin's work is considered pivotal by many researchers in the field.

Kounin's studies of classroom management began accidently when one day he reprimanded a student in his Mental Hygiene class at the university for reading a newspaper he had unfolded in front of him. His reprimand was completely contrary to what he advocated in the course, but it caused him to notice what he later called the "ripple effect": Other students in the class were adversely affected by his reprimand. Whispers stopped, concentration shifted from the instructor or the window to notebooks on the desks, and side glances at others ceased. Silence in the classroom was heavy. This experience, confirmed by subsequent research, showed a remarkable effect of teachers' efforts to maintain discipline in the classroom: Their *desists* (remarks intended to stop misbehavior) affected students who witnessed the event. The effect of the desist rippled out from the target student to influence the behavior of others in the class.

After investigating the ripple effect, Kounin and his colleagues went on to explore other important classroom management phenomena. They discovered that teachers were more effective when they had "withitness," the ability to be aware of what is going on in all parts of the classroom at all times. They also showed that making smooth transitions between activities and maintaining momentum within activities are essential to managing classrooms. The use of strategies for maintaining group alertness and increasing students' accountability was found to greatly increase students' attention. Students' attention was also increased through the use of various techniques for avoiding boredom. Taken together, the techniques researched by Kounin have provided a way to prevent discipline problems (Kounin, 1970a). Kounin claims that he discovered nothing new in his research. Rather, by studying videotapes of many classrooms, he simply learned what successful teachers did that their less successful counterparts did not.

Characteristics of Desists

The metaphor of a ripple to describe what happens when teachers issue a desist is an apt one. The effect of teachers' interventions spread out from the target student to other class members—first to those near the target student, then to those a bit farther away, and then in turn to those still farther. Kounin studied desists and the ripple effect in four different settings: college, high school, kindergarten, and summer camp. In his study of kindergarten children, Kounin found that he could describe desists in terms of three major characteristics: clarity, firmness, and roughness (Kounin, Gump, & Ryan, 1961). These characteristics help determine how great a ripple is created by a particular desist.

CLARITY

Clarity is a measure of the amount of information the teacher provides students during a desist. A teacher may, for example, yell for a student to "stop that." This command provides very little information. Nothing is specified about the nature of the inappropriate behavior nor what should be done to correct it. More clarity would be provided if the teacher instead said, "Lee, stop pushing José." Clarity is achieved in three ways:

1. by clearly specifying the inappropriate behavior ("Carlos, stop hitting Eric.")
2. by providing instruction about how to stop the misbehavior ("Carlos, take your seat.")
3. by providing a reason for the desist ("Carlos, you can't remain in class if you hit other students.")

Kounin found that students who witnessed a teacher desist another child's misbehavior with clarity tended to conform more and misbehave less. This tendency was true of the target student as well.

FIRMNESS

The firmness of a desist also influences the ripple effect. Firmness is the extent to which teachers convey the messages "I mean it" and "right now." If a teacher says, "Please stop talking, Julie," the directive will have very little ripple effect. However, firmness can be increased if the teacher (1) makes the desist more emphatically, (2) stops talking and looks at the student, (3) walks toward the student, or (4) touches or otherwise guides the student toward proper behavior (Kounin, 1970a). Firmness has less effect than clarity and is effective only with students who are misbehaving.

ROUGHNESS

The roughness of a desist has a different effect than its clarity and firmness. Roughness in a desist is the extent to which the teacher expresses anger or exasperation through scowls, remarks, threats, or punishment. Roughness fails to improve behavior. However, children do tend to be upset and anxious when witnessing a desist with roughness (Kounin & Gump, 1961). Roughness is sometimes thought to be just an intensification of firmness. However, its effects are different enough to merit its consideration as a separate characteristic.

In his college study, Kounin (1970a) found that supporting desists (those that offer help to students) and threatening desists (those that chastise students) produced ripple effects. Students who were not themselves targets of the desist were affected by it. Threatening desists, however, lowered students' estimates of the instructor's competence, helpfulness, likability, lack of authoritarianism, and fairness.

In his high school study, Kounin found that the type of desist had no effect on the amount of misbehavior exhibited by students who witnessed it. It did, however, create some emotional discomfort for them. The factor that did influence behavior was the degree to which the teacher was liked. High regard for the teacher, in connection with high motivation to learn, produced the highest level of work involvement and a minimum of misbehavior. Punishment was observed to have no impact in classes in which students had low achievement motivation. When teachers increased firmness, an inclination to behave better was found only among those students with high motivation to learn the subject. Students were more likely to approve of a teacher's methods of handling misbehavior and more inclined to side with the teacher than with misbehaving students if they were highly motivated to learn. In addition, students who liked the teacher were more accepting of the teacher's methods of controlling misbehavior.

Unlike desists in the other settings, desists in a summer camp produced no ripple effects and did not affect the amount of misbehavior in the participants. Kounin attributed this result to the view that misconduct at summer camp is more acceptable than at school. Obviously, what students feel is acceptable or unacceptable behavior influences ripple effects.

In general, younger students are more greatly affected by ripple effects when the desist has clarity and firmness. College and high school students are influenced by ripple effects according to how much they like and respect the instructor and how motivated they are to learn.

Using Desists Effectively

As Kounin continued his research efforts, he learned that the results of desists in an experimental setting were different from those that occurred naturally in the classroom. In experimental settings, he found that desists with different characteristics had effects that differed according to the grade level of the students and the circumstances. However, when students were studied in natural situations with teachers they had been with for a while, the characteristics of the desist made no difference in how they behaved. This finding suggested, of course, that other factors were involved. By careful study, Kounin determined that by themselves the attributes of the desist—clarity, firmness, and roughness—made no difference in classroom behavior. What did seem to matter was the teachers' ability to accurately monitor what was actually taking place in their classroom (their degree of "withitness"), whether they dealt with the most serious discipline infractions as the primary problems (correct targeting), and whether they chose an appropriate moment to issue a desist to the person who initiated trouble (correct timing). It also mattered whether teachers could deal with more than just one situation at a time ("overlapping"). Obviously, more than one activity takes place at one time in most classrooms. The ability of teachers to deal with more than one situation simultaneously determined whether a particular desist technique worked effectively (Kounin, 1970a).

WITHITNESS

▼ Brian was whispering to Jon during quiet study time. Ms. Tobler looked up and said, "Brian, stop that whispering!" The desist had clarity and firmness but made no difference. At the same time Brian was whispering to Jon, Ms. Tobler failed to detect Sonja and Jeff flipping spit wads at one another in another part of the room.

▼ Mr. Nielsen was helping Huia and Tim at his desk when he became aware of students whispering. He looked up in time to see Arlene lean over and whisper something in Georgia's ear. Mr. Nielsen said, "Arlene and Georgia, stop that." Whispering continued all around the room as Mr. Nielsen continued helping Huia and Tim. What Mr. Nielsen had missed was the fact that Francine had been making fun of Georgia and Arlene had just whispered to Georgia not to pay any attention to her. Mr. Nielsen was unaware of what was really happening in the classroom, even though class members were.

In both of these cases, teachers lacked what Kounin calls *withitness*, the ability to know what is going on in all areas of the classroom at all times. Teachers who have withitness appear to have "eyes in the back of their heads." Their uncanny ability to track even those activities students try to hide increases their effectiveness in stopping students' misbehavior. Students need to be convinced that their teachers know what is really going on (Kounin, 1970b). Otherwise, disruptive behavior persists. Students apparently are drawn to see how far they can go in creating problems for the teacher. If the teacher knows what is going on (is "with it"), there is no need to continually test the limits. The limits are known.

In developing withitness, teachers should make sure that each desist they issue is correct in terms of its targeting and its timing.

Targeting.   Mistakes in targeting are of two types:

1. The teacher desists the wrong child or an onlooker for misbehavior.
2. The teacher desists a less serious display of misbehavior while overlooking a more serious one occurring at the same time.

Sometimes teachers fail to track an entire sequence of their students' behavior and thus fail to properly identify the student who initiates a problem. Instead, they catch a student who is reacting to another's provocation. When teachers confront students who are just reacting to classmates, they encourage more such provocations. When real perpetrators can consistently avoid detection, other class members are less fearful that they may be observed if they too step out of line. In addition, the class is likely to make a joke of the teacher's ineptness in catching on to what is happening.

Ignoring a more serious classroom infraction and attending to a less serious one also limits the effectiveness of a desist. In the following example, the teacher makes a mistake in targeting:

▼ Nellie was sitting at her desk reading her library book even though she has been assigned to work on her genetics exercise. Mr. Hugie observed her for a minute and then ordered her to put her book away and get busy on the assignment. He missed the fact that Jared and Lurleen were at the back of the room trying to catch goldfish in the fish tank.

Likewise, if a teacher desists a child who was observed whispering to a neighbor while two other children fight in the back of the room, the teacher obviously is attending to the wrong target. Students react to mistargeting with increased misbehavior. They sense that their teacher is not really aware and are more willing to misbehave without fear of being caught. Teachers' credibility depends on selecting the most serious discipline problem on which to focus attention.

Timing. Timing is a critical aspect of withitness. Correct timing is determined by whether or not misbehavior is allowed to become more serious before the teacher takes action. The timing for a desist is correct if the misbehavior is no more serious at the time of the desist than at the time it started. The interval between the onset of the misbehavior and the desist is not the critical element in determining whether timing is correct or not; rather, it is the seriousness of the misbehavior.

It is a timing mistake to wait until misbehavior spreads before doing anything about it. For example, if a couple of students left their seats and went to the back of the room and were then joined by three or four others before the teacher intervened, the desist may be too late. Once the misbehavior spreads, it is much more difficult to deal with. When the two students started toward the back of the room, the teacher should have immediately requested that they take their seats.

Another timing mistake is to allow misbehavior to increase before it is desisted.

▼ Ms. Taylor was watching Reed and Reese as they discussed who had the right to use the swing first during recess. When Reed insisted that it was his turn, Reese replied, "You always say that. Every recess you think you get to use the swing first. It's my turn to be first."

Reed replied, "That's not true. You had it first yesterday. I'm going to use it first today." Without further argument, Reed grabbed the swing from Reese, causing him to slip and fall. As soon as Reese hit the ground, he bounced right up and started pounding on Reed with his fists, trying to get the swing back. When Ms. Taylor reached them, they were rolling around on the ground and pounding on one another.

Ms. Taylor waited too long to intervene. She should have made her desist before tempers flared.

It is critical that teachers handle students' misbehavior by directing their efforts at the proper student as quickly as possible. Correct targeting and timing are far more important than firmness and clarity. *The most effective desist will be well-timed and directed to the proper students with the necessary firmness and clarity.*

OVERLAPPING

▼ Ms. Kennedy had divided her class into two groups; students in one group worked on their science experiments, and students in the other group practiced the Thanksgiving play. Ms. Kennedy was listening to Nancy recite her lines when David and Jerry, who were supposed to be working quietly on their science projects, started talking loudly. "Nancy," Ms. Kennedy instructed, "I'm listening. Continue reciting. David and Jerry, get back to your seats and continue working on your science projects without making so much noise."

▼ Wally was reciting the names of the bones and muscles in the human body to Mr. Holmstead, his physiology teacher. Mr. Holmstead noticed that Deanna and Robert were making and throwing paper airplanes instead of reciting the names of the bones and muscles to one another. He left Wally and went to where Deanna and Robert were sitting. "Listen, you two!" he roared. "Stop this nonsense right now! I know you haven't finished learning the names of the bones and muscles already. Get back to work!"

How do these two desists compare with one another? In the first example, Ms. Kennedy is successfully handling both situations. She does not have to stop one activity to attend to the other. She allows one situation to continue and deals decisively with the second. Many teachers, like Mr. Holmstead, drop the learning activity in which they are involved to respond to misbehavior. During this delay, the students whose learning was interrupted may get distracted and find it hard to refocus themselves once the teacher returns. In addition, students elsewhere in the classroom may become more unruly as they witness the lack of withitness exhibited by the teacher.

Overlapping, the management of more than one activity simultaneously, does not consist exclusively of verbal directions given to students. A remark or a simple look can convincingly communicate to students that the teacher is aware of what is happening. Remarks and looks are more effective if they are given with clarity and firmness (Kounin & Gump, 1974).

Withitness and overlapping have been studied to determine both their individual and their combined effectiveness. These studies indicate that although withitness plays a somewhat more important role in classroom management, withitness and overlapping are significantly related. *The most effective desist will show that the teacher knows what is going on in the classroom; it will be properly timed and targeted and have firmness and clarity. It also will not interfere with other tasks the teacher is performing.*

▼ Ms. Sorensen was working with a group of students at her desk. Charlotte, a member of the group, was reciting a poem she had just memorized in preparation for the school poetry festival on Friday. Meanwhile, Brad and Norma left their seats near the door and moved to the window to watch some of their classmates playing on the softball diamond. As they watched, they pointed out the window and softly talked about what they were observing. At the back of the room, Dee, Hal, and Yusef were laughing out loud as Yusef threw one of Fern's shoes to Dee. With the first toss of the shoe, Ms. Sorensen motioned to Charlotte to keep reciting and then said, "Dee, hand Fern's shoe back to her. Dee, Hal, and Yusef, take your seats right now and finish the questions in chapter 15 that have been assigned. You must turn them in at the end of this class period." Then, looking over at Brad and Norma, she nodded at them as a signal to take their seats, too. Brad and Norma quickly went to their seats and began working on the assigned problems.

Ms. Sorensen terminated the distraction immediately without stopping Charlotte's recitation. Her desist was timed to avoid the possibility that the shoe-throwing episode would escalate and spread to other students. Her message was clearly and firmly given.

In addition, she attended to the most critical target situation first and dealt with it decisively, making it unnecessary to do more than nod her head to correct a less serious situation. Ms. Sorensen thus simultaneously demonstrated her withitness and her skill in overlapping. Students in Ms. Sorensen's class were given reason to believe that she knew what was going on throughout the classroom and could deal clearly and firmly with each situation according to its merits. If they were tempted to misbehave, few students in her class would want to risk detection, for Ms. Sorensen obviously had eyes in the back of her head.

Movement Management

In self-contained classrooms where students work together, teachers initiate, sustain, and terminate many activities every day, and they coordinate the movement of their students. Sometimes students must move physically from one place in the room to another—for example, going from a reading circle to lab tables or lining up to go to the library. At other times they must move psychologically, as when they change from one kind of activity to another—for example, from quiet seat work to a discussion or from a teacher-directed exercise to self-directed cooperative work. All these movements present potentially difficult management problems. How can teachers make these changes and still retain a reasonable amount of order in the classroom?

Some teachers have difficulty handling these simple transitions:

▼ Mr. Keller decided that it was time to finish math instruction and begin group reading. He said, "All right, class, put away your arithmetic books and take out your reading books. When you have your reading books in hand, go ahead and move to your reading groups." When about half the class were on their way to their new location, Mr. Keller realized that he had forgotten to tell them to bring a pencil and paper with them. Consequently, he issued new instructions: "Class, you will need a pencil and paper today in your reading groups. Please take one with you when you go." Some students were able to go directly to their reading group. But there was some pushing and shoving and complaining among those who had to return to their desks to pick up the necessary pencils and paper.

Mr. Keller should have asked students to bring pencils and paper with them before directing them to move to their reading groups.

▼ Ms. Merrill had just finished a discussion about pronouns and had instructed her class to take out their textbooks and begin answering the questions at the end of chapter 12. As her students began to take out their books, Ms. Merrill said, "I forgot to tell you how you did on yesterday's test. I have all the tests scored, but they are not all recorded in my roll book. Some of you did pretty well, but there were a number of you who scored quite low. There were six who failed the test entirely. I'll try to get your tests back to you tomorrow, but it may be Monday before I can manage it. I have to score the tests for the other classes too." There were some loud groans, and a few students started vigorously waving their hands in the air. "Please get started on your assignment," Ms. Merrill implored. "You have only until the end of the period to complete it." Students continued to talk among themselves. Finally, Ms. Merrill yelled, "All right now, get to work! I'm not going to accept any late assignments!"

Ms. Merrill would have had better classroom control had she said nothing about the test until she was ready to hand it back.

Both of these episodes exhibit misbehavior caused by transition problems. In Kounin's research, important relationships were found between students' behavior and the maintenance of momentum within and between lessons. The ability of teachers to properly pace the work of students and to retain momentum and move smoothly from one activity to the next had much to do with the effective management of students. When transitions were smooth, students' attention continued to be focused and task-oriented behavior was promoted.

Kounin identified two kinds of transition mistakes teachers make that encourage misbehavior in students: jerkiness and slowdowns.

AVOIDING JERKINESS

The jerkiness of teachers' actions thwarts the smooth movement from one activity to another and encourages confusion, unnecessary activity, noise, delay, and misbehavior. To avoid these problems, teachers must make smooth transitions by establishing routines, giving clear directions, and completing one task before beginning another.

Jerkiness produces stops or jarring breaks in the flow of learning activities. These breaks may be short, momentary interruptions or relatively long episodes. There are a number of management mistakes teachers make that are classified as jerky. They include stimulus-boundedness, thrusts, dangles, truncations, and flip-flops.

Stimulus-Boundedness.   A stimulus-bound teacher readily gets off the track during a lesson by reacting to other, relatively unimportant things that are going on at the same time. Mr. Bell may, for example, stop in the middle of his explanation of how to prepare drawings for his woodworking class and exclaim, "Gene, if you don't sit up straight, you will have back problems for the rest of your life." Gene may need help in learning to sit up straight, but interjecting this comment in the middle of a lesson causes a momentary halt, and smoothness is lost.

Teachers who are stimulus-bound seem drawn to unplanned and irrelevant stimuli. They react to or comment about almost any extraneous event coming to their attention. They are distracted from the ongoing activity and become preoccupied with superfluous events. The teachers in the following examples succumb to stimulus-boundedness:

▼ Ms. Gunnell was explaining techniques of writing shorthand when her attention was drawn to a can of soda pop that had tipped over and spilled its contents on the floor. "Whose soda pop is that on the floor?" she shouted. "Who put it there? It's by your desk, Maxine. Does it belong to you? Hurry and get some paper towels from the restroom and clean it up."

▼ Mr. Larsen was explaining that the edible part of a kohlrabi is really the stem of the plant when he noticed that there was no food in the guinea pig's cage. "Who was assigned to feed the guinea pig today? Was it you, Lianne? Here, let me get it some pellets. Look at it eat! Has this guinea pig had any food this week? It acts like it's nearly starved. We're going to have to assign someone to feed it who will be responsible."

▼ Ms. Brenchley had been reviewing for the next day's test for about 15 minutes when she noticed that Glen had laid his head on his desk and was apparently asleep. "Look at Glen," she said. "Looks like he didn't get enough sleep last night. You students need to make sure you get to bed early so you can be alert in your classes. Now look what Glen is going to miss. He won't be ready for the test tomorrow. I hope all of you get enough sleep tonight so you won't be dead-headed during the exam tomorrow."

Thrusts.   Thrusts also disrupt the instructional process. A thrust is a sudden interruption of a learning activity with an irrelevant announcement, order, statement, or question (Gnagey, 1975). Thrusts make teachers seem oblivious to the group's readiness to receive their messages or respond to their questions. The intrusion is made without consideration for what students are doing. Teachers should appraise a situation beforehand to determine whether an interruption will disturb the thought process of students or interfere with group tasks.

▼ Mr. Bingham's chemistry students had been working on their test for about 20 minutes when he remembered that he had not told them that they needed to turn in their science fair proposals by the following Friday. He broke the silence unexpectedly by saying, "Class, I need your attention for a minute, please. I forgot to tell you to turn in science fair proposals by next Friday. If you fail to get them in by then, you will be unable to participate. Remember now, get them to me by Friday. It's 20 percent of your grade this term."

▼ Ms. Condie was talking to her home economics class about how to get the most for their money at the grocery store. Rozanne had been asked to tell about her trips with her family to do grocery shopping. When Rozanne finished, Nat, Joan, and Sidney raised their hands to volunteer information about their own shopping experiences. Ms. Condie suddenly turned around to face the chalkboard and, ignoring Rozanne as well as the three other students, said, "Look here at the chalkboard. You need to write down this assignment. It will be due next week. How many of you are done with last week's assignment?"

Dangles.   Dangles also disrupt smoothness. A dangle is an interruption that occurs when a teacher who is involved with students in one activity suddenly begins another, thereby leaving the previous undertaking hanging in midair, and then returns to the original activity. Dangles can occur either at transition points or during an ongoing activity.

▼ Mr. Wolfgram said, "Class, look at these words on the board. They need to be copied in your notebooks. Let me define them for you as you record them." Mr. Wolfgram started toward the chalkboard and then stopped and went to his desk instead. For about 20 seconds he shuffled through some papers; finally finding the current attendance sheet, he placed it in his outbox. This mission accomplished, he returned again to the task of defining the list of words written on the chalkboard.

▼ Ms. Arnoldsen was leading a discussion about how to solve quadratic equations. "Marilyn," she said, "would you explain how you got your solution to problem number

8 and put your work on the chalkboard?" The class watched quietly as Marilyn went to the board and copied out her answer. As Marilyn put on the finishing touches and set down the chalk, Ms. Arnoldsen asked, "Who is absent today? Did Dale make it? Does anyone know why Carvel isn't here today? OK, Marilyn, go ahead and explain your solution to the problem."

Truncations.   If a learning activity is begun and then suspended indefinitely, a truncation has occurred. One might say that a truncation is a long-lasting dangle. The initial activity is left hanging while other matters receive attention. The smoothness of a lesson is destroyed when it is abruptly dropped in favor of some unrelated activity.

Flip-Flops.   Flip-flops also occur at transition points in a lesson when the teacher terminates one activity and then starts another, only to return to the original activity again.

> ▼   "Class," the teacher said, "it's time to put away your science textbooks and get out your math books. Put your science books in your desks out of the way." After the children had swapped their science books for their math books, the teacher said, "We need to make sure you know which science questions should be done at home tonight and which ones need to be completed during the lab tomorrow. Which questions should be done at home tonight?"

AVOIDING SLOWDOWNS

Lesson momentum keeps students interested and involved and well-behaved. When momentum is lost, management problems occur. Any behavior of teachers that clearly slows down the rate of movement in recitation activities is known as a slowdown. Slowdowns hold the class back and produce a sense that time is being wasted. They occur in the form of overdwelling and fragmentation (Kounin, 1970a).

Overdwelling.   Overdwelling results when teachers continue to focus exclusively on a single issue long after students have understood the point being made (Kounin, 1970a). Overdwelling—commonly referred to as preaching, pontificating, nagging, or admonishing—makes children think, "All right, all right, enough already!" Overdwelling used in stopping misbehavior or encouraging conformity is often called overkill.

Teachers sometimes overdwell when they call attention to students' misbehavior.

> ▼   Ms. Adair looked up just in time to see Clair flip a spit wad at Elaine. "Clair, you stop flipping spit wads right now! Don't you know you could have put Elaine's eye out? On top of that, when you put those things in your mouth and flip them around the room, you can spread disease. I don't know how I'm going to get you to stop annoying other students by flipping spit wads at them. You need to be more cooperative. You'll just have to come in after school and clean them up. I don't think it's right to leave this mess for Mr. Palmer to clean up. I hate walking around and stepping on these filthy little objects all day long. This just has to stop. You need to learn what it means to be a good citizen in class. Good citizens don't bother other students by flip-

ping spit wads at them. People can't study when they're being hit with projectiles. I think it's time you decided to be more responsible. The next time this happens you may just have to visit the principal."

Whenever teachers engage in preaching, unnecessary slowdown occurs. Lesson continuity is ruined and more misbehavior is stimulated.

Some teachers overelaborate the directions they give. They continue to provide explanations when most of their students already grasp the concept.

▼ Mr. Shipley had his art class making Old English letters. As he walked around the room, he noticed that Brent's lettering did not meet his expectations. "Brent," he cautioned, "you need to make your letters so they stand straight on your paper. Also, your curls are not as round as they should be. Look here, class. See Brent's letters. They are not straight on the paper, and the curls are too flattened. They need to be more rounded. Brent, let's see if you can get them right. I think if you will make a box around the area in which you plan to put your letter, you can make sure it stands up straight. If you were trying to sell your lettering to someone, they would not be very impressed. They'd just give it back to you and look for someone else to do the job. Remember, you must make your letters in a very professional way. I suggest you try to make a letter inside a box and then set it back from you a little distance and see if it is sitting straight. Remember to put complete curves on your letters. That's very important. Now, class, let's see how well you can do your lettering."

Overdwelling can also occur when teachers concentrate on one small part of a more complex unit or behavior.

▼ Mr. Hart wanted to get the attention of two of his students. He directed them to watch him: "Pauletta, Kathryn, you need to turn around and face the board. You can't possibly see how to work these problems if you don't keep your eyes on the board. Now sit up straight and watch me at the board. Stop being distracted by the people behind you. You need to focus your attention on the board and what we are doing in class. If you don't, you won't know what to do with these problems when you get home tonight and try to solve them."

Teachers can spend an excessive amount of time collecting or passing back tests, papers, books, or other materials. They may, for example, pass out worksheets one at a time instead of a row at a time. It would be quicker and more efficient to count out the number of sheets needed in each row and then hand this pile to the nearest student in that row.

Fragmentation.   Another type of slowdown, fragmentation, occurs when teachers break an activity into subparts when it could be carried out as a single unit. Teachers may, for example, call one child to the board at a time when they could simply ask an entire row to take their places at the chalkboard.

The teacher in the following example gives a direction and then breaks it into fragments.

▼ "All right, class, put away your geography books and get out your math books. I want you all to close your geography books. Put away your workbooks and your colored pencils. Remember to put your rulers in your desks, too. OK, close your geography books. Put them where they belong. You need to get them out of the way while you work on math. When you have done this, I want you to take out your math books. Take out your math books and put them on your desk. All that should be on your desks now is your math books. Turn to page 139. You will need a piece of paper and your regular pencil. Remember, I told you to put your colored pencils away. Now we will start on problem number 1. How many have a piece of paper and a pencil ready?"

Effective teachers avoid both jerkiness and slowdowns. They manage movement in their classes so that students participate and remain attentive. They keep lessons flowing smoothly. Kounin's research showed a very strong relationship between smoothness and momentum of the class, indicating that together these two factors improve classroom productivity and discipline. Maintaining momentum tends to be the more important of the two, but smoothness itself significantly improves learning and reduces disruptions (Kounin & Doyle, 1975).

Group Focus

Few teachers have the luxury of working with one student at a time. More often they work with an entire class. In ordinary classes, Kounin found that teachers who could keep students paying attention to the same thing at the same time had fewer disruptions and their students learned more. He called this attention *group focus* (Kounin, 1970a).

Group focus requires the participation of students who are not engaged in reciting during a lesson. Obviously, the more students who participate, the more involved they will be and the fewer disruptions they will cause. For example, a teacher who is teaching children to multiply two-digit numbers could have one student in class verbally give the answer to problems as they are solved while class members write their answers either on paper at their desks or on the chalkboard. Students who solve problems at their seats could be asked, at the teacher's signal, to raise the problem sheets up to be examined. Having everyone solve and give answers to problems makes it unnecessary for the group to wait for one of its members to respond. All students get a chance to test their skills.

To sustain group focus, teachers should keep students on their toes and help them maintain attention (Kounin, 1970a). Kounin recommends the following techniques for keeping a group alert:

1. Create suspense. Pause and look around before selecting a reciter, saying, "Let's see now, I need to find a person who appears to know the answer."

2. Avoid naming the student who will be called on until the question is asked. Randomly pick students to answer questions. Avoid patterns that allow students to predict when they will not be called on and therefore do not have to prepare an answer.

3. Intersperse questions that call for all students to respond in unison with those that require individuals to answer. For a response in unison, teachers might either have the whole group recite or ask all students who know an answer to raise their hands.

4. Alert those students who are not reciting at the moment to be prepared to react to the reciter's response. Students may be told to look for mistakes or to formulate differences of opinion. A teacher may ask, for example, "Who agrees with Don's answer? Jane, what do you think is the correct answer?" Students who are not performing at the moment are thus invited to maintain focus on the lesson along with the person who is reciting.

Teachers should also make it necessary for each student to learn all of the information taught in class (Kounin, 1970a). Several techniques can help students become more accountable for learning all of the subject matter:

1. Ask students to hold up their work so that it can be visually inspected. In Ms. Cutler's math class, for example, all students are provided with a set of numeral cards that can be held up to represent the answers they obtain in working math problems.

2. Require students to recite their answers to questions in unison.

3. Involve other students in a recitation. You could say, "Class, let's watch Kenny closely while he gives the multiplication facts for the sevens."

4. Ask children who are prepared to demonstrate their skill or knowledge to raise their hands. Then ask some of these children to demonstrate.

5. During a recitation, circulate and check the work of children who are not reciting.

6. Check the performance of students while they are performing.

7. Ask all members of the class to make written responses and then randomly ask a few selected participants to give their responses.

According to Kounin, keeping children alert is more critical to productive discipline than checking on them. However, both techniques for maintaining group focus are evidenced in the behavior of teachers who are successful in managing their classes (Kounin, 1970a).

Preventing Boredom

Students have a hard time maintaining interest in activities that are repeated too often. When their interest wanes, they become progressively more disruptive. The quality of their work also suffers. When students become bored, they may begin to make mistakes they would not otherwise make. They may work more mechanically and carelessly. When they work without thinking, they fail to get meaning from what they are doing and lose the continuity necessary to understand an entire concept or principle.

Students who are bored not only become less involved, but they may also cause disruptions in an effort to somehow break the monotony. They may daydream, poke their neighbor, tap their feet, or start talking with those around them (Kounin, 1970a). Educators erroneously consider short "attention span" to be the primary source of students' boredom. However, Kounin found in his research that children need a lot of variety to maintain attention. How long an activity lasts is not a crucial factor. Teachers need to create lessons that provide sufficient variety and move from activity to activity smoothly and at appropriate times. Kounin suggests that teachers can prevent boredom by providing students with meaningful, challenging work and introducing variety in their lessons.

MEANINGFUL, CHALLENGING WORK

Students need to feel that they are making progress in an activity and that the activity is worthwhile. It takes longer for students to become bored when they feel that they are accomplishing something useful. Kounin noticed that when students felt challenged during a lesson, boredom was delayed. When they were challenged, they felt that what they had done was important and meaningful. A challenging activity produced a greater sense of accomplishment than a routine, simple activity. It is not easy to provide students with an appropriate level of challenge. Some students may be overwhelmed with a task others find only mildly difficult. In some cases, work that is demanding to some students will be too easy and routine for their classmates. Teachers may have to issue different challenges to different students. The whole class can be alerted to a challenging task if teachers preface the activity: "Your next assignment, class, is going to be an interesting one. You will all find it to be helpful in creating better relationships with your friends. It will take some time and effort on your part, but you will find it very worthwhile."

VARIETY

Variety adds zest to life. According to Kounin, it does the same thing in school. He found that the greater the variety in teachers' lessons, the less rapidly satiation occurs. Variety can be created in a number of ways.

Content.　　Teachers can vary the content of the material being taught. Varying content is easier to do in self-contained classrooms, where several different subjects are taught. Teachers can move from subject to subject periodically. The greatest variety is created when dissimilar subjects follow one another. In secondary schools, varying content is more difficult. Teachers could conceivably add some variety to a single subject by having students study more than one topic at a time within that subject.

Difficulty.　　The level of intellectual challenge can also be varied. Tasks can vary from simple memorization to critical problem-solving and creative thinking. Varying the level of difficulty is an ideal way to prevent boredom because it corresponds to recommended strategies for deepening students' intellectual development as they move through the curriculum (Taba, 1967).

Presentation.　　Variation of presentation patterns can create interest in students. Even the most interesting approaches to teaching will eventually become boring if they are used continually. Teachers can use such presentation methods as demonstrations, labs, lectures, discussions, problem-solving sessions, role-playing, and classroom debates to add interest to their lessons.

Materials.   Some teachers add interest to their classes by varying the numbers and kinds of materials they use in teaching. Many teachers use only textbooks and worksheets. Other possibilities include slides and film strips, videotapes and motion pictures, audiotape recordings, live specimens, musical instruments, paintings, carvings, souvenirs collected in foreign countries, laboratory equipment, pictures—and the list goes on.

Group Structure.   Restructuring group configuration provides a way to create variety. Small-group work and independent study can be interspersed among whole-class activities. Sometimes students participate more fully in a class discussion when it is preceded by smaller group discussions. Teachers may start out teaching the whole class, then break the class into small groups for a time, and finally reconvene the entire class. Such reconfigurations create a great deal of variety: Students change their physical position within the classroom, the focus of attention shifts from the teacher to fellow students, and the different activities require different intellectual and social skills.

Preventing Discipline Problems

The Kounin model, which focuses on the smooth management of students in the classroom, is concerned primarily with preventing discipline problems. There are no provisions for correcting behavior problems once they arise. Consequently, it can be used in conjunction with other discipline models that have corrective components. Because Kounin's model is composed primarily of various techniques rather than principles, portions of it can be used with any of several different discipline approaches.

Schoolwide Discipline

Kounin makes no suggestions about schoolwide discipline. His recommendations pertain to the management of students' behavior in the classroom. In addition, his approach applies only to recitation. It offers no guidance for managing such activities as group projects. There is no delineation of principles that may apply beyond the specific situations in which his research was done.

Strengths and Weakness of the Kounin Model

STRENGTHS

1. The model is based on empirical research and documents teachers' behaviors in the classroom that either promote or hinder learning.

2. It shows that teachers' positive and negative influences may extend beyond the limits they intend.

3. It offers several techniques for making desists effective.

4. It stresses the importance of choosing the proper discipline problem to deal with and timing desists appropriately.

5. It helps teachers create the impression that they are aware of all that is going on in the classroom.

WEAKNESSES

1. The model is limited to use in classroom recitation sessions. It is not generally applicable to a broad range of classroom situations or teaching approaches.

2. It shows teachers how to avoid discipline problems but not how to solve serious difficulties.

3. Is not designed to help students become personally responsible for their behavior.

SUMMARY

The techniques advocated by Kounin are designed primarily for recitation sessions. They do not apply as well to other learning approaches. They are intended to help teachers maintain focus and interest in teacher-directed activities and to avoid possible disruptions. In directing classroom activities, teachers should routinely

1. communicate withitness to their students by being aware of what is happening in all areas of the classroom at all times.

2. show students that they can successfully deal with more than one issue in the classroom at once. They should show themselves capable of continuing the instructional program while dealing with potential discipline problems.

3. be able to deal with the most critical issue in the class when several problems surface at the same time.

4. be able to deal with problems in a timely way, before they escalate and become more disruptive and difficult to correct.

5. manage classroom activities so that there is a smooth transition from one activity to another.

6. maintain group focus through the proper application of alerting and accountability procedures.

7. create learning experiences that incorporate meaningful, challenging material in a variety of ways in order to reduce boredom.

CENTRAL IDEAS

1. The ripple effect, which is the effect on students who witness teachers correcting the misbehavior of other students, depends on the clarity and firmness of the desist along with the situation in which the desist takes place.

2. Teachers are judged to have withitness and consequently discipline more effectively when they correct more important misbehavior first and when they make corrections before the influence of misbehaving students has a chance to spread.

3. When teachers are able to deal with discipline problems while simultaneously handling other classroom duties (i.e., to use overlapping), they discipline more effectively.

4. Smooth movement from one activity to another reduces discipline problems.

5. Overdwelling—talking excessively or taking actions that are clearly unnecessary—can create discipline problems.

6. When teachers break activities into units that are too small, discipline problems are created.

7. Maintaining students' participation in learning activities aids good discipline. Participation can be encouraged by keeping students alert, making them accountable for learning the material, and helping them avoid boredom.

QUESTIONS AND ACTIVITIES

QUESTIONS TO CONSIDER

1. With which other discipline approaches are Kounin's procedures compatible?

2. To what teaching-learning situations do Kounin's procedures apply? What are some learning situations in which his procedures do not apply?

CLASSROOM ACTIVITIES

The following classroom situations could develop into problems unless the teacher intervenes. Have class members finish the descriptions, incorporating at least one of Kounin's procedures.

1. Rachel and AnnaBell have just gotten out of their seats during quiet study time and have made their way to the back of the room near the magazine rack.

2. Jon has just picked up the hall pass and is about to leave the room during an examination. At the same time, Martha has turned around in her seat and is looking at Solomon's test paper.

3. Students are supposed to be completing a worksheet at their desks. Several students are staring out the window. Another three or four students have turned around in their seats and are talking to their neighbors. Other members of the class appear fidgety and are shuffling papers and flipping pages in their textbooks.

4. Students have been participating in a class discussion. You want them to break into smaller groups and begin discussing a related topic.

5. As you write on the board, two students in the back of the room are throwing objects into the fish tanks. At the same time, two other students sitting at the side of the classroom farthest from you have begun constructing paper airplanes. In the middle of the class, two students are passing notes.

6. You are conducting a discussion. You want to keep your students focused on the matter at hand.

STUDENT APPLICATIONS

Describe a classroom situation and the manner in which you would use the following techniques recommended by Kounin to enhance learning and prevent discipline problems:

1. communicating withitness

2. dealing with more than one issue at a time

3. dealing with the most important issue first

4. preventing the escalation of problem behavior

5. ensuring smooth transitions from one activity to another

6. maintaining group focus by using alerting and accountability procedures

7. reducing boredom by giving students tasks at which they can succeed, subject matter that challenges them, and a variety of presentation methods

REFERENCES

Gnagey, W. J. (1975). *Maintaining discipline in classroom instruction*. New York: Macmillan.

Kounin, J. S. (1970a). *Discipline and group management in classrooms*. New York: Holt, Rinehart and Winston.

Kounin, J. S. (1970b). Observing and delineating techniques of managing behavior in classrooms. *Journal of Research and Development in Education, 4*(1), 62–72.

Kounin, J. S., & Doyle, P. H. (1975). Degree of continuity of a lesson's signal system and the task involvement of children. *Journal of Educational Psychology, 67,* 159–164.

Kounin, J. S., & Gump, P. V. (1961). The comparative influence of punitive and non-punitive teachers upon children's concepts of school misconduct. *Journal of Educational Psychology, 52,* 44–49.

Kounin, J. S., & Gump, P. V. (1974). Signal systems of lesson settings and the task related behavior of pre-school children. *Journal of Educational Psychology, 66,* 554–562.

Kounin, J. S., Gump, P. V., & Ryan, J. J., III. (1961). Explorations in classroom management. *Journal of Teacher Education, 12,* 235–247.

Taba, H. (1967). *Teachers' handbook for elementary social studies*. Reading, MA: Addison-Wesley.

10

The Jones Model: Fredric H. Jones

OBJECTIVES

This chapter is designed to help you

1. learn to make seating arrangements in the classroom that give teachers greater control
2. implement the praise-prompt-leave sequence of instruction
3. effectively use nonverbal language to set limits on students' behavior
4. describe how students react to limit-setting by their teachers
5. create a program of Preferred Activity Time that can be applied in a specific type of classroom

ASSUMPTIONS

1. Children need to be controlled to behave properly.
2. Teachers can achieve control through nonverbal cues and movements calculated to bring them closer and closer to students physically.
3. It is appropriate to pressure students to behave by reducing the time they are allowed to spend in preferred activities.
4. Reinforcing good behaviors will increase their frequency.
5. The involvement of parents and school administrators in classroom discipline helps the teacher gain control of students' behavior.
6. Stopping instruction to deal with discipline problems helps eliminate these problems.

Introduction

Fredric Jones is a psychologist who conducted research on classroom practices while working at the UCLA Medical Center and the School of Medicine and Dentistry at the University of Rochester. From this work he created his discipline model, which is now promoted in the Classroom Management Training Program he directs. Teachers who are trained in this California-based program go on to train their colleagues. Jones emphasizes the need for teachers to employ just enough of their physical presence in the classroom to ensure that students remain on-task and avoid disrupting their neighbors.

▼ LaVern glanced expectantly at Dale, wishing that he could work up enough courage to say something. He knew, however, that Mr. Bell was still looking straight at him. It was almost as if Mr. Bell could read his mind. Even when Mr. Bell was dealing with a commotion in some other part of the classroom, he would still look back at LaVern. His eyes seemed to be everywhere at once. No students escaped his attention if they were even the least bit disruptive in class. The look on his face always showed little emotion. It was hard to tell what he was thinking. Sometimes he would come right to your desk and stand there looking at you. LaVern always went right back to work rather than challenge Mr. Bell. The way Mr. Bell carried himself seemed to communicate his authority and let everyone know who was in charge.

This episode illustrates a few of the tactics Jones recommends for improving classroom discipline. He believes that classroom management procedures must be positive. They must affirm students while setting limits and promoting cooperation. Coercion must be avoided. Jones also believes that discipline procedures must be practical, simple, and easily mastered. They must ultimately reduce the teacher's workload. Teachers should use discipline techniques that take the least amount of planning and effort and involve the least amount of time and paperwork. Jones believes that it is erroneous to assume that discipline refers primarily to handling major crises. Instead, it involves the management of many small problems and potential problems. Teachers make 500 management decisions each day, which makes their work second only to that of air traffic controllers in complexity and stress (Jones, 1987a). Learning how to manage these many situations effectively is necessary if teachers are to avoid burnout before they reach age thirty-five. To help teachers cope with management problems, Jones recommends that they

1. properly structure their classroom,
2. learn how to maintain control in the classroom by using appropriate instructional strategies and by setting limits,
3. build patterns of cooperation, and
4. develop appropriate backup systems.

Classroom Structures

Many discipline problems teachers experience are the result of mismanaging various routines and procedures in the classroom. Rules may be misunderstood. Seating arrangements may hinder easy access to students, making it difficult to monitor their behavior. Interactions between teachers and their students may promote misbehavior. Successful teachers know how to manage their classroom and avoid these problems.

RULES, ROUTINES, AND STANDARDS

Jones believes that the following common misconceptions about rules create problems for teachers:

1. *Misconception:*   Students already know how to behave when they reach your class.

   Reality: They usually have a vague idea about rules, but in reality they wait to find out "your rules" first. Until rules are clarified, students go as far as they can to determine limits.

2. *Misconception:*   Teachers should avoid spending too much time going over the rules because doing so takes too much time away from the instructional program.

   Reality: Teachers should take whatever time is necessary to help their students understand class rules. It is reported that teachers who have the fewest discipline problems may spend most of the first two weeks of the school year teaching rules, routines, standards, and expectations (Evertson & Anderson, 1979).

3. *Misconception:*   Rules are general guidelines.

   Reality: General rules have their place, but they must always be backed up by specific requirements. Teachers must spell out exactly what they expect and how students can comply with these expectations.

4. *Misconception:*   Announcing the rules of the class will ensure that they are understood.

   Reality: Rules have to be taught. They have been taught only when they are properly understood. Informing students of rules and procedures will usually not give students a sufficiently clear understanding of what teachers desire. Students should be involved in a dialogue with their teachers regarding the rules.

5. *Misconception:*   If you do a good job teaching your rules at the beginning of the school year, you will not have to refer to them again.

   Reality: If teachers are to avoid discipline problems, they must reteach the rules periodically throughout the school year. Not only do students have a tendency to forget the rules, but they also need to have them reinforced occasionally. Otherwise, they will behave as if the rules were never given.

6. *Misconception:*   Discipline is essentially a matter of strictly enforcing the rules.

   Reality: Rules should not be enforced through dictatorial means. Students' cooperation must be enlisted to ensure compliance with rules. Good disciplinarians are relaxed and emotionally warm, not harsh like drill sergeants.

7. *Misconception:* Students inherently dislike and resent classroom rules.

   Reality: On the contrary, students appreciate teachers who systematically organize their classrooms. When rules are lacking, the resulting chaos makes learning difficult. Most students recognize the benefits of an orderly classroom and prefer teachers who exercise control through the proper use of rules.

Rules, routines, and standards are critical aspects of any classroom. Imagine a classroom in which there is no rule prohibiting talking out of order during quiet study time or during discussions and lectures. Or imagine what a chemistry lab would be like if students were not required to adhere to safety standards. In a chemistry lab, rules such as the following are absolutely essential:

1. Use proper safety precautions when inserting glass tubing into a stopper.
2. In the lab, always wear safety goggles to protect your eyes.
3. In the lab, always wear an apron to protect your clothes.
4. Avoid letting strong bases and acids make contact with your skin.
5. Do not dispose of chemicals by pouring them down the drain. Place them in the appropriate disposal receptacles.
6. Use all chemicals only in the prescribed way.

Students should be very familiar with the procedures to follow in case of fire, chemical spills, and chemical contamination of clothing, skin, or eyes. Rules are also necessary regarding lab cleanup as well as equipment and chemical storage. Sometimes special rules are necessary in labs where expensive equipment is used.

Jones believes that teachers should teach rules, routines, and standards as they would teach any other subject. This teaching is different from the usual practice of making a few pronouncements about rules during the initial class period or lecturing students after rules have been violated. Students should understand and be able to follow the rules. There should be no misunderstanding about how rules are to be interpreted. To enlist the support of students for the rules, teachers should conduct discussions in which students can express their views about (1) what characterizes a good classroom, (2) what their role should be, (3) what obligations and responsibilities both teachers and students have, and (4) what kinds of behavior can ruin a class.

SEATING ARRANGEMENTS

In addition to establishing rules, teachers need to arrange classroom furniture in ways that maximize their mobility and allow greater physical proximity to students. This proximity provides moment-by-moment access to each student. Teachers need to put the least distance and the fewest physical barriers between themselves and their students. Any arrangement that provides quick and easy access to all students is likely to be successful. The teacher's desk should not be in the front of the room. In this location it restricts the teacher's movement and reduces proximity to students. Students' desks should be located near the board. There should be just enough space to allow mobility for the teacher (Figure 10.1).

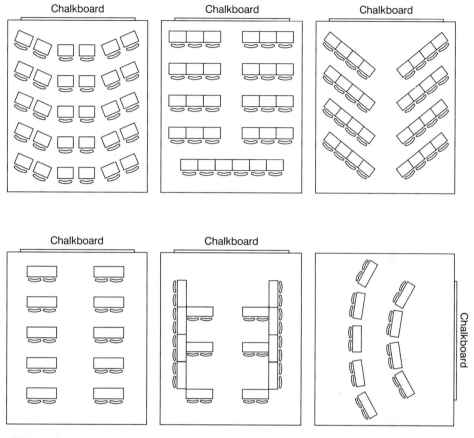

FIGURE 10.1
Accessible seating arrangements.

Some teachers believe that students should have the freedom to select their own seats in the classroom. Jones prefers to have assigned seats. Good students tend to locate themselves near the front, where they can participate more fully and thus get better grades. Chronic disrupters, on the other hand, are inclined to seat themselves near the back of the classroom as far away from the teacher's scrutiny as possible. This naturally-occurring seating arrangement is a potential powder keg as far as discipline is concerned. Wise teachers will seat potential disrupters close to them and place more conscientious students near the back of the room.

What kind of a seating arrangement can be made at the beginning of the year before you are sufficiently acquainted with students to know where to seat them? They should be seated either alphabetically or randomly and told that changes will be made in seating within a few weeks. If you forewarn students, you will encounter less resistance when actual changes are made. It is also wise to tell students that you intend to change seating periodically to help maintain a good learning environment.

STUDENT-TEACHER RELATIONSHIPS

Building positive relationships is a particularly critical task of teachers in their initial contact with students. Students are more susceptible to the influence of teachers they like and respect. If students respect the teacher, they are also more likely to enjoy the subject being taught and be more successful learning it. Positive student-teacher relationships are built on trust. Trust is promoted in an atmosphere of freedom. Children need to gradually receive more responsibility for making their own decisions in school. As they mature in an atmosphere of freedom, they will learn to make appropriate choices without coercion. Many teachers ordinarily perceive children as lazy—requiring force to get them involved in worthwhile activities—and naturally prone to misbehavior. Thus, many teachers feel that students need to be threatened and punished before they will behave well. However, with proper training most students can learn to be more self-governing and responsible.

To build proper relationships with students, teachers need to get as much information about their students as possible. On the first day of class, it is wise to have students provide basic information such as their name, address, home phone number, hobbies, and interests. This information can be recorded on an index card. Ice-breaking activities can be used to help teachers become better acquainted with their students. Students can be assigned to interview one another and then report on what they find. Teachers can help structure these interviews by giving students a list of topics to be covered. Teachers too can interview their students. Even in secondary schools, interviews could be completed in two or three weeks if teachers interviewed three students each day. Another excellent way for teachers to become acquainted with students is to take their photographs and post them on the bulletin board.

To develop relationships, teachers must not only learn about students but also allow students to become better acquainted with them. Teachers need to talk about themselves. Opening up to students helps them see their teachers as human beings with desires and goals similar to their own. Teachers can tell students about their interests and hobbies; some students may have similar hobbies and thus share a common bond. Teachers can share their teaching aspirations with their students, explaining why they chose the teaching profession and what gratifications they find in teaching. Teachers may discuss attitudes, feelings, and such matters of mutual concern as respecting others and taking personal responsibility for learning. Teachers also need to show their students that they are active, interested learners, not merely dispensers of information; students can easily detect the hypocrisy of teachers who do not enjoy learning.

Classroom Control

Rules define what the limits are, but they do not establish them. Establishing limits can be done only in the give-and-take of the classroom. Students by nature will test the limits. They need to find out how the rules will actually be applied. They know what the teacher said about the rules, but they need to see whether what was said was truly meant. For example, the teacher may say that whispered talking is allowed during quiet study time, but what level of noise will actually be permitted? Students have learned that different teachers have different levels of tolerance for noise. They want to know how far they can go. Teachers who "mean business" are able to give students the clearest picture of what they can and cannot do in the classroom. These teachers are more successful than their less direct counterparts.

Jones' initial attempts to define how teachers show that they mean business were not successful, mostly because he concentrated exclusively on verbal cues. Body language is also a subtle yet powerful way for teachers to communicate their intentions. When appropriate body language is integrated with spoken messages, a teacher's resolve is adequately conveyed.

Power, or control, is almost always an issue in the classroom. Students will assume all the power they can. It is very desirable to control one's own life in school in order to make it as pleasant as possible and avoid difficult learning situations. The question is, who is going to control whom? Jones, of course, believes that teachers must maintain control. Successful teachers know how to exercise interpersonal power in a way that is typically described as diplomatic, confident, and self-assured. In other words, they mean business. Interpersonal power is best exercised calmly. Conveying calmness establishes the ability of teachers to exercise control over themselves. Children commonly attempt to gain control of their teachers by getting them upset. Children almost always acquire control when teachers lose their tempers.

Jones believes that maintaining control in the classroom depends on two interrelated components: the teacher's instructional strategies and limit-setting.

INSTRUCTIONAL STRATEGIES

Teachers often lose control of their classes when they spend too much time with each student. While they are working with one student, others goof off. Teachers can escape this predicament by avoiding universal helping interactions and instead using the praise-prompt-leave sequence of instruction.

Avoiding Universal Helping Interactions.   In his research, Jones found that teachers commonly experienced discipline problems when they finished a lecture or discussion and began helping students individually at their seats. Students usually began immediately to ask their teachers for help. Teachers usually responded with a "universal helping interaction": They tried to

1. find out where a student was having difficulty

2. re-explain the portion of the lesson the student did not understand

3. supply the student with additional explanations and examples

Jones contends that this process ordinarily takes at least five minutes for each student. If the practice period lasts 30 minutes, no more than six students can receive help. While the teacher is helping these students, the rest of the class, particularly those who are unsuccessfully seeking help from the teacher, will talk and goof around. This result, according to Jones, helps explain why talking to neighbors in ways that are disruptive constitutes 80 percent of the discipline problems in a typical classroom. Not only does discipline break down, but the students who do receive help are unable to use the teacher's long, drawn-out explanations to successfully complete their work. The universal helping interaction is too slow and inefficient. Teachers tie themselves up for too long a period with too few students and leave too many students unattended and unrewarded for too much of the work period (Jones, 1987a).

Teachers should be aware of how most universal helping interactions between students and teachers are initiated and avoid getting caught up in them.

1. Asking students where they are having difficulty is the most common and straightforward means of initiating a helping interaction. Teachers often ask, "Where are you having difficulty?" or "What is it you don't understand?"

2. Teachers are often aware of the difficulties students experience and identify these difficulties as they offer to help. For example, they may say, "I see you are having trouble carrying the correct digit. Let me show you how it is done."

3. Focusing on the students' strengths before calling attention to the problems is a common tactic among teachers who are aware of the necessity of giving students support during feedback. They believe that giving good news first will diminish the negative effects of the bad news that follows. A teacher might say, "You did the first few problems correctly, but when you got to the ones requiring long division, you did them all wrong."

4. Some teachers express their exasperation with students in the way they use body language, such as shaking the head from side to side, as if to say, "I have never seen anything like this. How could you have worked these problems this way?"

5. Sometimes, before they help students, teachers give voice to comments that are simply derogatory (for example, "How can you be so stupid?"). Jones calls these comments "zaps and zingers." Considerable harm can be done to students to whom these comments are directed.

Using the Praise-Prompt-Leave Sequence.   In place of universal helping interactions, Jones recommends the three-step sequence of *praise*, *prompt*, and *leave* (Jones, 1987b).

The first step is to praise. In giving praise, the teacher reviews what the student has done right, which not only provides a positive experience for the student but also defines the starting point for new instruction. For teachers to become good at giving praise, they need to avoid the common habit of looking for errors in students' work. This tendency causes teachers to communicate dissatisfaction as well as frustration and exasperation. Teachers should build upon adequately completed work, not defects. They need to develop an aptitude for seeing the positive and make it a reflex action. Once the strength of a student's work is identified, appropriate words can be used to describe it. This language must be a specific description of exactly what is well done. Avoid statements such as "Nice job" and "You're off to a good start." Instead, say "You have organized this paragraph well. There are transitions between all the sentences."

The second step is to prompt. To prompt is to tell students exactly what to do next. Prompting should be clear and simple. Ordinarily, mastery of concepts involves many steps. Students, however, can perform these steps only one at a time. Teachers should, therefore, provide a prompt that requires a one-step performance. Asking students to perform many steps tends to produce cognitive overload. Teachers tend to bog students down with excessive, complex verbiage. They talk too much and explain more than students can keep straight at one time. Instead, teachers should prompt students about the next action to take and then encourage them to act on the prompt.

The third and final step is to leave. Once a clear and simple prompt is given, teachers should leave and turn their attention immediately to other students. They must not take time to observe how students act on prompts. Leaving will cause many teachers discomfort, given their inclination to stay at students' desks long enough to see how they respond to instructions. Even so, teachers must avoid the temptation to stay longer. Not only does leaving convey confidence in students' ability to act on the instruction given, but it also gives teachers more time to circulate in the class. With this system, teachers are able to see more students and see the same student more than once in one class period. At the same time, the teacher gains greater control by being able to move around the entire classroom more quickly.

LIMIT-SETTING

Along with particular instructional strategies, Jones believes that teachers must employ very specific, limit-setting discipline techniques (Jones, 1987a). These techniques primarily involve the use of body language designed to convince students that their teachers are in control even when provoked. Body language communicates a teacher's interpersonal power to students. The teacher's objective in using limit-setting techniques is to resolve the power issue and have students return to their work. Limit-setting always entails the same series of steps. How many steps are taken depends on how quickly disruptive students return to work.

Step 1: Having Eyes in the Back of Your Head.   The first step in limit-setting is to be aware of and simultaneously monitor the behavior of all students in the classroom. Sometimes this skill is called "withitness" or "having eyes in the back of your head." Obviously the seating arrangement in the room helps teachers exhibit withitness. They can also increase their effectiveness by placing themselves where they are able to see the entire class. In those instances when teachers cannot see the class, they must monitor it by listening. Most of us have learned to focus our attention on one thing at a time and block out other sensory information. As a teacher, however, you have to make a conscious effort *not* to filter out extraneous noises. They must learn to attend to everything that occurs in the classroom.

Step 2: Terminating Instruction.   Suppose that while you are helping one student you glance across the room and notice two other students talking to one another; you catch one of them looking at you. Some teachers believe that disruptions should not be attended to during instruction because this attention only reinforces bad behavior. Jones argues that discipline should always take precedence over other class activities and must be dealt with immediately. He believes that if you ignore the discipline problem, even temporarily, and return to giving instruction, you reinforce the discipline problem. He recommends that when you encounter a discipline problem while you are giving instruction, you should stop in mid-sentence, make a hand gesture to the student being helped to indicate that you are temporarily stopping instruction, and then proceed to deal with the problem. In addition to making a hand gesture, you may quickly ask to be excused: "Excuse me for a moment. I'll be right back."

Step 3: Turning, Looking, and Saying the Student's Name.   As soon as instruction has been terminated, you should turn from the student being helped and focus attention on disruptive students. *Turn around completely* and face the misbehaving students squarely. Turning to face students conveys the message that you are dealing with them exclusively. They have your full attention. Failure to face students squarely signals them that you are less than one hundred percent committed to disciplining them.

Next, *look them in the eye*. Your gaze must be unwavering. Do not allow your eyes to dart around or otherwise break contact. Darting eyes tell students that you are uncomfortable and anxious. It is also important not to show disgust or irritation. You do not want to convey anger. Instead, you want students to see you in complete control of yourself. A steady look that is free of emotion will communicate the desired message. Along with eye contact, you should maintain an appropriate facial expression. Facial expressions can send either the intended message or one that is contradictory and confusing. For example, if teachers smile in a particularly stressful discipline situation, they may communicate submission rather than limit-setting. A fiery look accompanied by a slight smile may be interpreted by students as "I don't want you to talk. I'd like you to go back to work, but I'm not going to insist on it." It is better to remain expressionless as you continue to maintain perfect eye contact with the student causing the most trouble. Even if students smile at you, be sure to sustain your expressionless look. You want to convey the message that you find nothing amusing about bad behavior and that you are simply waiting while the student decides what to do next. There are other cues you can give with your body. Some of these cues should be avoided. For example, hands on hips or folded arms usually indicate impatience or upset. Instead, let your arms hang comfortably at your side or, if your prefer, place them in your pockets.

Then *say the names* of disruptive students—only once and in a flat, matter-of-fact fashion. If your voice is bland, it will convey your calm and self-control. Learning how to remain calm and relaxed in response to provocations is the most crucial aspect of limit-setting, and yet it is the most difficult to master. Commonly it is forgotten when students do irritating things.

The limit-setting process explained so far may be all you need in many instances. After having said the students' names, you should wait while you take two relaxing breaths. Continue to stand directly facing the offending students and maintain your gaze. Sometimes students will try to deceive you. They may give you a smile to acknowledge that they are being observed and yet have no intention of going back to work. Without diverting your eyes directly, you should check under the offending students' desks to determine whether their knees and feet are back in the correct position for working. Unless they are, you have not accomplished the necessary task. It is wise to remember that students often play games with you. Jones likens limit-setting to playing poker: Teachers increase the bet until students "fold." Teachers need to continually raise the stakes until students decline to go further. In other words, proceed through the steps of limit-setting until disruptive students give in and go back to work. A rule of thumb in limit-setting is to go no further than is necessary.

Step 4: Moving to the Edge of the Student's Desk.   If after hearing their names students simply look at you and make no attempt to turn around and go to work, you should move in a relaxed fashion to the edge of the most disruptive student's desk (Figure 10.2). Move at the same pace at which you would take a stroll through your garden. Do not get in a hurry. Keep yourself relaxed. Under no circumstances should

FIGURE 10.2
Moving to the edge of the student's desk. The teacher, at the edge of the student's desk, looks the student directly in the eye.

you stop moving until you reach the student's desk. Position yourself with your legs touching the front edge of the student's desk. While taking two relaxing breaths, look the student straight in the eye. Do not repeat the student's name and do not repeat the class rules. Waiting at the student's desk will help you maintain your calm as well as give the student time to decide what to do. You should wait until the student goes back to work and remains working for a while.

Step 5: Moving Out.   The "moving out" phase of limit-setting is just as important as the "moving in" phase. When the disruptive student has returned to work, lean over and thank the student by name. Then continue to wait in front of the desk, watching the student work a little while longer. If another student was involved, go to that student's desk and wait there. Give this second student equal time to go to work. Take two relaxing breaths and thank this student. Watch the student work for a while. Take two more relaxing breaths. At this point, you should move away slowly. Go to the student you were helping at the time of the disruption, turn and look at the students who caused the disruption, and take two more relaxing breaths. The offending students will probably look up at you and correctly ascertain that you are still monitoring their behavior. This entire procedure conveys the fact that you mean business.

Step 6: Using Palms.   Sometimes students do not respond when you stand in front of their desks. If so, Jones recommends that you lean over at the waist and, while resting your weight on one palm, give the reluctant students a prompt—either verbally (telling them exactly what you want them to do) or nonverbally (motioning with the arm and hand for them to turn around) or both. A verbal prompt should be short and direct. For example, you may say, "Turn around in your seat, and finish doing the rest of your math problems." After giving these prompts, maintain your position, leaning on your palm. Take two relaxing breaths. If the student goes back to work, watch the student for a while, still keeping your position. Take two relaxing breaths before moving to the second student's desk to repeat the process.

   If the prompt does not produce the desired result, lean slowly across the student's desk and put both palms flat on the desk in such a way that you straddle the student's books and papers. Rest your weight on your palms with your elbows locked and take two or more relaxing breaths while maintaining continuous eye contact (Figure 10.3). This position will bring you eyeball to eyeball with the student. Do not say anything. Wait for a positive work response. If the student goes back to work, watch for two more relaxing breaths, thank the student, watch for two more relaxing breaths, and then move to the next student and repeat the process. When all students are working, move out as previously described.

   Sometimes during the limit-setting sequence, students will engage in various types of back talk, the purpose of which is to get control and to trap the teacher into exploring some side issue. There are several types of back talk, each of which can tempt teachers to react. Any reaction, however, just aids students in their quest for control. Jones identifies seven major types of back talk prevalent in the classroom:

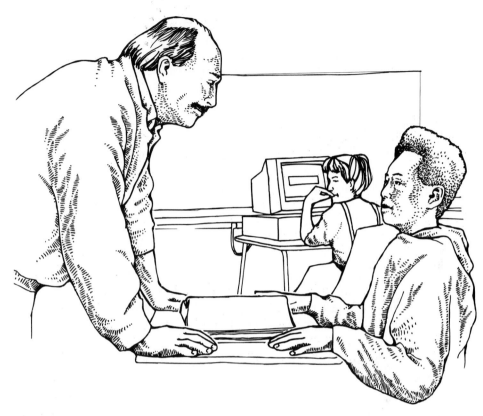

FIGURE 10.3
Using Palms. The teacher continues direct eye contact.

1. *Feigning helplessness.*   Students attempt to change the issue from discipline to instruction. Usually they offer a pained request for help, hoping that the teacher will bite. They may say, "I don't understand this. Will you show me how to do it?" Teachers easily get sidetracked because of their commitment to help students learn. When a student professes helplessness in order to sidetrack you, Jones recommends that you not provide help at that time. It is better to just look at the student and wait, saying nothing. You may eventually say something like "Keep working. I'll be back in a few minutes to help you." At this point, the less you say, the better.

2. *Denying responsibility.*   Students commonly profess innocence when they are caught misbehaving. They may say, "I didn't do it" or "Why are you picking on me? I was just sitting here." Responding to these comments only promotes conflict and further self-justification by students. Therefore, do not debate with them. Just relax, be quiet, and wait.

3. *Blaming others.*   "She started it!" or "He started it!" is the usual way children blame one another. Children know that blaming one another is an effective way to

get their teachers sidetracked. Teachers seem compelled to find out who started a problem so that they can punish the offender. Just remember, it does not matter who started the altercation. Knowing who initiated the disruption will not change anything. Remember, too, that students use this ploy to avoid doing their work.

4. *Accusing the teacher of professional incompetence.* Teachers have a tendency to take students' negative comments about their competency seriously. Students may say, "How am I supposed to understand? You didn't explain well enough." They may also accuse you of never making anything clear. Here again the motive is to get you sidetracked. Students know that their teachers take these attacks seriously. It may be true that some explanation was not clear. The quality of instruction is not the issue, however. Gabbing with neighbors is not the solution to misunderstanding what is taught. Keep in mind that students will claim not to understand as an excuse to avoid responsibility.

5. *Urging the teacher to leave.* Sometimes students tell their teachers to go away:

"OK, just leave me alone. I'll get back to work."
"Hey, just back away from here and get out of my face. I'm going to do this."
"I'll start doing this just as soon as you back away from here."
"Holy cow! Get off it, would you? Back your face out of here."

Students think that they can control a situation if they are the ones who tell others what to do. They depend on the shock value of such statements to get teachers to react to them. Obviously teachers must avoid the temptation to react to such directions.

6. *Hurling insults.* Students are gambling for high stakes when they use insults to throw their teachers off balance. Students may insult their teachers when they feel that they have very little to lose. When they insult teachers, students may act cocky or pretend to be offended or upset:

"Hey, who buys your clothes? I've never seen anything clash so bad."
"Did you know hair styles like yours went out during the Civil War?"
"Where'd you get that big wide tie? The last one of those I saw was on Nutsy Squirrel."
"Hey, move back a little. You've got bad breath!"

Even if you do have bad breath, you should stand your ground. Just relax and hold your position, leaning on the student's desk and looking the student straight in the eye. The issue is not whether or not you have bad breath. If you can avoid reacting, you will ultimately control the situation.

7. *Using profanity.* As a last-ditch effort to upset you, students may swear at you. Some profanity is considered mild and evokes a negligible response in most people. Some words, however, may have a tendency to provoke a reaction. If students call you names, you may feel it necessary to put them in their place. Most adults feel that young people should not be allowed to get away with name-calling. However, the purpose of profanity is to get you to react. It is better to relax, keep quiet, and wait. If you remain calm, you can control the situation and get the student back on-task. You can impose an additional sanction later if you deem it necessary. As the students file out of the classroom at the end of the period, call the

student by name and say that you want to speak with him or her. This action will make other students realize that they cannot get away with profanity in the classroom. Calling the student aside after class will also allow you to confront the student in private without an audience of peers. However, if the student "folds" in the face of your silence, self-control, and proximity, then detaining the student after class will probably be unnecessary.

Step 7: Camping Out in Front.   Suppose that you have completed the Palms step in the limit-setting process but the disruptive students continue to make excuses and blame others. Camping out in front may now be appropriate. Start from the Palms position, then bend your arm until your weight is resting on your elbow (Figure 10.4). Take two relaxing breaths, look at the student with indifference, and wait. This position puts you closer to the student and improves eye contact. If the student then stops fooling around and looks at you, take two more relaxing breaths and repeat the verbal prompt to turn around and get back to work. Repeating the prompt lets the student know that you are not accepting excuses. If work is resumed, thank the student, take two more relaxing breaths, and move slowly over to the next student and repeat the same procedure.

FIGURE 10.4
Camping out in front.

FIGURE 10.5
Camping out from behind.

Step 8: Camping Out from Behind. If, while you are camping out in front of one student, another comes to the rescue by making some comment, you may need to camp out from behind. This step may be necessary if students gang up on you and need to be separated. Move between the students, turn sideways next to one student, and lean on your elbow as you did camping out in front (Figure 10.5). If the student is on your left, lean on your right elbow and look straight into the student's eyes, take two relaxing breaths, and wait. If the student talks back, wait until the student is finished and then give a prompt to return to work. Thank the student, and then move out in the prescribed way.

Promoting Cooperation

What if limit-setting doesn't work? Many teachers may be tempted to nag, threaten, or punish. These temptations should be resisted. Punishment promotes alienation. It will not solve discipline problems.

RESPONSIBILITY TRAINING

Instead, teachers can promote cooperation through responsibility training (Jones, 1987a), which induces students to demonstrate good behavior voluntarily. Students do not cooperate without a reason. They will cooperate, however, if good relationships are established and incentives provided. Jones explains that establishing good relationships with students by itself is insufficient. It is, however, necessary. An incentive system must be devised to go with it.

Technically, Jones' incentive system is based on the concept of negative reinforcement. Incentive systems usually provide positive reinforcement as a consequence of appropriate behavior; the reward follows good behavior. In a system of negative reinforcement, however, students are given their potential reward in advance. Jones calls his reward system Preferred Activity Time (PAT). This PAT is given to the class as a whole in predetermined units (a week's worth, for example), which the students can retain by responsible learning behavior or squander through misbehavior. When a student misbehaves, the teacher starts a timer or stopwatch. The length of time the misbehavior lasts is then subtracted from the class' PAT. The stopwatch provides an exact accounting and eliminates possible controversy over how much PAT remains.

Jones also advocates that positive reinforcement in the form of bonuses be given when students conserve time. If students hurry to clean up the classroom or finish an assignment early, the teacher can reward them with additional PAT. It is wise to give students plenty of time to do their assignments so that there is ample opportunity to earn bonuses. Bonuses can also be earned, for example, if all students are in their seats when the bell rings.

To summarize, students are given PAT in advance, which they can either retain or squander. In addition, they can earn bonuses for completing tasks in less than the time allotted. A record of penalties and bonuses is kept at the teacher's desk or on the chalkboard. In operating this system, teachers should ensure that bonus opportunities more than offset opportunities for penalty. Otherwise, the system will fail.

Preferred Activity Time can consist of fun and games, either for educational purposes or purely for diversion. There should probably be a mix of various options. Time should be allotted for both individual and group activities. For individual activities, you might suggest that students bring games from home to play during PAT. Group activities may include team competition in any one of a number of formats. Games based on baseball, football, or basketball are very popular. In a foreign language class, for example, students on one team can reach "bases" by translating, spelling, conjugating, and using a given verb; if a mistake is made, a student on the other team can "catch" it for an "out." Appendix B lists many materials that describe activities suitable for PAT, and it indicates the grade levels for which the activities would be appropriate.

Certain problems in the class can be overcome by assessing a penalty without allowing for a corresponding reward. When a student routinely and unnecessarily interrupts instruction and asks for the hall pass to use the restroom, the teacher should readily comply with the request and then start the stopwatch. The amount of time it takes the student to go to the restroom is subtracted from the class PAT. When their PAT is thus reduced, students will begin using breaks between class periods to go to the restroom instead of asking for the hall pass during class. The age-old problem of not having a pencil can be similarly terminated. When students inform you that they have no pencil, ask whether someone has a pencil to loan and start your stopwatch. The number of pointless trips to the pencil sharpener can also be reduced. Place a can of sharpened, but short and grungy, pencils on your desk. If students need a sharpened pencil, have them retrieve one from the desk. Meanwhile, the stopwatch will run.

Other problems can also be handled with responsibility training. The technique has been successfully used with tantrum behavior, group divisiveness, short attention span, and other problems. It has also been used in a variety of school settings outside the standard classroom, such as passing in the halls, assemblies, chemistry labs, and specialized classes (gym, shop, typing, home economics). So long as the rules are known and the teacher takes away time using a stopwatch, students behave better.

OMISSION TRAINING

Occasionally PAT is ineffective with a few students who have special problems. For example, students with emotional disabilities may be angry or hostile and continually provoke teachers and other students. Omission training may be helpful for such students. In omission training, positive reinforcement is used instead of negative reinforcement; good behavior, not bad, is timed and rewarded. The unruly student is excluded from PAT. If the student behaves well for a predetermined period of time, a bonus is received that can be shared with the whole class. Bonuses can be earned with each subsequent time interval during which the student behaves properly. Four steps are followed in omission training:

1. Prevent any further confrontation by moving the student away from the rest of the class.

2. Determine a period of time—from 15 minutes to an entire day—that you believe is reasonable and appropriate for the student to behave.

3. Identify and communicate to the student the particular behavior you expect.

4. Explain the bonuses that can be earned.

Backup Systems

In rare instances, neither responsibility training nor omission training is successful. A backup system may be necessary (Jones, 1987a): Jones advocates the systematic application of negative sanctions. They are arranged hierarchically from lesser sanctions to more serious ones. Not only teachers but also administrators and parents are involved in imposing sanctions. Jones recommends that teachers manage their own backup systems as much as possible, pointing out that the participation of school administrators and parents is often unreliable. Involving parents takes time, and parents are frequently less than fully cooperative. The greatest drawback to sending students to the office is that the sheer number of students there prevents them from being effectively helped. After a trip to the office, students may return to your class more inclined to misbehave.

Several low-level sanctions can be imposed for misbehavior. They should be applied, in order, as the need arises:

1. *Warning.* Go to the student's desk and quietly say that you are sorry that the student has decided to continue behaving badly. Warn the student that if you return again, the result will be serious. Maintain eye contact and a relaxed manner. If the problem persists, go to step 2.

2. *Pulling the card.*   Pull the index card with the student's name and address from the card file while the student is watching. This should be done in a relaxed manner while maintaining eye contact with the student. It will be obvious that you intend to call the student's parents or guardian if the behavior does not stop. If this measure does not take care of the problem, go to step 3.

3. *Letter home on the desk.*   Go to the student's desk and use Palms as described in the limit-setting procedure. Breathe in a relaxed manner, and say that you are sorry that the student has continued being disruptive. Then return to your desk very slowly. When you get there, take out a pen and paper and begin to write a brief letter home. It should explicitly detail the student's inappropriate behavior. When the letter has been completed, put it in an envelope and walk back to the student's desk. Go to Palms and calmly say that the letter is to the student's parents or guardian. Inform the student that you will send it immediately unless a week passes without any repetition of the unacceptable behavior. Explain that at the end of a week, if there is no further misbehavior, the student may tear up the letter and put it in the wastebasket. The letter should be left taped to the student's desk in self-contained classrooms or to the teacher's desk if students move from class to class.

If students create more trouble, the teacher may have to impose mid-level sanctions:

1. *Time-out.*   The student is removed from the activity in the classroom. Time-out usually takes place in an out-of-the-way area in the classroom, but there may also be a special room designated for time-out elsewhere in the school. Sometimes time-out can take place in another teacher's classroom.

2 *Detention after school.*   Students have to make up the time lost by goofing off.

3. *Loss of privileges.*   Students are prevented from participating in activities such as sports, plays, and contests.

4. *Parent conference.*   Disruptive students and their parents meet with you after school.

There is also a list of high-level backup sanctions. These sanctions are the school's final effort to get disruptive students to change their behavior:

1. *In-school suspension.*   Students are placed in a designated room in the school outside the regular classroom. The room is monitored, and the students' regular teachers give them regular assignments, which must be completed there.

2. *Saturday school.*   Students attend school on Saturday to make up for time lost to unexcused absences and late arrivals ("tardies").

3. *Delivering the student to a parent at work.*   The child is delivered to the parent along with a message specifying the inappropriate behavior and the conditions for readmission to school.

4. *Asking a parent to accompany the student in school.*   The parent sits with and supervises the student all during the school day.

5. *Suspension.*   Suspended students are not permitted in school for a specified period of time.

6. *Police intervention.*   Law enforcement officers can be summoned when students are involved in criminal activity such as assault, theft, or drug-dealing.

7. *Expulsion.*   As a last resort, students may be expelled. Readmission after expulsion usually involves a series of meetings and approval by the board of education.

If limit-setting and responsibility training are effectively implemented, it should be unnecessary to impose negative sanctions from the backup system. These sanctions should be used only as a last resort. They are generally employed by school administrators, not classroom teachers.

Preventing Discipline Problems

Limit-setting is a corrective discipline procedure. Responsibility training, on the other hand, is designed to prevent discipline problems. With responsibility training, students are encouraged to work productively and not disturb the class. If they are disruptive, they lose part of their Preferred Activity Time. Loss of Preferred Activity Time is a deterrent to bad behavior.

Schoolwide Discipline

Jones considers discipline to be almost exclusively the responsibility of the classroom teacher. He recommends that students with behavior problems not be sent to the office to be dealt with by school administrators. Instead, he encourages teachers to apply the steps in his discipline approach. It is only when teachers have exhausted what they can do in the classroom that they should refer students to the office for administrative action.

Strengths and Weaknesses of the Jones Model

STRENGTHS

1. It specifies a set of steps to follow in dealing with discipline problems.

2. It tells exactly how far to go in applying discipline techniques.

3. It defines the role of the teacher as well as the role of administrators in discipline.

WEAKNESSES

1. It does not promote autonomy in students.

2. It is difficult for some teachers to apply the techniques as specified.

3. Some teachers are uncomfortable getting as physically close to students as the procedures dictate. Close physical proximity may also produce violent reactions in students, causing some parents to intervene on behalf of their children.

4. Preferred Activity Time may be less educational than Jones supposes.

5. Jones' insistence that discipline take precedence over instruction is contrary to what most educators would recommend. Many classroom disruptions are encouraged when teachers terminate instruction to focus on discipline problems.

6. Allowing the misbehavior of individual students to penalize the entire class may cause some students to be overly submissive and others to rebel.

7. Jones' approach promotes a "tattling" relationship between teachers and parents and can stimulate hostility between parents and teachers or the school.

8. It encourages teachers to be aggressive and controlling instead of helpful and supportive.

SUMMARY

Central to Jones' discipline system is the necessity of creating and teaching classroom rules to students. Students who have a role in creating classroom rules will have a greater inclination to follow them.

Control in the classroom is enhanced by proper seating arrangements. Students should be seated so that the teacher always has immediate access to the entire classroom.

Teachers ordinarily spend too much time helping just a few students, leaving the rest of the class time to invent mischief. This problem can be avoided if teachers apply the praise-prompt-leave sequence of instruction: praising students for what they have done right, prompting them on the next single step they must take to perform a task, and immediately leaving. Teachers can thereby more effectively control the entire classroom.

When discipline problems do occur, teachers must be skillful in limit-setting and responsibility training. Limit-setting involves a sequence of movements made by the teacher to limit disruptions by students. With this approach, teachers use their eyes as well as their physical proximity to students to deter bad behavior. The successive steps of limit-setting are applied only as students fail to respond appropriately to earlier movements made by the teacher. In responsibility training, students as a group are given a quantity of Preferred Activity Time, which they can either keep by behaving appropriately or squander through improper behavior. Preferred Activity Time gives individual students and groups of students the opportunity to participate in enjoyable educational activities such as games and contests.

If these approaches to discipline fail, backup sanctions may have to be employed, the most serious of which are suspensions and expulsions.

CENTRAL IDEAS

1. Seating arrangements that allow teachers open and quick access to all their students will help them maintain control in the classroom.

2. Limit-setting involves the use of nonverbal language and movements that put the teacher's eyes increasingly closer to those of the misbehaving student. Teachers should proceed through the series of limit-setting steps no further than is necessary to cause the student to behave properly.

3. Students use helplessness, denial, blame, accusations, insults, and profanity in an effort to thwart the loss of control they sense as the teacher sets limits.

4. Preferred Activity Time (PAT) is given to students as a negative reinforcer. They retain as much PAT as their behavior warrants or squander their PAT by behaving inappropriately.

5. When neither limit-setting nor responsibility training is successful in curbing students' bad behavior, omission training may be initiated. In omission training, students are rewarded for exhibiting desired behavior during predetermined intervals of time.

6. If students' behavior is still unacceptable after repeated efforts to help them change, parental as well as administrative assistance may be sought in the form of parent conferences, suspension, or, as a last resort, expulsion.

QUESTIONS AND ACTIVITIES

QUESTIONS TO CONSIDER

1. How is Jones' discipline approach similar to and different from Behavior Modification?

2. What inconsistencies are there between the procedures of limit-setting and of responsibility training and the backup sanctions of Jones' model?

3. How is Jones' model different from the traditional way in which teachers apply discipline in the classroom?

CLASSROOM ACTIVITIES

1. Prepare and show a video that depicts a teacher using Jones' limit-setting techniques. Stop the video and analyze each step in the process.

2. Have selected students demonstrate Jones' techniques for limit-setting. Have the class critique them.

STUDENT APPLICATIONS

1. Practice limit-setting with classmates. Concentrate on eye contact, relaxed breathing, and movement to and from a student's desk.

2. From the list of references for the Jones Model in Appendix B, prepare descriptions of games and activities you could use during Preferred Activity Time.

▼

REFERENCES

Evertson, C. M., & Anderson, L. M. (1979). Beginning school. *Educational Horizons, 57,* 164–168.

Jones, F. H. (1987a). *Positive classroom discipline*. New York: McGraw-Hill.

Jones, F. H. (1987b). *Positive classroom instruction*. New York: McGraw-Hill.

UNIT

3

Creating a Comprehensive
Discipline Program

To determine what discipline approach to use, you must first determine your personal philosophy and values. This determination will provide guidance as you decide which of the available discipline models is most attractive. An extensive analysis of existing theories is essential in this process. If you find that you consider the available models of discipline inadequate, you may decide to create one of your own. Then, armed with a discipline approach that has been carefully analyzed and mastered, you will be much better prepared to meet the challenges of the classroom.

A good discipline program should be comprehensive. Components designed to prevent as well as correct discipline problems are essential. In addition, a comprehensive discipline program should include schoolwide applications. This unit is designed to help you make these decisions.

11

Choosing a Discipline Approach

OBJECTIVES

This chapter is designed to help you

1. decide on a discipline approach to use in your teaching by applying your personal philosophy and values, establishing criteria, validating assumptions, and assessing the strengths and weaknesses of various discipline models
2. decide whether a single existing theory of discipline meets your expectations, whether a synthesis of two or more theories is more appropriate, or whether you need to create your own personal approach to discipline
3. decide which discipline orientation to use (theory-based, eclectic, or shifting)
4. select an approach to discipline that both corrects and prevents discipline problems and also has applications for schoolwide discipline

Introduction

This chapter illustrates the process of selecting an approach to discipline using the steps outlined in Chapter 2 and the information about the various discipline models presented in Chapters 3 through 10. In this chapter, a single model of discipline will be selected, and the rationale behind the selection will be explained. Chapter 12 illustrates the creation of a personal discipline approach from elements of several of the models along with additional compatible components.

Applying a Personal Discipline Philosophy

A philosophy of discipline should be consistent with your philosophy of education as well as your philosophy of life. For the purposes of illustration, let's consider a hypothetical teacher who has a discipline philosophy with the following components:

1. Children are born with a will to master their environment and achieve satisfaction of their basic needs.
2. The basic needs of children include self-determination, avoidance of control by others, love and acceptance, variety, and enjoyment.
3. Because of children's needs for self-determination and avoidance of control by others, discipline should provide children with opportunities to become self-governing.
4. Children can learn to be responsibly self-governed if they are given opportunities to make free choices and taught about behavioral consequences.
5. When children are allowed to be self-governing, they are less inclined to rebel and create discipline problems in school.
6. Discipline problems can thus be prevented to a great degree if children are allowed to be self-governing.
7. Children's sense of acceptance is best achieved when teachers accept them for what they are and allow them a greater degree of autonomous self-expression.
8. Discipline problems can be prevented if teachers help children satisfy their needs through acceptable means rather than allow children's disruptive behaviors to evolve.
9. Children can become responsible more readily if they learn not to give excuses and shift blame.

Behavior Modification, Assertive Discipline, the Jones Model, and the Kounin Model are all based primarily on teachers' control and therefore are the models least consistent with these philosophy statements. Before being discarded, however, they need to be evaluated in terms of how well they satisfy our hypothetical teacher's criteria and how valid their assumptions are.

Establishing Criteria

The following set of criteria will be used to evaluate the different discipline models:

A. Is the discipline model likely to help children become more self-disciplined and responsible?
B. Is it consistent with the view that children's motives are based on a self-directed effort to achieve autonomy, gain control of themselves and their environment, and achieve a high level of acceptance by others?
C. Is it helpful in promoting good self-concept in students?
D. Is it effective in promoting good classroom behavior?
E. Is it likely to help prevent discipline problems?
F. Is it consistent with an instructional program involving self-determined learning projects?
G. Can it be easily implemented?

H. Can it be readily learned?

I. Can it be applied in a schoolwide discipline program?

It should be readily apparent that criteria A and B are an outgrowth of the philosophy statements. The remaining criteria deal with more practical matters. It should also be pointed out that the list of criteria are arranged in order of importance. Whether decisions are made formally or informally, they are most often based on prioritized criteria. Otherwise, less important considerations may carry undue weight in the decision-making process. Deciding the order in which to arrange criteria is a matter of personal logic. For example, one might claim that criterion A is more important than criterion B because good classroom behavior is irrelevant if it is not voluntary; therefore, the more critical outcome of schooling is for students to become responsibly self-disciplined. The other criteria can be compared in a similar fashion and their relative importance determined.

Now let's apply the criteria to the different discipline models, assigning a rating to each discipline model based on the extent to which it satisfies each criterion. The ratings are given on a scale of 1 ("does not satisfy the criterion") to 5 ("completely satisfies the criterion"). Table 11.1 shows the results of such an evaluation. Keep in mind that deciding which discipline model best satisfies the entire set of criteria is not simply a matter of adding up the values in the table. Because the criteria have different degrees of importance, they need to be weighted accordingly. How different ratings are assigned is a matter of judgment and depends on your familiarity with the models. A few examples will be given here. It would be wise for you, however, eventually to create your own set of criteria and make your own judgments about how well each model satisfies them.

Reality Therapy/Control Theory was given a rating of 5 on criterion A because helping children become more self-disciplined is a basic principle on which the model works. Behavior Modification and Assertive Discipline were given a rating of 1 because, although they incorporate quite different ways of controlling students, they both assume that children require the control of teachers to behave properly. A rating of 1 was also given to the Kounin Model. Nowhere in the description of this model and its applications do self-determination and responsibility appear as factors; it is based entirely on control by the teacher. Even though responsibility is one of the expressed aims of the Jones Model, in its implementation it is oriented almost entirely toward control by the teacher, so a rating of 1 was given.

In terms of how well they help promote good self-concept (criterion C), four of the models received a rating of 5: Logical Consequences, Transactional Analysis, Reality Therapy/Control Theory, and the Ginott Model. The Logical Consequences model is designed to help children recognize that their misbehavior is the result of behavioral mistakes they make trying to satisfy their needs. Their frustrated efforts often produce poor self-concept. Through Logical Consequences, children are helped to regain a greater sense of adequacy through more need-satisfying behavior. Transactional Analysis gives children a way to interact with others successfully by avoiding crossed transactions and other behaviors that cause alienation. More positive interpersonal interactions promote a better self-concept. Reality Therapy/Control Theory fosters the development of a good self-concept by empowering children to regulate their own

Criteria	Behavior Modification	Assertive Discipline	Transactional Analysis	Control Theory	Logical Consequences	Kounin Model	Jones Model	Ginott Model
A. Self-discipline	1	1	4	5	4	1	1	3
B. Gain autonomy	1	1	4	5	4	1	1	3
C. Good self-concept	2	1	5	5	5	2	1	5
D. Good classroom behavior	5	2	3	4	4	4	3	3
E. Prevent discipline problems	2	2	3	5	4	3	2	3
F. Consistent with instruction	1	1	5	5	5	1	1	2
G. Easily implemented	4	5	2	1	1	4	4	3
H. Readily learned	4	5	3	1	1	3	3	3
I. Applied schoolwide	1	4	1	3	3	1	1	1

TABLE 11.1
Comparison ranges of different discipline models where 1 does not satisfy the criterion and 5 completely satisfies the criterion.

need-satisfying behavior. The Ginott Model recommends a number of tactics designed to be used by the teacher to promote good self-concept in students.

The other models are less likely to foster good self-concept. On the surface, it may appear that Behavior Modification improves children's self-concept by rewarding better academic performance. However, children exposed to reinforcement programs are unlikely to achieve a sense of well-being when their behavior is being manipulated by others. They realize that their behavior is being controlled and altered because others judge it to be inadequate. Similar criticisms could be made of Assertive Discipline, the Kounin Model, and the Jones Model. Assertive Discipline and the Jones Model are less helpful than the Kounin Model, however, because they are more punitive. They both advocate aggressive behavior by teachers and potentially abrasive teacher-student interactions. This friction is more likely to promote poor self-concept.

You will note from Table 11.1 that Behavior Modification and Assertive Discipline are ranked much better than Logical Consequences, Transactional Analysis, and Reality Therapy/Control Theory in terms of ease of implementation (criterion G) and ease of learning (criterion H). Learning to use Assertive Discipline is relatively easy, which perhaps explains its popularity to some degree. It also corresponds well with the need of many teachers and school administrators to maintain control of students. Behavior Modification is a little more difficult to apply correctly. Many teachers have the habit of mistakenly reinforcing misbehavior in their effort to curtail it. Learning to reinforce good behavior and ignore misbehavior does not come naturally. It may require considerable effort and training. The greater difficulty of using Logical Consequences comes from the requirement that teachers discover the operative motives of children. Because children either are unaware of their motives or deliberately hide them, teachers need considerable skill in asking questions and interpreting students' nonverbal responses. Transactional Analysis is even more difficult to learn and apply. Teachers have to be alert to the games students play and avoid getting involved in playing them. They must also avoid the natural tendency to express the Parent and Child ego-states and remain in the Adult. Reality Therapy/Control Theory perhaps has the highest difficulty level because teachers need a good deal of skill to interact with students who are attempting to avoid responsibility by making excuses, lying, and shifting blame. Helping children assume responsibility is understandably difficult if they have a long history of successfully avoiding it.

Once you have a fair idea of how the various discipline models satisfy the criteria, you can make a tentative decision. The data generated so far show that Reality Therapy/Control Theory most fully satisfies the first and second criteria. Behavior Modification and Assertive Discipline, on the other hand, are more easily implemented and learned (criteria G and H). Because a model's ease of implementation and learning are ranked as less important than its potential for helping students become responsibly self-determined, it is easy to conclude that Reality Therapy/Control Theory should be the model selected. This conclusion would be valid if in fact Reality Therapy/Control Theory could be implemented and learned adequately without too much difficulty. What is an acceptable level of difficulty? If the goal of helping students become more responsibly autonomous has a high enough priority, teachers may invest considerable time and effort to achieve the skill needed to apply it. However, if learning to apply Reality Therapy/Control Theory proves to be too difficult, this approach may have to be rejected. However much individual teachers may want to use a particular approach, their ability to learn how to use it adequately is a real limiting factor.

Examine the table again. It appears that Reality Therapy/Control Theory satisfies the criteria best. In addition to the strengths already identified, it has higher ratings in preventing discipline problems (criterion E) and correspondence with the intended instructional program (criterion F). Reality Therapy/Control Theory's closest competitor is Logical Consequences. If Logical Consequences could be more easily learned and implemented, it might be a better choice. However, compared to Reality Therapy/Control Theory, it is equally difficult to learn and implement. Therefore, according to the criteria specified and the rankings given, Reality Therapy/Control Theory is the most desirable approach—if it can be learned and implemented without too much difficulty.

Identifying and Validating Assumptions

A list of assumptions is given at the beginning of each of the chapters about discipline models (Chapters 3 through 10). You were asked to think about the validity of these assumptions as you read each of the chapters. The most important assumption that must be evaluated is either that students are able to achieve an adequate level of self-regulation or that they must be controlled by their teachers. Logical Consequences, Transactional Analysis, and Reality Therapy/Control Theory all assume that humans can become responsibly self-regulated. Behavior Modification, Assertive Discipline, the Kounin Model, and the Jones Model assume that they cannot. Behaviorists claim that humans are born as "blank slates," that they have no will and simply respond to reinforcing stimuli, so consequently they are at the mercy of the environment. It is therefore necessary for teachers to create an environment that reinforces more positive behaviors in students. Otherwise, by responding to various erratic stimuli, students are likely to behave unacceptably.

To determine whether the assumption of self-regulation is valid, examine evidence from three different perspectives (experience bases): personal experience, empirical evidence, and logical exposition. You may be personally acquainted, for example, with individuals who have left well-paying jobs and accepted positions with far lower pay in an effort to achieve a greater degree of autonomy. If we consider the power money has to satisfy most of our needs, such career moves seem to support the contention that humans have a will and are not just blank slates. But how does one account for the fact that so many people seem to be conditioned by their paychecks? Because not every person can be so conditioned, it can be concluded that those who are conditioned choose to allow the conditioning.

Empirical evidence for self-regulation is hard to obtain. Behavioristic studies usually show that individuals can in fact be conditioned. Conditioning is simply a matter of finding a sufficiently powerful reinforcer. Because humans have no will, behaviorists claim, they cannot resist the reinforcer. It is true that some children who have been conditioned by rewards later refuse to do their schoolwork without rewards. This refusal, however, does not show that they are unable to resist rewards. Rather, it shows that they have made a choice to work for rewards and not to work without them.

Glasser (1984) makes a logical argument in support of self-determination by examining the behavior that might be expected in connection with some common stimuli in the environment. A red traffic light signals us to stop, and so we do. A telephone rings and we answer it. The question is whether we just respond to these stimuli automatically or choose how we respond to them. Haven't you ever failed to answer the telephone because you were doing something more satisfying at the time? Wouldn't you run a red light if you were hurrying to take a seriously injured child to the hospital? Most people would not only run the red light but also ignore speed limit signs along the way. No doubt you would slow down as you approached a red light, for safety's sake, but the light in and of itself would not control your behavior. You would choose how to respond to the light stimulus.

The evidence cited here shows how the validation process works. It may not, however, prove conclusively that humans are not blank slates. Other sources may present evidence to the contrary. You should consider all available evidence and decide in favor of discipline models whose assumptions are best supported by the evidence. In our example, the evidence gives greater support to those discipline models that assume human beings to be capable of responsible self-determination. The assumptions about responsible self-determination that go along with Logical Consequences and Reality Therapy/Control Theory not only satisfy the criteria specified in the example but also can be validated.

The next step is to examine conflicting assumptions associated with Reality Therapy/Control Theory and Logical Consequences. Both models advocate helping children satisfy their basic needs as a way of promoting good behavior. With Reality Therapy/Control Theory, teachers can assume that nearly all students have a similar set of needs, which they must legitimately satisfy. When using Logical Consequences, on the other hand, teachers must find the current level of their students' needs. Only then can they help their students more legitimately fulfill those needs. Because finding the appropriate need level is critical to this model and because the need level is not always evident, teachers must interrogate students, asking them *why* they behave as they do. Unfortunately, many students are unaware of their motives or, if they are aware, do not want to disclose them. When students are unable or unwilling to discuss their motives, need determination becomes something of a guessing game that depends extensively on the teacher's skill in diagnosing various nonverbal cues. Because of the great potential for misdiagnosis, it cannot be assumed that teachers can accurately make this determination. The implicit assumption that teachers can consistently make accurate determinations must be judged invalid. In addition, a model designed to help students achieve a greater degree of responsibility should not include procedures that run counter to this purpose. For example, the practice in Logical Consequences of determining students' motives by asking them *why* may encourage them to give excuses, a result that is incompatible with helping them assume responsibility for their own behavior.

Another technique used in Logical Consequences that may promote less responsibility development than Reality Therapy/Control Theory is the practice of restricting misbehaving students to two behavioral options. Children who insist on leaning back in their chair may be told to choose between sitting with all four chair legs on the floor or sitting with two legs permanently raised off the floor. In the application of Reality Therapy/Control Theory, children are asked to explore a wide range of consequences for behavior and are permitted to choose behaviors that produce more satisfying consequences. Students are thus given a greater degree of self-determination.

Thus, our hypothetical teacher finds that an examination of the assumptions underlying each model gives the most support to Reality Therapy/Control Theory.

Sometimes additional information about the strengths and weaknesses of different models can help in validating assumptions. Lists of such information are included near the end of each of the chapters about discipline models (Chapters 3 through 10). As you validate assumptions, you may wish to re-examine these lists.

Considering Options

In deciding on a discipline approach, you have three options from which to choose. You can

1. use a single existing discipline model

2. synthesize components of different models

3. create your own discipline approach

If you decide on a single model, you are using a theory-based orientation (refer to Figure 2.2), and you must carefully apply the principles of that particular theory. Our hypothetical teacher decided on a theory-based orientation.

However, after going through the decision-making process outlined in this chapter, you may find that the model you select as best is still unsatisfactory. You may then decide that you prefer to use elements of a number of models (an eclectic orientation). If you decide on an eclectic orientation, you will need to select from among the various models those elements that suit you best and recombine them into an approach suitable for disciplining a variety of different kinds of children in a variety of circumstances (Charles, 1989). Or you may adopt a shifting orientation, in which case you would select a number of models and apply them in some systematic way depending on various factors such as the degree of self-control exhibited by students. If you decide to use a shifting orientation, you will select perhaps six or eight discipline models that differ in terms of the relative amounts of control exercised by teachers and autonomy enjoyed by students. Some of the models will be based on management theories (which assume that children's development depends on external influences), some on nondirective intervention theories (which assume that children's development depends on internal influences), and others on leadership theories (which assume that children's development depends on an interaction of both internal and external influences). The model you use in the classroom at any particular time depends on how much control you need to exercise to maintain good classroom discipline. In general, you will use various techniques from the different models as the situation seems to dictate (Wolfgang & Glickman, 1980).

After examining the various options, you may prefer to create your own discipline model. Your created model should have a theory-based orientation. That is, you must first devise a set of principles upon which to base your model. Next, you need to formulate procedures that put your principles of classroom discipline into practice. You will need to provide for prevention as well as correction of discipline problems. Your model should also be applicable to a schoolwide discipline program. Chapter 12 gives a detailed example of a discipline approach created from some compatible elements of several discipline models plus several new components.

SUMMARY

The most critical task in choosing a discipline approach is determining your personal philosophy and style of teaching—to what degree you plan to exercise control in the classroom or encourage autonomy in your students. You also need to decide whether you prefer an orientation to discipline that is theory-based, eclectic, or shifting. Criteria can then be prepared to help you choose among the various discipline models. The assumptions behind each of the models considered should then be identified and validated. The discipline model selected should not only correct discipline problems but also prevent them and provide for schoolwide discipline as well. If you discover that none of the models is satisfactory, you may need to create an approach of your own. Creating your own model will most likely involve putting together some elements of two or more models plus some of your own ideas.

CENTRAL IDEAS

1. The relative amounts of control you plan to exercise in the classroom and autonomy you intend to allow your students is the first issue that you must resolve in making a decision about what discipline approach to use.

2. Criteria are statements that provide standards of judgment for deciding between alternatives.

3. Assumptions accompany all human proposals and activities. Their validity must be determined if teachers are to avoid making poor decisions.

4. Consistency is the critical aspect of a theory-based orientation to discipline. Teachers who prefer an eclectic orientation instead use flexibility as their guiding principle.

QUESTIONS AND ACTIVITIES

QUESTIONS TO CONSIDER

1. What is the function of a personal philosophy of education?

2. What must be done to create a functional educational philosophy?

3. How can you be certain that the discipline approach you select is an appropriate one?

CLASSROOM ACTIVITIES

Have the class divide into groups according to the discipline approach they favor. Have each group prepare a defense for the approach they have selected and present it to the class.

STUDENT APPLICATIONS

1. Write a set of statements that reflect your personal philosophy of education. Include a statement regarding your view about the issue of teachers' control and

students' autonomy. Decide which discipline orientation you prefer: theory-based, eclectic, or shifting.

2. Prepare a list of prioritized criteria. Use them to determine which of the discipline models you prefer.

3. Make a list of assumptions for each discipline model and validate them. Use this information to further clarify which discipline model is most appropriate for your use.

4. Consider the extent to which the model you favor corrects discipline problems, prevents them, and allows for schoolwide applications.

5. Make a final decision about which discipline approach you prefer. If none of them is deemed satisfactory, begin assembling ideas for a discipline approach that would satisfy your expectations.

REFERENCES

Charles, C. M. (1989). *Building classroom discipline: From models to practice* (3rd ed.). New York: Longman.

Glasser, W. (1984). *Control theory: A new explanation of how we control our lives*. New York: Harper and Row.

Wolfgang, C. H., & Glickman, C. D. (1980). *Solving discipline problems: Strategies for classroom teachers*. Boston: Allyn and Bacon.

12

Creating a Personal Theory of Discipline

OBJECTIVES

This chapter is designed to help you

1. identify the components of a comprehensive discipline program and describe the relationship of these components to one another
2. understand how criteria are used in creating discipline procedures
3. specify what makes curricula relevant
4. explain how satisfying students' needs can reduce discipline problems
5. solicit valid input from students about the instructional program
6. involve students in creating rules and expectations
7. encourage useful input from students about the teacher's role in the classroom
8. improve students' behavior by guiding them through the process of exploring their previous commitments to the rules
9. improve students' behavior by guiding them through the process of exploring their intentions
10. avoid colluding with students who do not want to accept responsibility for their inappropriate behavior

Introduction

Undoubtedly the most frightening prospect for beginning teachers is the possibility that they may be unable to teach effectively because there is so much misbehavior in their classrooms. Even veteran teachers are often perplexed by discipline problems. Most teachers have no comprehensive theory of discipline to apply consistently. Instead, they commonly use various ideas about discipline picked up from disparate sources. Teacher training may not do much to alleviate this problem. Training in discipline for many teachers is often very meager, and many teachers embark on their careers without having mastered an effective approach to discipline. Instead, they are armed with a list of *dos* and *don'ts* and an almost sure inclination to react inappropriately to inflammatory situations in their classrooms. This lack of preparation will certainly magnify the difficulties experienced by first-year teachers.

This chapter is designed to help prospective teachers design their own program of discipline. As an illustration, a comprehensive discipline program will be outlined that follows a single set of principles. It is comprehensive because it will be applicable not only in the classroom, to prevent as well as to solve discipline problems, but also on a schoolwide basis. A good discipline model must have an explicit set of guidelines and accurate, predictable explanations for a wide range of human behaviors and interactions. The more a model can explain and predict, the more valuable it is. Models of this kind can be used to deal with a wider variety of school problems. They can provide a better understanding of how discipline problems develop and how they can be prevented.

Another attribute of a good discipline model is utility—the ease with which teachers can use it in the classroom. Most teachers should be able to apply a model while they are teaching, without making special adaptations. It should, in fact, be an integral part of and be based on the same principles as the instructional program.

An Example of a Comprehensive Discipline Program

The discipline model outlined here is based on the philosophy that students should increasingly achieve greater autonomy over what they study and how they behave in school. This approach should most appropriately be called a synthesis. It draws most heavily on Glasser's Reality Therapy/Control Theory; it also incorporates from Transactional Analysis the teacher's practice of speaking from the Adult ego-state and from Behavior Modification the recommendation to avoid reinforcing students' misbehavior. Some new ideas are also added.

The following criteria have been established for this discipline program. The program must:

1. provide for students' autonomy,
2. help students learn to be increasingly responsible and self-directed in terms of both discipline and the program of studies,
3. correspond well with the instructional program,
4. promote good self-concept in students,
5. develop a greater sense of cooperativeness among students,
6. prevent as well as correct discipline problems,
7. promote increased learning,
8. help students achieve greater consistency between their intentions and their behavior,
9. help teachers avoid collusion (collaboration between students and teachers for deceitful purposes is a common way in which discipline problems are perpetuated), and
10. promote better schoolwide discipline.

THE ROLE OF THE HOME

Various home experiences have an influence on children's behavior. If parents spend little time at home, children may seek unsuitable social experiences elsewhere, experiences that sometimes have devastating consequences. Even when parents are at home, parent-child interactions may be laced with conflicts. Factors such as divorce and poverty, as well as physical and mental abuse, can adversely affect children's ability to function properly. Children from severely dysfunctional families in particular face enormous adjustment problems at school.

Four aspects of dysfunctional families will be discussed briefly in this section:

- damage to self-concept
- attention deprivation
- love deprivation
- excessive control

Damage to Self-Concept.   The development of self-concept in children begins long before they start attending school. The confidence with which children enter school will have been either enhanced or diminished by various home experiences. Children are able, at an early age, to perceive their own helplessness when compared with larger and more capable adults (Harris, 1967). This perception is perhaps the reason why children so readily seek adult approval. Children's outlook on life depends generally on how successful parents are in helping them shift from feeling helpless to feeling confident about themselves. The very foundation of children's growth depends on their achieving a positive image of themselves as they form a personal identity. Achieving this image involves developing a sense of personal control over their lives. Dysfunctional families provide little or none of the emotional support children need to develop this control, and children from such families experience extreme personal problems (Biehler & Snowman, 1982). The success in school of children from dysfunctional homes is greatly limited (Purkey, 1970).

Attention Deprivation.   Children who do not get enough attention at home often compensate by seeking attention from their teachers. Unfortunately, many children receive their parents' attention only when they misbehave. If they do not disturb parents unduly, they are ignored. These conditions encourage unacceptable behavior and discourage acceptable behavior. Children from such homes discover that their bad behavior is a sure way to get the attention they crave. When children learn these behavior patterns at home, they tend to repeat them in school. If teachers of these children do not recognize these patterns, they can fall into the same trap of attending only to the children's misbehavior.

Love Deprivation.   Love deprivation is similar to attention deprivation. In fact, children usually consider attention to be an indication of how much they are loved. They feel unloved when parents are too preoccupied to give them sufficient attention. Some parents have the mistaken idea that the *quality* of time spent with children can make up for the lack of *quantity*. Quality time is obviously critical. However, children often interpret the lack of time spent as lack of caring. Children deprived of love often cause discipline problems as they try to satisfy this need. They may become so preoccupied in their quest that they gain very little from school.

Excessive Control.   A history of excessive control at home may also create discipline problems in the school, particularly when the level of control has been extreme. Human beings need freedom; they want to control their own lives. They also want to control others (Glasser, 1984). This conflict is particularly challenging in the rearing and teaching of children. As children mature, they increasingly seek freedom from adult control. Conscientious parents ordinarily allow and even encourage their children to assert their independence as the children demonstrate an ability to use it wisely. However, some parents not only fail to teach their children to act independently in appropriate situations; they actively try to stifle all independent thought or action in their children, which they regard as signs of rebellion. The conflict between the children's desire for freedom and the parents' unwillingness to allow it may actually encourage the children to rebel. Rebellion at home may extend to the school and other areas of society. In dysfunctional homes, parental control may take the form of abuse, whose symptoms can show up in children as extreme rebellion, criminal behavior, or withdrawal.

THE ROLE OF SOCIETY

Family influences and social influences on discipline problems are usually interrelated. Rejection at home, for example, may encourage children to search elsewhere for acceptance. Rejected children are often attracted to gangs, even though—or perhaps because—certain gangs flout accepted behavioral norms. A gang may satisfy a child's need for attention and for an identity. Gang members often demand and receive greater allegiance from one another than from their families. This allegiance further alienates children from their families and solidifies their gang identity. As evidence of their worthiness to join a gang, children are sometimes expected to participate in acts deplored by the rest of society—an armed robbery or a mugging, for example—and they may be periodically required to repeat such acts in order to confirm their commitment to the gang's value system. Such participation is designed to force members to choose between the gang and society and to reinforce loyalty within the gang. Gangs tend to be territorial, and conflict between gangs or within a gang usually revolves around turf, privilege, or property. The conflict can turn violent. When gangs become established, school officials may have considerable difficulty dislodging them.

A problem often associated with gangs, but certainly not limited to them, is drug abuse. Using or selling illegal drugs not only influences students' behavior directly but also alters the general atmosphere of the school. Drug abuse and its associated violence have become so severe in many schools that school officials must enlist the help of law enforcement personnel to maintain order.

Peer pressure, which is part of everyday life at school, contributes significantly to shaping students' behavior. If their peer group considers school a joke, students may go

This sample discipline program is based on the following assumptions:

1. Children can learn to govern themselves autonomously.
2. Children's basic needs include love and acceptance, control, freedom, and fun.
3. Children will collude, shift the blame, lie, and otherwise try to avoid accepting responsibility unless they are taught appropriate alternatives.
4. Children's needs are met better through cooperative learning than competitive learning. Cooperative learning improves students' relationships and reduces discipline problems.
5. When children realize that their intentions differ from their behavior, they will change their behavior to conform to their intentions.
6. Children will learn to be more responsible if they are taught to apply problem-solving skills to real-life problems in an atmosphere of freedom.

PREVENTING DISCIPLINE PROBLEMS

It is obviously wise to have a successful preventive discipline program. If discipline problems can be prevented, many of the difficulties experienced by teachers will be avoided. Discipline problems tend to escalate once they appear. In a well-conceived preventive discipline program, problems will not have a chance to grow and become increasingly difficult to overcome. A good preventive discipline program has several important characteristics:

1. It provides for students' needs (love, control, freedom, fun) in the instructional program.
2. It encourages students to communicate what they would like to learn and how they would like to learn it.
3. It involves students in establishing explicit rules and expectations.
4. It allows students to help determine the role of the teacher.
5. It fosters the establishment of good relationships between students and teachers.
6. It helps students learn how to evaluate their own academic performance.

Providing for Students' Needs.   Human needs include control, freedom, and fun along with love and acceptance (Glasser, 1984). The misbehavior of students is often an indication that one or more of these needs is not being met. Students are often unable to satisfy their needs in school. The same may be true at home or in other social settings. Because children spend so much time in school, teachers have a unique opportunity to help them more fully meet their basic needs and enjoy a more satisfying school experience. In the preventive discipline approach described here, helping students satisfy their basic needs is an important way to prevent the problem behaviors that often result when needs go unmet.

Adults usually consider children's need for control to be illegitimate. It seems presumptuous to allow students to assume control when they often seem out of control and rebellious. However, solving the problem of rebellion in students will not be achieved by restricting their behavior. Their unruliness is a product of having too few opportunities to govern themselves. This problem can be solved only by allowing students more control and responsibility, not less.

A student's need for freedom is difficult to provide for in school because students are normally assembled in large groups and expected to pursue common goals. The curriculum and the rules of behavior are usually dictated, giving students little or no leeway. These restrictions are necessary, it is believed, because students are inherently irresponsible. Teachers tend to believe that students will choose to misbehave if given the freedom to do so. However, to reduce discipline problems, teachers should avoid restricting students' options and instead help them expand their range of choices and make their choices wisely.

Students are customarily told that learning is difficult and that to be successful in school, they have to work hard. Most teachers do not believe that they have any obligation to make learning fun. In fact, teachers themselves generally consider learning to be hard work, not fun. Yet anyone who observes young children learning in an unstructured environment must admit that they seem to be having fun. In fact, from a very young age, children seem compelled to learn and spend much of their time engaged in learning, all the while enjoying themselves immensely. Unfortunately, however, the longer students spend in school settings, the less they like learning. In fact, school can turn some children off from learning altogether. How can this change be explained? One major factor is that learning in school is quite different from natural learning. For one thing, students are expected to learn what is assigned instead of what they consider interesting. Strict schedules must be followed. When compared to natural learning, completing school assignments is a drudge. It does not need to be so. Learning in school can be just as exciting as learning that occurs naturally. When it is, fewer discipline problems exist. When learning is not fun, students get bored and start looking for some other activity to entertain them. Usually they misbehave. Teachers can prevent discipline problems by allowing students to pursue many of their own personal interests.

One of the prime requirements for teachers is that they love their students. If students do not feel genuinely loved and accepted, they will react negatively. Love is demonstrated through actions (pats on the back, handshakes), words (use of the student's name, compliments), and attitudes (fairness, kindness). Excessive control, anger, and cutting remarks express a lack of love and respect. Love helps prevent discipline problems; negative expressions promote them. Teachers should generally be warm and caring and positive toward their students. Some teachers stand at the door and greet their students as they come into class. Others keep a checklist to remind them to initiate positive interactions with their students. Attending students' activities and making comments about how well students perform can be a very effective way to show that you care.

Involving Students in Determining the Curriculum.   When instructors teach interesting classes, they experience fewer discipline problems. When students are not bored and when they are fully involved in learning, they devote less time to misbehavior. Greater interest can be anticipated from students if they have a significant role in deciding what they learn. If students are involved in making curriculum decisions, teachers have less difficulty in motivating them. Teachers can then capitalize on the existing legitimate interests of students rather than attempt to impose on them a predetermined program of study, however well-planned it may be.

Students' interests can be ascertained by asking them directly, observing them in unstructured situations, and encouraging them to express their likes and dislikes. During the first day or two of class, students should be asked to supply their teachers with a list of their outside interests and hobbies. These lists not only provide insight into students' personalities but also can suggest unusual learning opportunities and stimulate better student-teacher relationships.

Teachers usually do not allow students to make decisions about the curriculum. It is supposed that students have insufficient training and experience to decide these matters. In addition, it is commonly believed that students will base their choices on how easy a subject is or express interest in areas of study that have no legitimate place in school. It is true that students have a meager knowledge of most subjects and are consequently unprepared to make valid decisions about their relative importance. However, to prepare students for making wise decisions, teachers can teach them the relative significance of various alternatives.

Teachers should first undertake with their students a comprehensive examination of possible topics and then help them consider the implications associated with each topic. For example, some topics prepare students for further schooling or college whereas others by themselves provide essential, practical knowledge. Some courses are part of a sequence and, therefore, are relevant only to those students who plan to take the advanced courses. Sometimes topics have current relevance or interest and as time passes may become less useful. Some things are important for everyone to understand; others are simply "nice to know." Armed with information such as this, students can make better choices. In the process of making their selections, students should help create a list of topics of general interest for the entire class as well as lists for individuals and small groups. In most courses, it is unnecessary for all students to study all the same topics.

According to an old adage, you can lead a horse to water, but you cannot make it drink. Likewise, you cannot force children to learn. A particular topic may be considered important by teachers, but it will be taken seriously by students only when the students themselves decide that it is important. Sometimes students may express no interest in a particular area of study because they are unaware of its relevance. Teachers need to help students put subjects in context. Once students know more about how one topic is interconnected with others, they will be better able to judge its relative value. Ironically, sometimes the very topic most resoundingly rejected by students who are given no choice is the most enthusiastically embraced by those who are allowed to choose for themselves.

Not only must students be able to make choices regarding the curriculum, but teachers must also help them obtain resources and then provide instruction that is interesting and lively. Discipline problems can be prevented to a great extent when these conditions exist. One excellent way to make the curriculum more relevant is to arrange cooperative learning experiences for students. In some types of cooperative learning, students decide what they learn and are invited to make their selections applicable to their own interests. Cooperative learning can help avoid the debilitating effects of competitive learning.

The following discussion illustrates how a teacher can involve students in determining the curriculum for a biology class:

Teacher Class, over the next few days we will be discussing our program of studies for the year. In a class such as biology there are many different topics, some of which may be more significant or interesting to us than others. Because there are far more good topics in biology than we have time for, we will need to choose as a class what we would like to study. We will probably find that there are a number of topics we all want to investigate and others that interest only a few of us. It is perfectly all right if the entire class works on some topics and then we break into small groups to study others. I have given each of you a sheet containing a rather long list of possible topics. At the bottom of the list are a number of blank spaces where you can write in other suggestions. We will create our program of studies from all the topics listed and put it in some reasonable sequence. Probably the first thing you need to do is to expand the list so that topics you are interested in are included. To help you look for possibilities, I have divided you into groups. At the table where each group is sitting I have deposited a number of copies of *Scientific American, Science News,* and some other periodicals. There is also a folder containing news articles about biological subjects I have collected over the past year or two. During this class period, you are free to browse through these sources and discuss with your group the topics that seem most appealing to you. When we meet tomorrow, we will discuss your suggestions and start making decisions about our biology curriculum. Remember, as you look for possible topics, try to judge their significance. If we are all going to take the time to study a particular topic, it should be significant as well as interesting. The significance of a topic can often be judged by whether it (1) has received much attention, (2) has important health considerations, (3) involves important ecological concerns, (4) allows active participation by class members, and (5) involves a fundamental biological topic. These criteria have been included on your sheet so that you can refer to them as needed. You should decide on the topics you prefer and arrange them in order of importance. Remember, some of you may feel strongly about a particular topic, but others may not share your interest. Take note of those topics so that they can be studied in small groups. Now let's get started. If you have questions, I will come around and try to answer them.

The teacher must decide how long this activity should last. As many class periods should be taken as students can productively use. When this phase has been completed, the process can continue.

Teacher Each of the lists your groups have compiled has been placed on the board. Notice that the more popular topics have been listed first. Now we need to decide as a class what would be the most profitable topics

	to study and how to put them in the most meaningful sequence. As you look at the lists on the board, which areas of study appear to be the most important ones?
Karl	It looks to me like AIDS probably leads the list, with ecology, evolution, reproduction, and immunity all coming in a close second.
Joyce	It looks like quite a few people want to study heart attacks and strokes too. I think they may be more interesting to the class than some of the other subjects. Maybe we can study a unit on diseases first.
Teacher	Joyce, you've made a good suggestion: grouping areas of study based on how they are related. Diseases sounds like a good grouping. Let's look at each one a bit more and decide what we may need to study as background for each of the diseases suggested so that we can get a more complete understanding of each. AIDS, of course, is caused by a virus. What areas need to be studied before an investigation of AIDS would be meaningful?
Naomi	Obviously, we need to learn about viruses, but I think we need to learn about other things like bacteria so we see how viruses compare.
Aaron	Well, if we're going to study bacteria and viruses, we probably need to learn more about cells. Viruses and bacteria are cells, aren't they?
Teacher	Well, viruses don't carry on all the functions of a cell, but they do infect cells, and therefore the study of cells would help us understand how viruses function. What do we need to learn about the function of cells?
Camille	I know there are a lot of chemical things that go on in cells. Perhaps that would help us.
Teacher	Yes, a lot of chemical reactions take place in our bodies that you will need to understand.
Verlyn	From what I read in *Science News*, some of the diseases we want to study are thought to be inherited. High cholesterol is probably an inherited problem. So are many kinds of cancer. I read somewhere they think even alcoholism and depression may have genetic origins. There are probably a lot of diseases that are inherited. Our class is particularly interested in diseases, so I think we should spend a lot of time studying genetics. We should also study bacteria and viruses a lot. I think these subjects are all related.
Teacher	How many members of the class like what has been said so far? Does anyone have an opposing view?
Roger	I am really interested in studying diseases, but if we do that, we won't have a biology course like the one they expect you to have had when you go to college. I want to make sure I get what I need to prepare me for college.
Teacher	How can we make sure we study what we are interested in and still cover the topics Don believes will prepare us for college?

Celia	I don't know how many of you plan to go to college, but I don't. I really want to learn how to take care of myself and avoid some of these diseases. I think we can study the topics Roger is worrying about as background for studying the more interesting and important topics.
Teacher	As we go along, let's make sure we remember to look at this question. At the present time we have expressed an interest in studying diseases, particularly those aspects of disease that pertain to subjects such as cytology, or the study of cells, microbiology, chemistry, and genetics. These are all bona fide subjects in most approaches to the study of biology. Let's go on and suggest additional topics now and continue to make comparisons.

Other topics need to be dealt with in a similar manner until the entire content of the course has been outlined. Similar discussions can be held to address questions about how the various topics are to be studied, including such issues as the frequency of labs, grouping, evaluation, and field trips. The desired outcome of these discussions is that students will feel good about both the content and the form of instruction. They need to be actively involved, so that they will feel a high degree of commitment for what is proposed. This commitment gives students a greater incentive to work and teachers a more effective means of dealing with any misbehavior that arises. Students who fail to enthusiastically learn what they agree to learn can have their previous commitments brought to their attention. This eventuality should be rare if students are genuinely involved in deciding their own curriculum. Fewer discipline problems can be expected.

Involving Students in Establishing Rules and Expectations. Once the curriculum has been agreed upon, teachers should next guide their students in formulating rules. Rules are a necessary part of any successful preventive discipline program. Students need a specific understanding of what behavior is acceptable and unacceptable in the classroom. Like the curriculum, rules should be jointly established. Students' ownership of rules depends on whether or not they have genuinely helped create them. If they do not accept rules as their own, students will not feel compelled to follow them. When students have been involved in formulating rules, they can also be relied upon to help enforce them. In fact, they may take care of most necessary enforcement.

A word of caution is needed when students help enforce rules. They can sometimes become too negative and punitive. They should, therefore, be taught that because punishment has little logical connection to rule infraction, it is unacceptable. Punishment is usually applied arbitrarily and with negative emotion and should therefore be replaced with consequences. Consequences follow logically from the rules and can be interpreted by students as appropriate and fair. Students should help determine consequences. Unless they do, they will refuse to accept them, and the consequences will fail as a deterrent to misbehavior.

The process of determining rules and consequences is illustrated in the following discussion:

Teacher	As a class we have determined our goals and the topics we wish to study during the coming year. I personally believe the curriculum we

have made will provide excellent opportunities for learning. But sometimes, as happens in almost any classroom, learning can be disrupted. As a class we need to be aware of these potential disruptions and how to prevent them. If they ever occur, we need to decide what to do about them. What kind of behavior will prevent us from achieving our learning goals?

Steve	I think talking too much is the biggest problem.
Ann	I believe the biggest problem isn't how much we talk but when we do it.
Teacher	So, Ann, what do you have to suggest about when to talk in class?
Ann	If we just talk one at a time during discussions and don't whisper to one another during lectures, things would be much better.
Rachel	Yes, and if there was no loud talking during quiet study time, we would all be able to concentrate better.
Chuck	I have a problem with that. During quiet study time I like to ask other students questions and get their help.
Tina	Well, Chuck, that can be done quietly.
Teacher	How many believe quiet conversation won't interfere with learning during quiet study time? *(Most hands are raised.)* I see most of you believe that it will not interfere. Let's try it for a week and then evaluate ourselves. Now, Ann suggested that just one of us talk at a time during discussions and that we refrain from talking during lectures. How do you suggest we accomplish this?
Roger	I suggest we raise our hands and have you call on us.
Elaine	I don't like that. It makes me feel like a first grader. Can't we just be sensitive to one another and then be careful not to speak when someone else is talking?
Rosanne	That doesn't work. I've been in other classes where we tried to do that. It's always too noisy. It sounds good, but it just doesn't work.
Teacher	Are there more comments about this issue? *(The class is silent.)* How many prefer to raise their hands during discussions? *(Most hands are raised.)* It looks like most of you would rather use this method. Here again, this issue can be reconsidered later if you wish. Now, in the event that any class member disturbs our learning activities by talking, what should be the consequence?
Glen	I think they should be kicked out.
Teacher	What do you mean by "kicked out"? Where would they go and what would they do?
Glen	I haven't thought about that. I just think they shouldn't be allowed in class when they're too noisy. Couldn't we just sent them to the principal's office?
Teacher	Do you think Ms. Brenchley would want to handle problems like this, problems that we as a class could handle ourselves? What could we

	do that would not involve the principal but would be fair and appropriate?
Dolores	Couldn't you just move the person who is talking to a new seat? In one of my other classes the teacher did that and it worked well.
Teacher	Would you like to have your present seating be a privilege you could forfeit by talking and disturbing the class? *(The students indicate general agreement.)* Where would you suggest the disruptive person be seated?
Camille	I'd make them sit up by your desk.
Teacher	You have created your own rules for this class. Now it sounds like you want me to enforce them for you. Wouldn't you rather take care of these problems yourselves?
Jay	I would. I would like to have a seat designated that is right in the center of the classroom, where the person is surrounded by a discipline committee. It would be their job to make sure no more disturbances took place. If the person is still noisy, I suggest they be sent home and required to bring their parents to class and petition the discipline committee to get back into class.
Teacher	Would others like to comment about Jay's plan?
LaRetha	I think that is one of the best ideas I have ever heard. I think we should do it. We could at least try it for a while and see how we like it.
Aaron	I like it, too, but we would have to be sure the discipline committee took their responsibility seriously. Maybe we could all take turns serving on the committee. It doesn't sound like it would be much fun.

In this discussion, the teacher tries to have students consider some important points of a preventive discipline program. Other points would also be brought up and discussed. The end product should be a few good rules, and students should have a role in enforcing these rules with appropriate consequences. The rules should be an outgrowth of the students' previously established learning goals.

Involving Students in Determining the Teacher's Role.   Once students have established classroom rules and procedures, it is appropriate to discuss the role of the teacher:

Teacher	So far we have discussed your learning goals and how you will handle disruptions. It is time to discuss some things I might do as your teacher to help your learning be more profitable. Does anyone have any suggestions?
Tina	I think we need lots of breaks from learning. I think we should have a party every Friday. *(This suggestion is followed by cheers and laughter. The teacher just looks at the class and waits for additional responses.)*
Renaldo	That's pretty stupid, Tina. Occasional parties are all right, but having one every Friday is a joke. You can do your partying after school.

Shon	I'd like to have parties, too. Maybe we can have one every month.
Teacher	Does anyone know the policy of the board of education regarding parties?
Jing	We all know that. We've heard it a hundred times. We are permitted one party each semester. I don't see how this discussion is related to the question you asked. Would you mind asking it again?
Teacher	I thought you might have some suggestions about things I could do to help you be more productive learners.
Karl	I like review sessions when I learn. Also, I hate surprise tests. I like to know when I'm being tested.
Terry	I agree with Karl. I also think we shouldn't have any homework over the weekends. Then we can come to school on Monday rested and ready to go to work.
Rachel	I like these suggestions. I also think we should have a better idea of what is going to be on the tests so that it isn't just a big guessing game.
Bob	I'd prefer it if we didn't have tests at all. I get so tense during tests that I can't remember anything I've studied. *(Several students chime in their agreement.)*
Teacher	If we didn't have tests, how could your work be evaluated and grades assigned?
Chuck	I wish we could do away with grades too. I hate them!
Naomi	Well, I like tests and grades. If you studied harder, you'd like them, too.
Teacher	Obviously, some of you like to be tested and others do not. Perhaps some of you could take tests while others had some alternative evaluation.
LaRetha	I do much better writing papers.
Karl	I would rather have oral tests.
Teacher	Now let's see what's been said so far. You have expressed a desire for various forms of evaluation. That can be arranged. You also indicated you wanted to avoid weekend homework and unannounced tests. I think these are appropriate requests. How many prefer we make these adjustments? *(All the students raise their hands.)* Is there anything else that you think would help you learn better?
Kulei	I would like to have more interesting lessons taught. Sometimes I really get bored in school.
Teacher	The class has already decided which topics it would like to study. Are you truly interested in learning about these topics?
Kulei	Yes, but I just want you to be a real interesting teacher.
Teacher	*(to the entire class)* What responsibility are you willing to assume as class members to make the lessons interesting?

Felecia	I think we should always be prepared, so that our discussions are based more on the questions students have.
Kim	I find if I have done some reading on the subject being discussed, I am interested and don't have to depend on the teacher to get me involved.
Teacher	How many would be willing to be prepared for class and come with questions to pursue in our discussions? *(All the students raise their hands.)* I would be willing to be as well prepared as I can be. I can't guarantee that I will always teach interesting lessons, but because you can regulate this to some extent by how involved you are in learning, perhaps everyone will be more interested and satisfied if you all search for questions you would like to have explored in class. That way the things that interest you the most can be investigated.

When students are trying to contribute suggestions about the teacher's role, they may make demands that cannot justifiably be met. Students who make these suggestions should not be humiliated or ridiculed. It is better for teachers to let other students react or to raise associated questions that need to be explored. Teachers must avoid being coercive and vetoing students' suggestions.

Fostering Good Relationships.   Whether or not teachers experience discipline problems in their classes depends to some extent on the relationships they have with their students. If students like their teachers, they will be less inclined to create trouble. The best relationship to establish is one of mutual respect. Such a relationship will develop when teachers help their students become more personally responsible and self-determined. If teachers are well prepared and personable in their relationships with students, avoiding all abusive behavior, they will gain more respect.

Helping Students Evaluate Their Own Work.   When teachers do all the evaluating in school, students tend to take less responsibility for their efforts and accomplishments. In fact, students develop an external locus of control when they are evaluated exclusively by teachers. An external locus of control is an outside influence to which accomplishments are attributed; success, some students believe, is the result not of effort but instead of fate or luck. Students react this way because they always have to depend on their teachers to determine the quality of their work and teachers often grade inconsistently. Helping students evaluate their own work helps them become more responsible and self-directed. The result is better discipline.

CORRECTING DISCIPLINE PROBLEMS

A comprehensive discipline program must not only prevent discipline problems but also provide a way to correct them. The first step a teacher might take if the discipline program fails to prevent problems is to talk with misbehaving students individually. In this discussion, the teacher can help students explore the commitments they have made about their behavior and determine whether or not they intend to honor those commitments.

Exploring Commitments.   The following example is based on the principle, on which the discussion of prevention was based, that students should exercise autonomy and personal responsibility. Assume that a student named Moana talked excessively and loudly during discussions and quiet study time even though she had previously agreed not to do so. She had been subject to actions by the classroom discipline committee but had reacted by shouting to her friends across the room and ignoring the pleas of the committee to follow the class rules. When her mother came to the class to get her readmitted, Moana got into a screaming match with her and the whole negotiation process broke down. Subsequently, this discussion took place between the teacher and the student:

Teacher	Moana, what did you do with Alice today in class during quiet study time that disturbed students around you?
Moana	I was just asking her to help me with the homework.
Teacher	What other instances are there when you have interfered with the learning of other class members by shouting to Alice and others while they were working on their projects?
Moana	I don't know.
Teacher	What about last Friday? Who were you talking loudly with just before the bell rang?
Moana	I was talking with Ralph.
Teacher	What did you agree, along with the rest of the class, about talking loudly during quiet study time?
Moana	I said I wouldn't do it, but I felt like the rest of the class was forcing me to agree to that. I really didn't accept it.
Teacher	Would you like me to write you a hall pass so that you can visit with the counselor and try to arrange to change classes? Perhaps you can find one where disruptions are more acceptable.
Moana	No. My friends are all in this class.
Teacher	What must you do so that you can remain in this class?
Moana	I guess I'll have to be more quiet during quiet study time.
Teacher	Is that what you intend to do from now on?
Moana	Yes.
Teacher	What will be the consequences if you fail to do what you stated you intended to do?
Moana	I guess I will have to find another class.

Exploring Intentions.   Sometimes students will not have made commitments with other class members to refrain from certain behaviors such as talking. In these cases, students' intentions can be explored and compared with their behavior. Most students do not intend to cause trouble. It would be unusual for them to admit that they intentionally disrupted their classes. More often, they will give an excuse and claim that someone else or something else is to blame. The fact that children do not intend to cause annoyance can be used as a powerful tool in helping them behave more productively. The strategy is to have them first state what their true intentions are and then to compare their intentions with their behavior and its consequences. Let's observe what a teacher might say in the case of a student who talks disruptively to nearby classmates during class discussions. This discussion should take place privately, outside of class:

Teacher	Carvel, what were you doing in class today during discussion that interfered with the lesson and disturbed other students?
Carvel	I didn't do anything. I was just asking Jake something about what you said during class discussion.
Teacher	When you talk loudly with other students during discussions, what negative impact does it have on the learning of fellow classmates?
Carvel	I guess it makes it harder for some of them to learn, but sometimes I have a question I would like to ask so that I can understand better what we are talking about.
Teacher	What are your intentions about disrupting the class?
Carvel	Well, I don't mean to cause any trouble.
Teacher	You indicate you don't intend to interfere with the learning of your classmates, but when you talk out loud during discussions, what disruptive influence are you having?
Carvel	I guess I keep them from learning, but I don't really mean to do this.
Teacher	So how does your behavior compare with your intentions?
Carvel	Not very well.
Teacher	What do you need to do, then?
Carvel	I need to make sure I don't talk out in class again.
Teacher	If you did have a question, what could you do differently?
Carvel	I could present it to the entire class.

Avoiding Collusion.   Sometimes students will deliberately provoke their teachers in an effort to cause a reaction, particularly when they either have failed to complete an assignment or are trying to avoid one. If students can get their teachers to react negatively, they can excuse themselves for their own failure and irresponsibility. When teachers respond negatively to students' provocations, they usually get involved in collusion. Collusion is a cooperative, but negative, exchange between individuals that allows both parties to excuse personal irresponsibility (Warner, 1980). For example, suppose that a student comes to class without completing an assignment due that day. To provoke the teacher, the student may say, "It wasn't possible to get the assignment done last night. The explanations you gave yesterday were not clear. I don't know how you could have expected us to complete the assignment with the little bit you taught us." Or the student may decide that stronger language is needed to elicit a reaction from the teacher and therefore speaks more bluntly, perhaps adding a bit of profanity: "I don't know when I've seen a stupider assignment than the one you gave us. It stunk like hell!"

Many teachers take the bait and reprimand the student for using vulgarity. If teachers sense that the assignment or their teaching is substandard, they may rise to defend the assignment the student has labeled stupid; in trying to excuse their perceived inadequacy, they end up participating in collusion. Some teachers reciprocate by calling the student stupid. Reactions such as these help students avoid accepting responsibility for their own failure. Students who claim that an assignment is bad can justify not doing it because the teacher's loss of control somehow invalidates anything the teacher requires. Students thus escape having to shoulder their academic responsibilities.

What could the teacher have said to avoid collusion when the student first started the provocation? Assume that the unfinished assignment was to solve several physics problems. The teacher could more profitably have said, "OK, let's look at the first problem." Then, addressing the provoking student directly, the teacher could have asked, "What does the first sentence of the problem say?" From here the teacher could guide the student through the problem to a successful solution and then say, "The other problems are exactly like this one. Start working on them and see if you can finish two or three by the end of class."

The recommended reaction for the teacher in this case is to help the student do the most responsible thing, which is to solve the problem set. The teacher should not react to the student's provocation. Neither should the teacher attack the student nor accept the blame for poor teaching. None of these reactions will help students assume responsibility for themselves.

SCHOOLWIDE DISCIPLINE

It is a common practice for teachers to have the school principal deal with discipline problems they feel unable to take care of themselves. The belief that discipline problems should not interfere with the instructional program justifies this practice in part. It is hard to defend having the entire class wait while the teacher corrects the misbehavior of one student. However, when students are sent to the principal's office, the teacher may be unable to predict potential outcomes. The student may return to the classroom, but the principal may give no indication of what actions were taken. Unless teachers and administrators understand and coordinate their disciplinary measures beforehand, what is done in the principal's office may be contrary to what the teacher is trying to accomplish. It is therefore essential for administrative disciplinary actions to be consistent with discipline in the classroom. Otherwise, success will be limited. Schoolwide discipline must be based on the same principles as classroom discipline.

Two types of problems are dealt with in schoolwide discipline programs: problems in the classroom that are referred to the principal's office by teachers and problems that take place in locations other than classrooms. Discipline problems referred to the office should be coordinated by teachers and administrators. In these cases it is particularly important to maintain consistency of discipline. Otherwise, students may be sent different messages and become confused, or they may begin playing teachers and administrators against one another.

Hallways, school grounds, buses, lunchrooms, auditoriums, and gymnasiums are often sites for fights, vandalism, drug abuse, and other related problems. These problems can best be handled as part of the schoolwide discipline program. Some of these problems are serious enough to require the involvement of law enforcement officials. Fighting, vandalism, and drug abuse not only are disruptive to the functioning of the school but also may be punishable crimes. Even though a school discipline program may not itself provide for punishment, the school should not protect students from the consequences of actions that violate the law, even if such actions take place inside the school. The potential danger to other students of crimes such as drug abuse and possession of weapons may be sufficient cause to expel the guilty parties permanently.

A few years ago in an inner-city high school there were many fights among students every day. Some of these fights involved deadly weapons. A new principal who had been assigned to the high school was determined to eliminate this problem. He decided that if any students took part in a fight, the police would be called and the students involved would be handed over to them. They would be permanently barred from returning to school. They might attend other schools in the district, but under no circumstances would they be permitted to return to that particular high school. If they attended another high school, they had to arrange their own transportation. During the first year these procedures were implemented, there were only two fights. Obviously students could see that no excuses would be accepted and that the administration would not back down. Actions of this kind may be necessary if discipline has deteriorated to such a point that students are endangered. In this case, the principal took it upon himself both to determine the rules and to enforce them. Ordinarily it would be better to involve a committee of students in creating rules and the entire student body in enforcing them. When teachers and administrators make the rules, students feel less inclined to follow them.

When rules are formulated by committees of students and ratified by the entire student body, greater acceptance can be expected. Students will also be more likely to police themselves. Such involvement is consistent with the classroom discipline approach outlined in this chapter.

SUMMARY

The three-part discipline program described in this chapter provides for students' self-determination and responsibility and is based on other important criteria as well. It provides an example of how you may formulate your own discipline program by borrowing some ideas from various theories and including some of your own. It describes procedures to prevent as well as correct discipline problems and includes applications for schoolwide discipline. Each of these components has been designed to be consistent with the others.

The preventive component includes the practices of

1. allowing students help determine what they learn in order to make it more relevant to them

2. having students help create the rules of conduct
3. involving students in defining the role of the teacher
4. improving student-teacher relationships
5. teaching students to evaluate their own academic performance
6. ensuring that students satisfy their needs in the school in legitimate ways

The corrective part of the discipline program includes provisions for

1. exploring commitments
2. exploring intentions
3. avoiding collusion

Exploring commitments enables students to reflect on the promises they have made to classmates and to change their behavior accordingly. When students explore their intentions, they compare their actual behavior and its consequences with their intended behavior. They are then helped to alter their behavior until it fulfills their intentions. In all interactions with students, teachers must avoid collusion—interpersonal entanglements that are used by students, and sometimes by teachers, to avoid responsibility. Teachers can then assist students to become more productive and responsible.

The schoolwide discipline program is designed to deal with problems that originate in the classroom as well as those that have their origin in other school locations. If school administrators become involved in classroom discipline, their actions must be consistent with those of teachers. Students should be involved both in creating school-wide rules and in helping to enforce them.

CENTRAL IDEAS

1. All aspects of a well-organized, comprehensive discipline program should be consistent with a single set of principles.
2. Students whose needs are satisfied in the school will be less likely to rebel.
3. The relevance of the curriculum can be determined only in consultation with students.
4. Students will apply themselves more enthusiastically to their studies when they have helped determine the curriculum.
5. Students will follow rules they have helped create more readily than rules imposed on them.
6. Students are more likely to improve their behavior when they are asked to recognize and accept previously made commitments to follow rules.
7. Students often fail to realize that their behavior and its consequences are inconsistent with their intentions. When they are asked to compare their behavior and intentions, students will adjust their behavior to coincide more completely with their intentions.

QUESTIONS AND ACTIVITIES

QUESTIONS TO CONSIDER

1. What special problems are inherent in creating a schoolwide discipline program?
2. What difficulties might be encountered in creating a personal approach to discipline?
3. What does a comprehensive discipline program consist of and how can such a program be applied consistently?

CLASSROOM ACTIVITIES

1. Have class members bring a set of criteria to class upon which to base a discipline program.
2. Have small groups of students with similar criteria get together outside of class to create a description of a discipline program that is consistent with their criteria.
3. Have each of the groups present its discipline program to the entire class. After each presentation, class members can provide a critique. (Or have each group provide other class members with a written description of its discipline program a few days prior to the critique session so that everyone can study it and give more thoughtful responses.)

STUDENT APPLICATIONS

After analyzing various discipline theories and creating a list of criteria, prepare a description of a discipline approach that satisfies your criteria and that draws upon various theories as well as your own ideas.

REFERENCES

Glasser, W. (1984). *Control theory: A new explanation of how we control our lives.* New York: Harper and Row.

Warner, T. (1980). *Self-betrayal.* Unpublished manuscript, Brigham Young University, Department of Philosophy, Provo, UT.

Classroom Management Approaches and Procedures

Classroom management procedures are an important complement to any discipline program. They contribute to an environment that enhances learning and minimizes the chance that discipline problems will occur. Teachers need to select from among the various classroom management procedures those that correspond most closely to the discipline model they use.

Any classroom management program must make provision for several important factors that affect proper discipline in the classroom:

- the physical classroom environment
- the instructional program
- teacher-student relationships

In this unit you will study the effects of the physical environment, time management, lesson management, and teacher-student relationships on the atmosphere of the classroom.

CHAPTER

13

Classroom Management and Instruction

OBJECTIVES

This chapter is designed to help you
1. appreciate the value of maintaining consistency between educational philosophy and the instructional program, including discipline
2. understand the problems created by competitive learning
3. apply specific cooperative learning approaches
4. identify the stages students go through and the adjustments teachers must make when the classroom learning environment is changed from one that is controlled by the teacher to one that allows more freedom for students

Introduction

Teaching is one of the most complex of all human activities. It is estimated that elementary school teachers are involved in more than 500 separate exchanges with individual students during a single day (Jackson, 1968). At any given moment in time, teachers must choose which among many actions and interactions to give their attention to. This multiplicity makes teaching much more difficult than is commonly assumed. Doyle (1986) contends that classrooms are difficult to manage because they are multidimensional, simultaneous, and unpredictable. To complicate matters further, the classroom environment is immediate and public—that is, teachers must perform right now, right here, in full view of everyone.

Teachers must deal with many dimensions within the classroom: managing and reacting appropriately to large numbers of students, participating in daily routines and special events, carrying out mundane tasks. Because of the number of people involved, any occasion can have multiple consequences that may require different reactions from the teacher. The behavior of any one participant has the power to influence how other participants react, and the reactions of teachers certainly influence how students behave. Many interactions in the classroom all take place at once. When teachers are engaged in instruction, they also have to keep track of time, monitor and react to students in a variety of contexts, and make last-minute changes in instructional formats and presentations, simultaneously pacing their lessons appropriately and managing students' behavior. Even in the most well-managed classroom, teachers cannot foresee nor plan for every contingency. Classrooms are dynamic places. The human interactions that take place in them are often unpredictable. Teachers consequently have an enormous task in making sure that their lessons are interesting to students and that students remain involved and are not distracted.

Discipline problems are rare in classrooms in which children are involved and interested and in which they are appreciated and loved. Unfortunately, in many classrooms these conditions do not exist. Goodlad found in an extensive national study of schools that students generally have far too few self-directed, meaningful educational experiences. In addition, he found that their learning experiences rarely go beyond mere memorization. Memorized facts are usually taught without any conceptual context, and students are seldom permitted to deepen their level of understanding by exploring the implications of important concepts or applying those concepts in real-life circumstances. Most learning does little to arouse students' curiosity or stimulate them to solve personal problems. The subject matter is ordinarily viewed by students as irrelevant to their personal struggles and development (Goodlad, 1984).

The relevance of learning any particular subject depends on the learners. Commonly, however, students have little to say regarding their educational program. Ironically, the longer children are in school and (presumably) the more mature they become, the less they are called upon to decide what they learn. Children in kindergarten have more to say about their program of studies than do high school seniors (Goodlad, 1984). It is clear that more self-determination may be kept from older students for fear that they will somehow abuse it. Yet they stand at the threshold of life where personal decision-making is not only important but absolutely essential. Where else but in school will they learn to function adequately in our complex world? How will they learn to live responsibly? These children sense their growing capacity to choose their own destiny and, therefore, assert their right to control it. Teachers need to provide students opportunities to do so.

What can be gained by letting children make decisions about what they learn and how the classroom is managed? How can they possibly know what they should learn in school? There are two ways to answer these questions.

The first requires an examination of school practices as they currently exist. Eighty percent of what is learned in school involves rote memorization (Cunningham, 1987). This activity is of questionable value given the fact that 65 percent of what is learned is forgotten in about a month (Cronback, 1965). In addition, many students refuse to memorize the information required. They do not consider such facts sufficiently useful nor the competition to acquire them to be worth the effort. Without meaningful learning opportunities and the motivation to become involved, what most students learn is of low quality (Glasser, 1990). Much of the school curriculum is also out of date soon after it is taught. For example, the sum total of scientific knowledge doubles about every 5.5 years at the current rate, which is also accelerating. By the time the average medical student completes training, half of all the information acquired in medical school is obsolete (Cross, 1985). The knowledge explosion has created so much valuable information that determining what should be learned in school is, to a large extent, arbitrary. With a little coaching, students themselves can make adequate selections.

Greater personal motivation is the second reason why it is wise to let children have a significant role in deciding what they learn. Greater effort can be expected from students who are allowed to help determine their own curriculum. More learning will consequently take place. In addition to information, students must learn to make better decisions, an ability that is critical for living in our complex modern world. When children complete school, real-life situations demand responsible autonomy. How will students learn to be self-determined if during school their freedom is consistently held in check? How will they ever learn to make responsible decisions if during school they are not permitted to decide even routine matters? How will they maintain an interest in lifelong learning under such conditions? Children not only need to have the opportunity to make decisions, but they also need to be taught how to make decisions effectively. Children should be engaged in projects in which thinking and problem-solving play a central part. There are many complex problems that confront children: dysfunctional families, peer pressure, the development of an identity, sexuality, love, acceptance. Without the help of knowledgeable and caring adults, children often turn to alcohol and other drugs to escape their problems. These problems, however, can be used as an integral part of the learning process. Sensitive teachers can assist students in developing important thinking skills in an atmosphere of freedom while at the same time helping them find valid solutions to their immediate problems. Students thus attain a growing sense of personal autonomy and thereby are empowered to make their own choices in a responsible manner. Better behavior can be expected from these students.

Consistency Between Discipline and Curriculum

Consistency between philosophy and practice is one of the least talked about yet most important educational considerations. Because consistency often has such a low priority, it is natural to expect inconsistency from teachers in both teaching and discipline. Maintaining consistency between various educational practices, however, has several important benefits.

First, students have an easier time interpreting expectations. If they are led to believe that they have some degree of independence and then experience excessive domination and control, they will be justifiably confused. Although students' confusion and associated dissatisfaction are not commonly considered significant, they do have a direct bearing on how successful students will be in school and how well-disciplined they will be. Preoccupation with issues of freedom and control often provides the basis for students' unrest and commonly thwarts students' learning.

A second benefit of maintaining consistency is better educational practice. When consistency is emphasized, greater effort is given to clarifying principles and applying them appropriately. If principles and practices are thought out more thoroughly, instruction is improved. In determining principles to apply in educational practice, teachers can take advantage of the careful thinking and research of others that is available in the literature.

Maintaining consistency also has a positive impact on teachers' commitment. This third benefit is perhaps the most convincing reason to support the application of educational philosophy to the development of school curricula. When teachers are committed, they are more likely to create good educational programs. Committed teachers ensure that their students are successful. Commitment comes when teachers determine for themselves the principles they will apply in their teaching.

Cooperative Versus Competitive Learning

One of the most critical decisions teachers make is whether they will provide their students cooperative learning opportunities or use traditional competitive learning methods. The decision to use cooperative or competitive learning depends on whether freedom or control is emphasized. This question also forms the basis on which to decide the kind of discipline to be used. When education is based on the principle of autonomy, cooperative learning can be incorporated in the instructional program and a discipline approach such as Logical Consequences, Transactional Analysis, or Reality Therapy/Control Theory used. When control by the teacher is emphasized, competitive learning along with Behavior Modification or Assertive Discipline can be employed.

In competitive learning, students usually work independently and then take competitive examinations for their grades. Because the number of high grades is often limited, only a few students can obtain them. This scarcity encourages students to look out for their own interests and to avoid helping their peers. In some instances, students sabotage the efforts of one another for the sake of grades.

Competition may be used with a number of different curricular formats. The traditional subject curriculum is the most common one. This traditional approach is convenient because the information students are required to memorize can be efficiently measured on written tests. Test results are objective and easy to score. The normal curve is the basis of competitive grading; students are given particular grades in specified proportions. Students who are not successful in getting high grades are prone to give up trying and instead use various defense mechanisms to avoid a sense of failure.

Cooperative learning, on the other hand, makes the success of each student dependent on the achievement of group members. Group members are encouraged to cooperate rather than compete. All cooperative learning approaches encourage group interdependence. In some instances, the learning program is regulated so that students are able to learn what they need to know only from one of their peers. In other cases, students are unable to complete their learning projects without help from others. In some cooperative learning approaches, the grade given to individual group members is a group average; this method of assigning grades, of course, is supposed to stimulate group achievement. Students exercise varying amounts of autonomy in deciding what they will learn. Some approaches give students a choice about the nature and pace of what they learn. Students may even decide when and how they are evaluated in some cases.

The following sections describe some of the more prominent and carefully researched cooperative learning approaches.

JIGSAW II

In Jigsaw II, material to be studied is prepared in written narrative form. The subjects for which this approach is most appropriate are social studies, literature, and science. The reading material for Jigsaw II is usually a story, biography, or chapter in a book. Students work in heterogeneous teams; that is, the class is divided into groups whose members are at different achievement levels and sometimes represent a mix of ethnicity, gender, or other factors. Team members are given "expert sheets" that list different topics to focus on in the reading. Topics cover themes that appear throughout the reading selection rather than only once. For example, in *Huckleberry Finn* a good topic would be the use of satire; a section of the book would be selected that included several instances of satire. After everyone finishes reading the material, students from different teams who have the same topic meet in an "expert group" to discuss their topic for a period of about 30 minutes. The original teams then get together and members teach their teammates about the topic on which they are "experts." A sample expert sheet on the topic "Early American Explorers" is illustrated in Table 13.1.

When teams are confident that they are prepared, quizzes are given that cover all the topics. Individual quiz scores are added together and become team scores. Individual improvement scores may also be given to encourage students to help one another make improvements in their learning. In addition, students on high-scoring teams may receive certificates or be recognized in some other way for their achievements.

Sometimes it is wise to include outlines to help guide group discussion. These outlines include the points students should definitely consider in discussing their topics. A sample discussion outline is illustrated in Table 13.2.

Initial Jigsaw II teams consist of four or five members and should be heterogeneous. Expert groups may be formed randomly, but they may be structured to include high, average, and low achievers. If the number of students in the class exceeds twenty-four, you may want to have two expert groups for each topic. Expert groups should have no more than six members. Discussion leaders should be appointed for each group. All students should eventually have an opportunity to be the discussion leader (Slavin, 1986).

TABLE 13.1
A sample expert sheet.

Early American Explorers

Read pages 45–91 in the materials packet.

Topics:

1. How were the early explorers instrumental in determining what trails would be used in early pioneer migrations?

2. What was the role of early explorers in settlement of specific areas of the American West?

3. Which early American explorers had the greatest impact on the western migration in America? Explain why.

TABLE 13.2
A sample discussion outline.

Topic: What was the role of the mountain men in the settlement of the American West?

Discussion Outline

1. Characteristics of the mountain men.
2. The life lived by the mountain men.
3. The mountain men's relations with the Indians.
4. Areas mountain men explored.
5. Influence of mountain men in the settlement of the West.

ORIGINAL JIGSAW

Original Jigsaw resembles Jigsaw II in most respects, but there are some important differences. In Jigsaw II, each student looks at all of the reading material. "Experts" are appointed to study the material in more detail and then teach team members. In Original Jigsaw, however, each student reads a different section of the material than other team members. This division has the advantage of making each team member the possessor of unique information. The value of each team member's contribution is thus increased. The only access other team members have to the information is from that person. Another advantage of Original Jigsaw is that less time is required because the readings are shorter; only part of the total unit is studied by each team member. More time, however, may be required in the teaching phase because team members will be completely unfamiliar with the rest of the material (Aronson, Blaney, Stephan, Sikes, & Snapp, 1978).

One of the difficulties with Original Jigsaw is that each individual section of the material must be written so that it is comprehensible by itself. Existing materials, however, are rarely written this way. Most written materials require other related sections or chapters to be read in sequence. In some instances, supplementary materials can be added to textbooks to make them suitable for Original Jigsaw.

Original Jigsaw makes less use of quizzes than Jigsaw II. In addition, team scores and improvement scores are not used. Students are given individual grades based on personal achievement. The achievement of high-scoring students is not given special recognition in Original Jigsaw.

CO-OP CO-OP

Sometimes teachers, particularly those in social studies and science, may want their students to locate their own materials and then share them with the rest of the class. In such cases, Co-op Co-op may be used. In this cooperative learning approach, students are encouraged to explore their own interests in the subject. They are exposed to an initial set of lectures, readings, or other experiences designed to stimulate their curiosity, but they should not be led to specific topics to study. They need to have some initial interest in the topic and be motivated to learn more about it. This initial interest helps sustain them while they learn. The amount of time needed for this first step depends on how long it takes students to identify an area to investigate and how varied their interests are in the topic.

Once students have developed an interest in some aspect of the topic, they are ready to begin the process of team building. Students are assigned to heterogeneous teams of four or five members and then given various exercises designed to stimulate group cohesiveness.

When teams begin working successfully together, they are allowed to select a topic for investigation. Teams are encouraged to select a topic among those of interest to the whole class. They should then discuss the various possibilities among themselves and settle on the most desirable one. The teacher should monitor these discussions in case two teams decide to study the same topic. They should be encouraged either to split the topic or to select different ones. If important topics are not selected, teams can be encouraged to consider them.

As soon as the learning teams have identified their topics, they divide up the labor by having each team member select a mini-topic for detailed study. Each mini-topic should provide a unique contribution to the team effort. Some mini-topics are more involved and complex than others, requiring some students to accomplish more than their teammates. This variation is acceptable so long as each member does in fact make an important contribution to the group. The acceptability of each mini-topic can be determined by (1) allowing students to evaluate the contributions of other team members, (2) requiring all team members to base their papers or projects on their own topic, or (3) having the teacher monitor the contributions of individual team members.

Once mini-topics have been decided upon, students work individually. Teammates do their assigned work with the understanding that others on their team are depending on them to cover all important aspects of their mini-topic. The preparation of mini-topics may take different forms, depending on the nature of the unit being covered. It may involve library research, data gathering, experimentation, or the creation of tangible products by means of writing, painting, or building.

As soon as team members have completed their individual work, they present what they have learned to their team. After these individual presentations, the team members discuss what they have learned and begin to formulate a total team presentation. They must try to fit the various mini-topics together like a puzzle into a coherent whole. As they link the mini-topics, they may discover that various pieces are missing that have to be researched and added. During these deliberations, students may be assigned different roles. One student may take notes while others criticize or commend the various presentations. After problems have been identified, researched, and corrected, the group is prepared for its total team presentation.

In the total team presentation, all the mini-topics must be synthesized into a coherent whole. It is expected that this presentation will be more than a series of reports on each of the mini-topics. Students are encouraged to make presentations in some form other than lectures. They can create displays and demonstrations, act out skits, and lead class discussion to help other classmates learn the topic. If team members reach different conclusions about their topic, they may be encouraged to engage in a debate in front of the whole class as the format for their presentation. During team presentations, the teams should have control of the classroom. They are responsible for how the time, space, and resources are used. Following each presentation, it is wise to sponsor a question-and-answer session so that a fuller understanding of the topics may be obtained. Additional follow-up activities in which team members share their experiences of researching the various topics may also be helpful.

Finally, team presentations need to be evaluated. This evaluation takes place on three levels:

1. team presentations are evaluated by the whole class
2. individual contributions to teams are evaluated by teammates
3. each individual's learning is evaluated by the teacher

The form of the evaluation may vary. Some teachers prefer formal evaluations; others favor a less structured approach. Self-evaluation may be a viable option. The class should have a significant role in determining the form of the evaluation (Kagan, 1985).

STUDENT TEAMS ACHIEVEMENT DIVISIONS (STAD)

In Student Team Achievement Divisions (STAD), students are assigned to four-member teams. Teams are mixed in terms of gender and ethnicity and matched to other teams as closely as possible in terms of achievement. Teachers make lesson presentations while students faithfully record what is taught. Students then work within their teams to make sure that all team members have mastered the content of the lessons. The objective of each team is to increase the achievement level of all its members. Certificates or other awards are given to teams on the basis of team improvement. Points are given for individual improvement and added together to form a team score. It usually takes from three to five class periods to cycle through a unit of instruction, from the teacher's presentation to team practice to test.

First, teams are given a unit of work in the form of instruction by the teacher, discussions, reading, worksheets, etc. Next, team members work together to complete appropriate assignments and worksheets. They study the material together and quiz one another until they feel prepared to take the test. Each student is then tested without help from team members. Team scores are posted and awards given to the highest-scoring team. Awards may include special privileges, free time, or recognition in a newsletter or on the bulletin board. Sometimes more exotic kinds of awards may be given. Some teachers keep team totals for several instructional periods and then give a special award to the overall winner.

STAD is usually organized so that each team member may earn up to 10 points for the team. A 30-item test is commonly used to determine students' performance. On each test, students are given one team point for each point they score above their test average. For example, a student with an average of 20 who scores 25 on the test gets 5 points for the team. Students who have perfect scores get the full 10 points regardless of past performances. High-achieving students have an incentive to help their less able peers because their own achievement level can only be enhanced by the improved performance of teammates.

STAD has been successfully used with most subjects—mathematics, English, social studies, science, the arts, and others—at most levels—from the second grade to the university. It is most appropriately used with topics that have well-defined objectives with single right answers. Mathematical computations, language usage, geographical facts, and science concepts work well. Teachers do not have to prepare special materials. They can use whatever they like.

The composition of teams may be changed periodically so that class members have an opportunity to work with other students. Caution should be exercised in changing team members, however. After teams gain cohesiveness, they may feel unhappy about breaking up. In addition, competition between teams often leaves team members unable to work with students they have formerly competed against.

TEAMS-GAMES-TOURNAMENTS (TGT)

Teams-Games-Tournaments (TGT) is similar to STAD except that weekly tournaments replace tests. The success of any individual is linked to the success of the group. Students compete against individuals from other teams who are at their achievement level. Achievement levels are subject to change from week to week through a "bumping" procedure. This weekly procedure is designed to match tournament participants on the basis of their performance. Those with similar scores from the previous week find themselves competing at the same tournament table the following week. Children who achieve at consistently high levels stay at the "high" table; those who achieve at consistently low levels stay at the "low" table. In between, considerable movement is possible each week from table to table. For example, a student who scores highest at one table is moved the next week to the next higher table. Here the student may score the lowest and end up back at the original table the following week. There are usually three participants at each tournament table. The winners at each tournament table bring sixty points to their team regardless of the achievement level of the participants. Students at low achievement levels can thus have as great an impact on total team scores as students at higher levels.

As in STAD, there is no necessity for teachers to prepare special curricular materials. Instead, they give regular instruction and assignments. Students usually spend a week studying and drilling one another in preparation for the tournament. The tournament games are usually played in a format similar to that of a TV quiz show. Questions are written on cards and placed on the tournament table. Students take turns choosing cards and answering questions. At the conclusion of the tournament, all scores are added up and the winning team receives special recognition or awards.

TGT is a little more time-consuming than STAD. Some time must be spent before each tournament determining the achievement levels of team members so that they can be matched to compete with other students at their level. It is also necessary to prepare question cards each week and supervise the tournament. Despite these possible drawbacks, TGT is a positive experience for most students and can enhance students' learning. Teachers report that TGT provides more excitement in the classroom than other learning approaches. Even reluctant learners tend to get caught up in the tournaments and become interested in learning. Probably much of this success is due to the fact that they are competing with students of their own ability instead of with their more able peers. They can readily see that they have some chance of success and that their efforts to prepare for tournaments will be rewarded (Slavin, 1986).

Generally it is recommended that teams stay together for about a six-week period. During this time the team that accumulates the greatest number of points should receive an overall award or recognition. Again, teachers should be sensitive to the problems that accompany the breaking up of teams. Team competition solidifies relationships between team members, but it has a tendency to cause alienation between teams. When team members become so involved in helping one another succeed, interpersonal commitments are created that are not easy to dissolve. The very quality of mutuality sought in teams is what tends to make breaking them up difficult. The longer teams are together, the more bonding occurs. The longer competition exists between teams, the more competitive team members feel against other teams. In some instances, some students come to dislike members of opposing teams. Therefore, if teams must occasionally be reorganized, perhaps the time between reorganizations should be reduced and the fact that reorganizations will occur publicized well in advance.

Teachers may want to use TGT for only part of their instructional program, which is easy to do. A science teacher may, for example, use TGT for three days and have students spend the rest of their time in the lab. TGT can also be used in conjunction with STAD. Tests can be given and tournaments held on alternate weeks. STAD scores and TGT scores can be obtained for a particular unit of study, and then both scores can be added together to determine final team scores. This combination provides a better base from which to assess learning because, although TGT may promote enthusiasm, it does not provide as much information about students' performance as STAD does. In STAD students answer all the test questions, whereas in TGT they answer every third question.

LEARNING TOGETHER

Learning Together is similar to Co-op Co-op. Students are organized into heterogenous teams, each of which has a project or task to complete. Team members are usually assigned a role based on their interests and ability. For example, one team member may act as recorder while others write, research, or create artwork. The teacher should concentrate on helping students perform tasks at which they will be successful and yet encourage students to do things that initially may be uncomfortable for them. In this cooperative learning approach, there is no competition between teams. Each team can attain as high a level as they are able and willing to reach. The object is for teams to help one another do their best. When the project or task is completed, it is graded and all members of the team receive the same grade. The ability of students to capitalize on their particular talents is one of the strengths of this type of cooperative learning strategy. Because the project or task is split into different parts, individual students can do what they are most qualified to do. Hopefully, a better project can be produced when students share their talents. A greater sense of pride is possible for all students when they take part in excellent projects.

One unique aspect of the Learning Together approach is the freedom students are given in deciding how they complete their projects or tasks. Students are allowed to decide how they will approach their topic and what they will specifically do for a final project. In choosing a topic or an approach, students may determine how they are evaluated as well. Projects could conceivably take the form of written work, dramatic presentations, videotape productions, demonstrations, experiments, contemporary applications of traditional artistic methods, or other creative activity.

One of the objections to Learning Together often raised is that grading is not equitable. When children work on nonconventional projects, it is difficult to make valid comparisons of the quality and quantity of work done by each individual. Students are commonly the first to complain that the grading is unfair, particularly when a few students do most of the work. In cooperative learning, because the success of the group depends on the commitment of all team members to do their part as well as they can, teachers usually establish conditions such that students have to take personal responsibility for their assignments. In fact, after students have been exposed to group grading for a while, they consider it more fair than competitive grading (Johnson & Johnson, 1985). Some teachers have modified group grading to take into account the efforts of students instead of depending exclusively on some measure of achievement. Other teachers have permitted students to evaluate themselves and others in their group. These efforts are no doubt responsible, in part, for the more positive attitudes of students toward grading in cooperative learning.

For a comparison of various cooperative learning approaches, see Tables 13.3 and 13.4.

TABLE 13.3
A comparison of cooperative learning approaches: Organization.

Cooperative Learning Approach	Role of Team Members	Expectations for the Team	Selection of Topics by Students	Interteam Competition
Jigsaw II	Teaching one another common materials	Emphasizing materials	No	No
Original Jigsaw	Teaching one another different materials	Getting materials	No	No
Co-op Co-op	Researching and teaching different materials	Getting materials	Yes	No
STAD	Drilling one another on teacher instruction	Practice	Yes	Yes
TGT	Drilling one another on teacher instruction	Practice	No	Yes
Learning Together	Working at different roles self-selected materials	Performance of chosen role	Yes	No

TABLE 13.4
A comparison of cooperative learning approaches: Team roles.

Cooperative Learning Approach	Materials	Amount of Material Studied by Team Members	Appropriate Subjects	Means of Evaluation
Jigsaw II	Book, chapter, story, or biography	All material	Social studies, literature, science	Quizzes
Original Jigsaw	Materials prepared by the teacher	Individual selections	Social studies, literature, science	Quizzes
Co-op Co-op	A variety from which students select	Individual selections	Most subjects	Various means
STAD	Regular classroom materials	All material	Most subjects	Quizzes and improvement scores
TGT	Regular classroom materials	Individual selections	Most subjects	Tournaments
Learning Together	A variety from which students select	Individual selections	Most subjects	Various means

Autonomy Versus Control

In school, as in many areas of life, the degree of autonomy an individual exercises is an important issue. Cooperative learning can promote self-determination in students, so it might be expected that schools would provide students more such opportunities to learn how to be responsibly autonomous. In practice, however, control by teachers increases as children go through school (Goodlad, 1984). The more control children experience, the more they rebel. The more they rebel, the more inclined teachers are to be controlling. These reactions can become a vicious circle.

In the controlling environment of school, most children learn to depend on their teachers to tell them what to learn and how to learn and also how their performance will be evaluated. Helping children who have been conditioned to dependency assume more control over what they learn and how they behave in school is difficult to accomplish. Researchers have discovered that students go through stages of adjustment as they abandon their reliance on control in favor of more self-determination. It is best to learn greater autonomy gradually (Boud, 1981).

When students are given autonomy in school, they at first feel threatened. Situations that involve novelty, uncertainty, or lack of familiarity create personal stress and leave them disoriented. Under these conditions, children are hesitant to participate. They continue to rely on external standards to guide their behavior and tend to base their responses on previous experience. Students may show apathy toward the new approach, or they may argue for a return to a system with more guidance by the teacher. During this entry stage, teachers can best support learners by creating a reliable environment with explicit norms and standards. Behavioral consequences should be clear.

As students experience more autonomy, they develop a greater sense of themselves as individuals capable of acting independently in environments at first regarded as unreliable and unsupportive. At this point, students may perceive themselves as autonomous and independent of the control of others but prefer to carry out individual activities within group settings. Learners in this stage—the reactive stage—often express dissatisfaction with group disorganization and confusion. They are often involved in conflicts and arguments with others about group functions. Teachers can support learners in the reactive stage by encouraging expressions of individual feelings and opinions and by not demanding strict adherence to standardized behavioral norms.

When learners start to feel confident about themselves as accepted members of the group and learn to accept the individuality of others, they move to the next stage—the proactive stage. Learners in the proactive stage see themselves as involved in activities that lead to mutuality, cooperation, and negotiation with others. They tend to search for an understanding of others in relation to themselves and begin to develop shared norms and values for group behavior. Learners at this stage engage in fewer individual activities and are less inclined to argue with peers. They like to participate with class-mates and enter into discussion with them. Learners in the proactive stage are best helped by teachers who accept and encourage cooperative and collaborative behavior in preference to individual performance or competition.

When students have learned to reconcile the perspectives of others with their own, they have reached the final stage—the integrative stage. At this stage, learners have a sense of balance between themselves and others and between working at group or indi-vidual tasks and maintaining interpersonal relationships with others. Learners are able to understand and integrate multiple standards of behavior, multiple interpretations of experience, and multiple sources of information. Learners at the integrative stage are best supported by teachers who encourage the development of internal standards to guide personal behavior and who openly share information about themselves and their feelings and values. These teachers are also willing to act as co-learners and to value and accept individual performance and group activities simultaneously.

Learners who have been conditioned to control by their teachers must move through these stages during the course of learning activities in which they experience greater autonomy. This progression can be facilitated by teachers who initially provide some structure and direction but eventually encourage independence and finally inter-dependence in group learning (Boud, 1981).

Group Learning and Group Dynamics

Managing group learning is ordinarily much more complex than directing a class as a whole or as individuals. During lectures or discussions involving the whole class, teachers can more readily monitor the behavior of students, and they usually direct the entire class toward a single goal. When the focus is on individual instruction, students are ordinarily confined to their seats for the purpose of writing or solving problems of one kind or another. In group learning, however, students may be working on quite different projects simultaneously and moving around the room to accomplish these tasks. Given the social needs of children and the fact that individuals behave differently in groups than they do alone, this mix of activities creates a potential for discipline problems. Group learning activities can hold many surprises, and teachers usually need to have special skills to regulate them properly.

Glasser (1984) indicates that the purpose of most human behavior is to satisfy needs for love and acceptance, control, freedom, and fun. Students participating in whole-class activities are commonly required to restrain their need-satisfying behavior and comply with the teacher's expectations and directions. However, their needs and the desire to satisfy them remain. The needs of many students are also unmet as they participate in individual activities such as seatwork. Teachers should remember that their students do indeed have needs and should be given an opportunity to satisfy them as they learn. However, it is critical that students' needs be satisfied in legitimate ways that do not promote misbehavior.

Opening up instruction to small-group learning provides more opportunities for students to legitimately satisfy their basic needs in school. To be successful, these learning experiences must be carefully organized and the cooperation of students must be obtained. Group leaders have to be identified and their efforts directed toward group cohesiveness instead of divisiveness. If group leaders involve one another or the teacher in power struggles, discipline problems will proliferate and learning will be inhibited. Teachers should not engage students in struggles for control. Some teachers are inclined to undermine students who attempt to seize power or discredit them. It is far better to promote the role of these students as leaders and give them the means to exercise their leadership in positive ways.

The role of the teacher as a member of the classroom group can be either positive or negative as well. There are several roles, however, that teachers must avoid. One of these roles is that of detective. Teachers who try to catch students misbehaving will find themselves spending a disproportionate amount of their time at this task, and policing student misbehavior often has the predicted result of stimulating more misbehavior. Teachers should also avoid the role of judge. This role sets teachers apart from the group and makes them an adversary, which nullifies their effectiveness in the group. The powerless victim is another role teachers should avoid. Students will neither respect nor accept the leadership of teachers who fail to take their responsibility as teachers seriously.

Teachers need to ensure that their role does not interfere with the leadership roles they are trying to encourage in students. Teachers do not necessarily have to direct and control everything that takes place in the classroom. It is far better for them to play the role of mentor and confidant. Teachers need to teach leadership and problem-solving skills to their students and then give them enough latitude to develop these skills in practical classroom situations. (See the discussion of thinking skills in Chapter 1.) Students are more likely to become involved in classroom activities when they are given an opportunity to satisfy their needs for freedom and control under the expert tutelage of their teachers.

When the effectiveness of the instructional program depends on the ability of students to help make decisions about what is learned, it is absolutely critical that they be equipped to make these decisions validly. An educational program is required that provides students opportunities for learning higher-level problem-solving skills. A necessary ingredient in learning problem-solving skills is freedom. As Blackham and Silberman (1975) affirm,

> there is little question about the desirability of extending autonomy and freedom of choice to everyone; the problem is determining when and how much. The ability to act independently and make wise and appropriate choices is learned just like any other facet of behavior. . . . A child needs not only experience, but the right kind of experience. And he needs a wise guide who can steer him clear of danger and who encourages, prompts, and reinforces behavior that is adaptive and successful. (pp. 4–5)

▼

SUMMARY

Few students feel sufficiently successful in competitive classrooms. All students would like to get As, but As seem to be reserved for just a successful few. Often patterns of success or failure are established early in life before various skills have had a chance to mature. In some cases, children enter school already able to do some of the things school is designed to teach. Some children, for example, already know how to read and are immediately singled out by teachers and reinforced. The early ability to achieve what teachers are looking for is a good guarantee of continued success. The sooner children show promise, the more likely they will be to garner a disproportionate amount of recognition by the teacher. As these children go through school, the achievement gap between them and their "less able peers" gradually widens.

Cooperative learning provides hope for altering this unhappy situation. It provides a way for students to assert themselves without the discomfort of always being compared with their peers and found lacking. Properly organized cooperative learning can help all children experience success and feel more accepted in school. Classrooms thus become more exciting places to learn because students have greater control over what they learn and because the atmosphere in which learning takes place is more fun. In cooperative learning programs, teachers can capitalize on the motivation students already have for learning by involving them in decisions about what they learn and then allowing them to pursue their own interests in their own style.

Students will also establish better relationships with their peers and learn how to get along more successfully with them. When children report what they consider to be their most significant school experiences, they rarely tell of something they have done alone. More often they report experiences involving others, such as winning a basketball game or participating in a school play. Almost never do they report receiving an A or completing a difficult assignment for a class as their "moment of glory" (Slavin, 1986). Succeeding in group activities is far more exhilarating than solitary success. It is apparently more satisfying to succeed when it involves helping others become success-ful as well. Unfortunately, most cooperative experiences in school are confined to phys-ical education classes and extracurricular activities. Rarely do students have these experiences in academics.

Cooperative learning holds the promise of making school more satisfying and excit-ing and at the same time improving the achievement levels of all students. It precludes the causes of discipline problems associated with the competitive classroom, so many classroom disruptions may never materialize. In addition, when group support is elicit-ed, many potential problems can be prevented and those problems that do arise can be solved much more easily. Cooperative learning is likely to be more fulfilling than regu-lar competitive learning because cooperative learning can better provide the diversity and self-determination necessary to satisfy students' varied needs (Savage, 1991).

CENTRAL IDEAS

1. When educational practice is consistent with educational theory,
    a. students will be better able to interpret expectations,
    b. the instructional program will be improved, and
    c. teachers will increase their commitment.
2. Competitive learning limits students' success and promotes poor self-con-cept.
3. In Jigsaw II, students work in heterogeneous groups to learn materials writ-ten in narrative form. Original teams send team members to expert groups to learn specific topics, which they then teach to original team members. Individual scores on tests become team scores.
4. In Original Jigsaw, not all team members read all the material; instead, ex-perts are appointed to study various sections of the material and teach it to team members. These experts are the only source for learning the material.
5. In Co-op Co-op, students are allowed to select their own topics within established guidelines. Each member of the team decides which part of the topic to study. Team members teach one another and then together prepare a presentation for the whole class. Presentations are evaluated by team members as well as the instructor.
6. In Student Teams Achievement Divisions (STAD), the class is divided into heterogeneous teams. The instructor presents lessons, and team members study the lesson content together. Scoring is based on how much team members improve their performance on tests.
7. Teams-Games-Tournaments (TGT) is similar to STAD except that in TGT team members compete against members of other teams who are at their achievement level. Tournament games are played in a format similar to that of a TV quiz show.
8. Learning Together is similar to Co-op Co-op. Students' roles on the team depend on their interests and abilities. All team members receive a collec-tive grade on their work.

9. Students go through several stages of development as they gain autonomy in the classroom, moving from dependence on the teacher to independence to interdependence. The role of the teacher changes according to the stage of the student.

10. Teachers can capitalize on the inherent interests of students by allowing them to choose what they learn. If teachers alone determine the curriculum, they have to motivate students to learn what they otherwise would not or what they may initially refuse to learn.

QUESTIONS AND ACTIVITIES

QUESTIONS TO CONSIDER

1. What kinds of curricula are most appropriately used with the different cooperative learning approaches?
2. How are different cooperative learning approaches similar or different in terms of
   a. the types of materials used?
   b. the amount of freedom exercised by students?
3. What is the function of self-determination in classroom learning?

CLASSROOM ACTIVITIES

Divide the class into teams. Using Co-op Co-op, have each team study a different cooperative learning approach.

STUDENT APPLICATIONS

Organize a series of lessons that can be taught with different cooperative learning approaches.

REFERENCES

Aronson, E., Blaney, E., Stephan, C., Sikes, J., & Snapp, M. (1978). *The jigsaw classroom.* Beverly Hills, CA: Sage Publications.

Blackham, G., & Silberman, A. (1975). *Modification of child and adolescent behavior.* Belmont, CA: Wadsworth.

Boud, D. (1981). Toward student responsibility for learning. In D. Boud (Ed.), *Developing student autonomy in learning* (pp. 21–37). London: Kogan Page.

Cronback, L. (1965). *Educational psychology*. New York: Harcourt, Brace and World.

Cross, K. P. (1985). The rising tide of school reform. *Phi Delta Kappan, 66,* 167–173.

Cunningham, R. T. (1987). What kind of question is that? In W. W. Wilen (Ed.), *Questions, questioning techniques, and effective teaching* (pp. 67–94). Washington, DC: National Education Association.

Doyle, W. (1986). Classroom organization and management. In M. C. Wittrock (Ed.), *Handbook of research on teaching* (3rd ed., pp. 392–431). New York: Macmillan.

Glasser, W. (1984). *Control theory: A new explanation of how we control our lives*. New York: Harper and Row.

Glasser, W. (1990). *The quality school*. New York: Harper and Row.

Goodlad, J. I. (1984). *A place called school*. New York: McGraw-Hill.

Jackson, P. (1968). *Life in classrooms*. New York: Holt, Rinehart and Winston.

Johnson, D., & Johnson, R. (1985). The internal dynamics of cooperative learning groups. In R. Slavin, S. Sharan, C. Webb, & R. Schmuck (Eds.), *Learning to cooperate, cooperating to learn* (pp. 103–124). New York: Plenum.

Kagan, S. (1985). *Cooperative learning resources for teachers*. Riverside: University of California, Department of Psychology.

Savage, T. V. (1991). *Discipline for self-control*. Englewood Cliffs, NJ: Prentice-Hall.

Slavin, R. (1986). *Using student team learning* (3rd ed.). Baltimore: Johns Hopkins Team Learning Project, Center for Research on Elementary and Middle Schools.

14

Classroom Management and Teacher-Student Relationships

OBJECTIVES

This chapter is designed to help you

1. improve your relationships with students and thereby improve classroom discipline
2. understand how students' self-concept problems are promoted in the school
3. explain what teachers can do to keep their students from developing poor self-concepts
4. affirm diversity in culture and language and provide instruction for minority students that increases the chances of success in school for them and for all students
5. understand the nature of gender bias and how to eliminate this problem from school learning materials as well as from teaching practices

Introduction

▼ Cheryl took her seat next to the window and immediately began talking with Lois about the previous night's basketball game. Cheryl was a drummer in the marching band, and Lois was in the color guard. Their conversation centered on half-time activities. Cheryl wanted to know whether Lois had seen Blair at the game, but before Lois could answer, Ms. Cherrington called the class to order. Cheryl muttered to Lois under her breath, "I don't feel like being in class today." Lois nodded in agreement as she crossed her arms on her desk and laid her head on them.

As Ms. Cherrington began the lecture, Cheryl found her mind wandering back to Genene's performance at the game. Genene was one of Ms. Cherrington's "pets." Cheryl laughed quietly and then muttered to herself, "Genene, you can never remember anything. Why can't you, for once, get through a routine without messing up?" She laughed again, loudly enough this time to be heard by those around her, and they turned to see what was so funny. Ms. Cherrington tapped her desk with her pencil to direct the attention of the class to the front of the room. "Who can remember the definition of a simile?" she asked, ignoring the disruption. The students turned back around in their seats as Ms. Cherrington went on with the lesson. Cheryl was still unable to concentrate, however, and her mind soon wandered again. This time she began beating her pencil on her desk as though she were playing an imaginary snare drum. Ms. Cherrington continued to talk as she walked down the aisle past Cheryl's desk. As she went by, she calmly took Cheryl's pencil from her hand and laid it quietly on the desk. She then continued on to the back of the room. "I'm going to ask a very important question about similes," she said, "and I want Allen, Ruth, David, Cheryl, Blaine, and Claron to be prepared to answer it." She paused a moment. "What effect do similes have when you use them in stories?" She paused again and then asked, "Blaine, can you tell us?" Blaine just shook his head. "Cheryl, do you have an answer?"

"I guess they help add life to the story," responded Cheryl.

"Yes, you're right, similes often do add life to stories," said Ms. Cherrington. "Can you think of an example of a simile from the story we read yesterday in class and explain what its effect was?"

Ms. Cherrington was obviously trying to get Cheryl involved in the lesson without causing her any embarrassment. When her classmates turned to look at her, Ms. Cherrington skillfully redirected their attention. Obviously sensing that Cheryl was having trouble concentrating, she tried to bring her back to the matter at hand without putting her on the spot. Teachers like Ms. Cherrington are greatly appreciated by students not only because they avoid embarrassing their students but also because they seem genuinely to care about them.

Successful teachers have good relationships with their students. Good relationships not only lay the groundwork for students' learning, but they are also the keystone of good discipline. Many discipline problems are prevented because teachers have good relationships with their students and teach interesting and relevant lessons. Positive teacher-student relationships have been shown to produce more positive responses by students in school (Aspy & Roebuck, 1977) as well as higher academic achievement (Brophy & Evertson, 1976). High-achieving students are much more likely than low-achieving students to believe that their teachers approve of them (Morrison & McIntyre, 1969).

Improving Student-Teacher Relationships

Some teachers do not realize that learning and discipline can be appreciably improved by creating better teacher-student relationships; many of them therefore do not actively work on improving relationships with their students. Some teachers are afraid to encourage friendships with students, fearing loss of control in their classrooms. However, being friendly with students actually promotes more positive behavior on their part.

ASSESSING ATTITUDES

One of the first things teachers might do to improve relationships with students is to make an assessment of their own attitudes and behaviors toward students. They should ask themselves questions such as:

- Am I courteous toward students?
- Do I listen carefully to students' questions and requests?
- Do I listen to students and respect their opinions?
- Do I control my temper when students behave improperly?
- Do I like to be with students?
- Do I treat students fairly?

It is also helpful to discover the attitudes of students toward teachers and the subjects they teach. Teachers should ask students such questions as:

- How relevant are the topics covered in this class?
- What topics do you like the most?
- What topics do you like the least?
- Do you believe that the teacher likes you?
- Does the teacher take the time necessary to help you understand difficult concepts?
- Does the teacher treat you courteously?
- Does the teacher have any distracting habits?
- Does the teacher listen to suggestions made by students?
- Do students' needs and interests receive the teacher's attention?

IMPROVING COMMUNICATION SKILLS

Teachers' communication skills are a critical factor in creating and maintaining good student-teacher relationships. Good communication usually helps establish a warmer and more friendly atmosphere in the classroom. Communication involves sending as well as receiving messages.

Sending Messages.   We all send messages both verbally and nonverbally, but we are generally less aware of the nonverbal than of the verbal messages. However, our nonverbal messages are often very powerful and may even distort the accompanying verbal meaning. Children often become adept at reading the nonverbal messages of their teachers. Children often discover through experience that nonverbal cues are more dependable than verbal information. For example, a teacher who claims to care for students may have a tone of voice or mannerisms that contradict the verbal message. Voice inflections can convey the message that teachers consider students to be dumb or smart, manageable or rebellious, cooperative or antagonistic (Jones & Jones, 1986). Teachers need to make their nonverbal messages congruent with their verbal ones.

Teachers can improve relationships with their students by not making coercive demands and by letting students feel that the classroom belongs to them as well as to the teacher. Teachers often insist that students comply with their demands unquestioningly. Students are told where they may sit, what they should learn, when they must submit papers and other work, when they can go to the bathroom, and so on. Some of these demands may be helpful, but others are made exclusively for the convenience of teachers. Sometimes demands are made simply to control. Consequently, students are made to feel that the classroom belongs to the teacher. Teacher-student relationships can be improved if teachers help students realize that they share the classroom and can help determine procedures that are necessary for successful learning there.

Teachers need to speak courteously to their students. Commonly used expressions such as *thank you, please,* and *excuse me* are absolutely essential. Courteous teachers not only enhance relationships with students, but they also serve as important role models. Many children speak rudely and even abusively to one another and to adults. They need to realize that such mistreatment interferes with the relationships they wish to establish.

Teachers should be genuinely concerned for their students. They need to find out about the activities of their students outside of class and show an interest in what they are doing. In some cases, teachers will find common hobbies and activities that can establish closer relationships with some students.

Receiving Messages.   Effective communication also involves receiving messages. Teachers can communicate genuine interest simply by paying attention to their students, maintaining eye contact and listening carefully to what they say. Listening skills are extremely important to teachers because they help students feel significant, accepted, and respected. Teachers who listen effectively can help students clarify their feelings and resolve personal conflicts. Unfortunately, some teachers listen halfheartedly to their students and provide superficial answers to students' questions, particularly questions that involve emotions. Rather than try to understand the emotions being expressed, many teachers try to sidestep the situation, often by suggesting that students have little reason to be emotional. Teachers thus avoid having to deal with the discomfort they feel when faced with students' emotions (Ginott, 1971).

As teachers listen to their students, they should give their undivided attention and in an empathetic and nonjudgmental manner seek to understand what is said. With such teachers, students learn (1) that their feelings are acceptable, (2) that their feelings can be expressed openly, and (3) that they can clarify and come to understand feelings that are at first confusing and frightening (Jones & Jones, 1986). This assurance reduces the tension and anxiety associated with emotions and also increases the chances that their expression will be productive. When feelings are not dealt with openly, they often are expressed in the form of anger, vandalism, or truancy.

Self-Concept and Discipline

The relationships teachers establish with their students have an influence on the development of students' self-concept, which in turn affects discipline in the classroom. Students with a poor self-concept not only fail to perform well in school, but they are also more likely to display unacceptable behavior (Purkey, 1970). Teachers often claim that students who do not perform well are simply unmotivated, that some students just do not want to learn anything. However, students are in fact never unmotivated (Covington & Beery, 1976). They may not be motivated to do what teachers want, but it can never truly be said that they are unmotivated. When students are required to learn what they have no interest in learning, they often do not apply themselves and fail as a result.

In school, one's success or failure depends on achievement, which in turn depends on one's level of performance. This preoccupation with performance begins surprisingly early in children's school careers. Schools are particularly adept at teaching children, at a very young age, that achievement determines their relative position among their peers. Before children have spent much time in kindergarten, they already are aware of the place they occupy. They can tell you the brightest and dullest of their classmates with comparative ease and often point out this fact with relish (Weiner & Peter, 1973). In the beginning school years, academic performance is influenced primarily by learning readiness. Children whose parents emphasize reading and other school-related tasks enter school far better prepared to succeed than those whose early experiences fail to promote these skills. As children move through the school system, differences in their performance become more pronounced and visible. These differences are emphasized by the grades they receive. Special privileges are reserved for children who are academically talented. This emphasis on schoolwork tends to reinforce the self-concept of students: Children who experience initial success will continue to do so, and children who are unsuccessful at first will continue to follow a pattern of failure.

Parents too usually place considerable importance on school success, so children are often under pressure from both the school and their parents to be high achievers. If children are low achievers, their self-worth is threatened. They fear that if they fail in school, they will not be worthy of love and approval. This fear is not unfounded. In our society, human worth tends to be equated with achievement. In practice, people are considered to be only as good as their socially-valued achievements (Covington & Beery, 1976). The feelings of inferiority that accompany failure can cause lifelong problems.

Schools, however, allow the possibility of success for only a fraction of the student population. These are the students who get the As and Bs. To some degree, most other students feel a sense of failure (Levine, 1988). The possibility of failure is a constant threat to these students. When they do fail, they may attribute their failure to an innate lack of ability.

The threat of failure and its attendant lack of self-worth is difficult for children to accept. In their anguish and frustration, they often resort to defense mechanisms. Children employ at least two strategies for maintaining a sense of self-worth when they believe that their chances of academic success are low: avoidance and overstriving.

AVOIDANCE

Sometimes children decide that if they cannot be sure of succeeding, they can at least protect their dignity by orchestrating their own failure. They accept the premise that they are prone to fail, but they attempt to reject the implication that their failure stems from inability. To avoid this implication, children may arrange circumstances so that their failure can be blamed on something other than a lack of ability. They rationalize that their failure is not an indication of their potential and therefore is not a real measure of their worth. These children become expert at keeping their actual ability a secret (Covington & Beery, 1976). They hide their competence by not performing and not participating. Such students are sometimes referred to as underachievers. They make a virtue out of failure to do work that, they claim, is unimportant.

In addition to nonparticipation, failure-avoiding children use other techniques to protect themselves from feelings of unworthiness. They come late to class, claim not to have heard what the assignment was, feign illness, pretend to be busy, and daydream. Because there are usually strong sanctions for not trying, these children often combine nonparticipation with false effort (Birney, Burdick, & Teevan, 1969). If children appear to be making an effort, we usually forgive their lack of productivity because as a culture we value "trying." To convince teachers that they are really doing their best, these children feign attention during class discussions, giving the outward appearance of thinking or adopting quizzical expressions. These efforts are deceptive because the students are not really trying to succeed, only trying to avoid failure. This deception involves a balancing act for students. They must calculate correctly in order to escape punishment and at the same time avoid putting forth too much effort. They do not believe that they could succeed if they really tried. If they should study hard and still do poorly, they could no longer blame failure on lack of participation. Instead, their ability could be called into question. They therefore try to protect themselves from discovery. When children count their success only in terms of avoiding failure, their learning is impeded. When learning is limited by lack of involvement and deception, the result is detachment, apathy, and passivity. These children become disenchanted with school and often spend their time being disruptive.

In trying to avoid failure, some children attempt to maintain a sense of personal worth by establishing impossibly high goals for themselves. Teachers are often inclined to hold high expectations for their classes, so they unwittingly collude with these students by supporting their impossible goals, virtually ensuring that they will fail. The children can then claim that their failure to achieve such high goals reveals very little about their ability. If the standards are sufficiently high, their failure seems comparatively small. If only the most able students can reach such goals, then these children cannot be blamed for their failure to achieve them (Covington & Beery, 1976).

Setting goals too low is another technique of failure-avoiding children. They like to achieve easily attainable goals for the same reason that they pretend to work for unreachable goals—neither failing at a difficult task nor succeeding at an easy one reveals much about their real ability. Both approaches help children avoid having to demonstrate what they really can do. These children know that the level of success they are striving for is not real. However, it is a level at which they feel they can at least appear to be successful. They commonly announce their low expectations publicly. In doing so, they have the added advantage of appearing modest (Birney, Burdick, & Teevan, 1969). No one can accuse them of bragging.

Such children know that they can achieve at a higher level. They consequently do not find satisfaction in their performance. Their self-respect is an illusion. However, they prefer this illusion to the possibility of disclosing their presumed lack of ability by doing their best and failing.

OVERSTRIVING

Overstriving is another tactic used by children to maintain their self-respect (Martire, 1956). These children try to escape failure through hard work. Instead of working for success, however, they are working against failure. Like underachieving children, overstriving children have the devastating belief that the sole measure of self-worth is school achievement. And like underachievers, they constantly try to fulfill the role they have created for themselves. They too may be plagued by the ultrahigh standards they set. The interesting thing about overstrivers is that they get high grades. They appear successful. However, their success is a burden. With each new achievement comes the need for increased performance to reach the next level of accomplishment. Therefore, achievement becomes successively more elusive, requiring an ever-increasing level of effort. Sometimes these children learn to fear success as much as they do failure because it signals yet another escalation of self-imposed demands. Still, they continue to strive until little additional improvement is possible. Often the pressure these children experience is intensified by teachers who encourage them to keep striving. They are told that they can be even more successful by trying harder. Teachers have no reason to doubt the value of this admonition. They have verified it repeatedly in the past. When the pressure mounts, however, these children come to loathe failure. They never view failure as simply part of the learning process, a stepping stone to ultimate success. Instead, they interpret it as evidence of their worthlessness. School, therefore, becomes a place of conflict for the overstriver. On the one hand, there is cause for optimism because of past successes. On the other hand is the ever-present specter of failure created by the escalation of demands.

Helping Children Improve Self-Concept

Improving children's self-esteem is not an easy task. A poor self-concept is resistant to change. Once children establish a poor concept of themselves, they tend to retain this negative perspective. Sometimes these negative views are unintentionally strengthened by actions taken to help children overcome self-concept problems. For example, it is commonly believed that students' negative self-concepts can be overcome if the children are given the opportunity to experience success. It seems logical that if the original difficulty is the lack of success, then providing success experiences should rectify the problem. Teachers assume that once children get a taste of success, they will continue to seek it.

However, failure-avoiding students are largely unresponsive to success. Indeed, they appear almost calculating in their rejection of potential success experiences provided for them. Once they see themselves as failures, success loses its reward value. Success is not expected, so when it does occur, they believe it to be a consequence of luck or fate instead of effort. What many teachers fail to realize is that success-oriented children attribute success to ability and failure to lack of proper effort, whereas failure-prone children attribute their failure to lack of ability and whatever success they may occasionally achieve to the momentary generosity of teachers and others, lucky guessing, or unusually easy tasks (Weiner & Kukal, 1970). But in reality, although they may try to hide it, these children are aware that their lack of success can be attributed to themselves. Teachers who try to entice such children to try harder to succeed fail to realize that they cannot afford to believe that success comes from their efforts or abilities. To accept such a thought would undermine their sense of well-being. If they continue to believe that their success occurs because of luck, then their lack of success does not have to be attributed to inability.

Failure-prone students believe that if they experience success, teachers and parents will expect them to continue being successful. However, children with low self-esteem feel unable to meet such an expectation, particularly when they believe that their success has been achieved through luck anyway. These children want to be successful, but they fear that if they evidence limited success, they will be obliged to repeat it on demand. Feeling unable to do so, they frequently act counterproductively to keep success from happening. They sabotage their own work when they find themselves in danger of succeeding (Aronson & Carlsmith, 1962).

What can be done about this problem? The most obvious and necessary measure to take is to adjust the present competitive system in school. The disabling effects of competition are certain. Because of it many students experience poor academic performance and consequently suffer low self-esteem. The long-term effects are enormous. When children are evaluated exclusively by their teachers, they usually conclude that teachers are the only source of valid assessment. Because the evaluations of various teachers are rarely equivalent, students may learn that their grades depend more on luck than effort. One solution to this problem is to allow students to do more self-assessment. When children learn to evaluate their own performance, they no longer have to depend solely on an outside source of affirmation, and they develop a more realistic and honest image of themselves. Self-assessment can also provide more consistency in grading and thus reduce the variability inherent in the evaluations given by different teachers.

Students who believe that their efforts influence their performance are said to have an internal locus of control. Individuals who believe that what happens to them is a matter of luck or fate have an external locus of control. People with an internal locus of control are more likely to accept responsibility for what they do. Those with an external locus of control are more likely to display helplessness, avoiding blame by giving excuses and lying. They are also much more likely to misbehave and to make excuses for their bad behavior. To help children become more internally controlled, teachers need to show them (1) how consequences relate to their actions, (2) how outcomes can be predicted based on personal actions, and (3) how choosing and planning can result in desired outcomes (Curwin & Mendler, 1988).

Overstriving students must learn to focus on success rather than on fear of failure. The first step is for teachers to stop insisting that overstriving students can and ought to improve themselves by trying harder. These children also need to realize that failure is not a permanent condition. They must understand that incorrect responses can be changed and improvements made without leaving an indelible mark. Mistakes should be viewed as stepping stones to future learning rather than immutable consequences.

Cultural Diversity and Interpersonal Relationships

Cultural differences—such as socioeconomic status, ethnicity, gender, language, exceptionality, or religion—have the potential for creating enormous discipline problems for teachers. In modern society it is increasingly typical to have children from different cultural backgrounds in the same classroom. To effectively work with such diverse student populations, teachers must learn about a variety of cultures and the special problems children from each of these cultures face in everyday life, especially in school. Teachers must take into account differences in cultural norms and learning styles along with specific language problems. The burden placed on teachers can be daunting.

Over the years, government and school officials have sought to assimilate minorities into the dominant American culture. The American commitment to equal opportunity for all has been the primary force behind these efforts. Various laws have been passed in an effort to achieve these ends:

- Title VII of the Civil Rights Bill, which prohibits discrimination based on race, color, national origin, or gender
- Title IX of the 1972 Education Amendments, which prohibits denial of full participation in all educational programs and activities on the basis of gender
- Public Law 94–142, the Individuals with Disabilities Education Act, which mandates educating children with disabilities to the maximum extent possible in the least restrictive environment

Unfortunately, despite these efforts, only limited assimilation has been achieved.

There are different theories about how assimilation takes place. One of these, the Anglo-conformity theory, holds that an individual's ancestral culture is renounced in favor of the behavior and values of the Anglo-Saxon core group. This theory is the one that has been commonly accepted and upon which most school practices are based. A second theory, the "melting pot" theory, contends that disparate cultures from all over the world could be assembled in "America's divinely inspired crucible" and somehow merged into a single, unique American culture to which all cultural groups would contribute. This admixture has never occurred. Instead, the specific cultural contributions of the various groups have been limited by the dominant culture (Gordon, 1964).

In reality, neither the melting pot theory nor the Anglo-conformity theory successfully accounts for what has taken place in America. Cultural pluralism provides a better explanation: Enough subsocietal separation has been maintained to guarantee the continuance of various ethnic cultural traditions and the existence of various subgroups without interfering with the operation of general American civic life. When minorities are not assimilated into the dominant American culture, they tend to maintain their own ethnic communities and participate peripherally in the larger cultural life in which they have been denied full membership.

AFRICAN-AMERICAN STUDENTS

The culturally-related behaviors learned by minority children and brought with them to school can create significant problems for their teachers as representatives of the dominant Anglo culture. For example, African-American children have learned that looking directly at the person who is disciplining them is considered a sign of disrespect. Many teachers, however, may insist that a child look directly at them when they are talking. Such conflicting expectations create great difficulty for the child.

Even more significant problems can occur for the teacher who is unaware of such street-corner games as "ribbing," "jiving," and "playing the dozens." These games have been part of Black culture for many years and provide a way for youngsters to test their parents or teachers and to gain status among their peers. Disadvantaged youngsters in particular participate in these games as a means of developing survival skills and achieving a mental toughness that makes them in some ways more capable than their more affluent counterparts. They become skillful in dealing with such diverse individuals as building superintendents, pimps, corner grocers, bill collectors, juvenile authorities, social workers, and school personnel.

Ribbing.   Ribbing is a verbal game of taunting, denigrating, or making fun of someone. Clothing or body parts, particularly the genitals of the male, or matters related to sex are usually the focus of the taunting; at other times, attention is turned to the social status of the person or the person's relatives. For example, a teacher broke up a fight between two students and then asked what had happened.

One of them said in a whiny voice, "Doran say I be clean 'cause it Mother's Day."

The teacher looked puzzled. "So what? Is that any reason to start a fight?"

Later on, one of the class members explained that "Mother's Day" is the day the welfare check comes. The purpose of this rib was to imply that the other student's family received public assistance and that the student was dressed well only because the mother's check had arrived.

Sneakers have been a big target for ribbing because they are a high-prestige clothing item. A student must wear the "correct" sneakers or suffer the ribbing of other children. One student may say to another, "I see you got your brogans on." This apparently innocent remark is designed to denigrate the wearer because the sneakers are old, worn out, less expensive, or a less popular brand (Foster, 1986).

Jiving.   Jiving consists of a number of verbal coping and survival techniques created by urban African-American males to manipulate, persuade, or hustle others. Jiving is also used as a verbal and physical technique to avoid difficulty, to accommodate some authority figure, or, in the extreme, to save oneself or someone else from being injured physically or psychologically. These manipulative jiving games usually are successful because of the preconceptions and expectations different ethnic groups have of one another. White people, for example, often stereotype African-Americans as either hedonistic, aggressive individuals or as shuffling children requiring help. African-American youngsters know of these preconceptions and fulfill them as a means of manipulation. An authority figure may be placated with gestures, facial expressions, style of pronunciation, and body postures that the individual believes will be deemed sufficiently subservient (Foster, 1986). An example of jiving is given by Cleaver (1968):

> Then one day we were out driving and I ran through a red light just a little too late and this motorcycle cop pulled me over.

"Say, Boy," he said to me, "are you color-blind?" I didn't want a ticket so I decided to talk him out of it. I went into my act, gave him a big smile and explained to him that I was awfully sorry, that I thought that I could make it but that my old car was too slow. He talked real bad to me, took me on a long trip about how important it was that I obeyed the laws and regulations and how else can a society be controlled and administered without obedience to the law. I said a bunch of Yes Sir's and he told me to run along and be a good boy. (p. 168)

One form of jiving is called woofing. How teachers react to woofing may determine how long they remain in the classroom. Woofing can take such forms as

- blocking a teacher in the hall
- positioning oneself in front of a teacher
- yelling and making menacing movements while arguing about a grade
- standing and staring at a teacher

For the woofing to work, the person being woofed on must become intimidated. If children can woof hard enough and long enough and are willing to back it up, few people will push them. Woofing can be terrifying for an unsuspecting teacher (Brown, 1969).

Sometimes jiving takes the form of signifying. Signifying usually begins when one child approaches another and says something inflammatory such as "Do you know what Sam said about you?" The individual doing the signifying keeps up this kind of questioning until the other person is provoked to go after Sam.

Playing the Dozens.   Playing the dozens has the reputation of initiating more fights and disruptions at school than any other activity. Playing the dozens has also been described as the most prolific source of stabbings and shootings (Foster, 1986). Often the opponent is accused of incest, homosexuality, cowardice, uncleanliness, or some form of physical or mental inferiority. Sometimes playing the dozens is used to exploit another child's weak point, such as a family member who is in jail or who has had a child out of wedlock. The form it takes with most schoolchildren, called "talkin' about moms," involves general insults about the opponent's mother.

How teachers react when youngsters play the dozens on them is crucial. They may lose the respect and confidence of the entire class if they are unable to respond properly. Usually these youngsters respect the teacher who can best them at their games without losing dignity and without coming down hard on them. Foster (1986) tells of his own experience learning how to deal with a student who was playing the dozens on him. One of his students publicly announced that he had had sex with Foster's mother the night before. Foster responded by telling him to "cut the crap" and get back to work. Other class members then began to react vociferously.

"You afraid of him?"

"Shit, hit him, man!"

"Go upside his knot."

"Why you let him say that about you moms? Shit."

Foster finally caught on and responded appropriately. He said, "Why should I be mad? He can't be talkin' about my mother, 'cause I know my mother. At least I know who my mother is." The student sulked off to his seat and got back to work. Foster reports knowing that he had succeeded in dealing with the situation when one of his students "put out his hand for some skin."

Culturally, many teachers are unprepared for the level of skill in playing these games that is achieved by many of their students. And yet if they are to work successfully with African-American children, it is essential that they know not only the games but also how to react appropriately. These games are played for their effects, for the verbal skills they develop, and for the physical and psychological protection they afford when they are brought to a successful conclusion. Teachers will generally be unable to change a practice that is so culturally ingrained. It is far better to learn how to react in a suitable way and avoid the devastating consequences of not being street wise.

HISPANIC STUDENTS

Children from the Hispanic community encounter an entirely different set of problems in the classroom than do African-American children. These problems stem primarily from language barriers and differences in family life. For example, Hispanic children have a motivation for achievement that is tied directly to the family. Whereas Anglo children achieve for themselves, Hispanic children achieve for their families (Ramirez & Price-Williams, 1976).

Language difficulties are a significant problem for Hispanic children. It is understandably hard for children who do not understand the dominant language to be successful in school. However, even after they gain some facility with the language, these children continue to suffer "voice" problems. Voice refers to the influence of the community and culture upon the understandings and thought processes of its members. Even though Hispanic children may use the English language in what appears to be its proper form, their understanding of word meanings reflects the culture they have grown up in rather than the dominant Anglo culture. For example, Puerto Rican children asked to respond to the English word *respect* most often spoke of concrete relationships with authority figures (Walsh, 1991):

> Respect is if the teacher say to you shut up, you have to respect. The same thing with your parents, the teacher, the pastor; if they say to you, you have to respect.

> When my mother talk to me, I don't talk back. . . . When she hit me, I go to my bed and I let my mouth shut as I should because if I'm smart to her, she will smack me.

The same kinds of definitions were also obtained in Puerto Rican children's responses to the Spanish word *respeto*. However, Anglo children made no such direct reference to the sense of authority and honor for their elders when they were asked to respond to the word *respect*. Instead, their responses were less subservient:

> Like you don't do anything bad to it or bother it.

> Having manners.

Several Anglo children even described the word *respect* broadly as treatment due them or attention they could count on:

Respect is when like your mother respects you and stuff, she takes care of you.

Like when you go to your aunt's house you expect her to respect you.

The Hispanic children had not adopted an Anglo-like voice when speaking English or defining English words. Their use of English appeared to be an extension of the Hispanic voice they had already established. It is generally thought that once children learn to speak English, they also think in English. It is also assumed that children learn not only to speak English words but also to grasp their significance, use, and contextual appropriateness in varying situations. However, in children for whom English is a second language, the native tongue appears to exert a continued and significant influence. The predominance of a culturally-based perspective on meaning is generally ignored by English-speaking teachers and school officials. Unfortunately, teachers who fail to understand the cultural voice in which Hispanic children speak find the responses of these children garbled, bothersome, and exasperating. When these children discover that their teachers do not understand, they develop negative reactions, not only to their teachers but also to the whole educational process and to the entire culture and language the teachers represent. Or they may decide that their parents have raised them in an inferior environment and subsequently reject their own culture (Christian, 1978).

For many Hispanic children, the school produces discord between the home and school. It places the cultural norms of the majority in opposition to the sociocultural and linguistic realities of these children. The school thus invalidates the inner voice that had previously defined the children's existence. As a result, the children internalize pieces of reality from two opposing worlds and in the process lose their sense of direction and identity. They may devalue their own cultural heritage and language and at the same time feel rejected by the dominant American culture.

The feelings of inadequacy created by these conditions are often amplified in the interactions of minority children with peers from the dominant culture. At the same time minority students are learning to disparage their own language, their culture, and their social group, majority students are also thinking negatively about them. Majority students often believe that Anglo culture and language is superior to that of minorities. Such beliefs form the basis for perpetuating inequities in school, in the workplace, and in other areas of society (Saville-Troike, 1980).

NATIVE AMERICAN STUDENTS

Native Americans also find themselves in cultural conflict when they enter the schools. Native culture differs from the predominant Anglo culture in significant ways. For example, to Native Americans, exactness of time is generally of little importance. In Anglo culture, time is of the utmost importance and punctuality is considered a virtue if not a necessity. Native Americans hold that because the future is uncertain, preparing for unknown eventualities is an inappropriate activity and an unhealthy approach to living. Non-Native Americans put money into insurance, fret over savings and investments, and do many other things that make little sense to Native Americans. Native Americans value patience. One's ability to wait is important. Anglo culture admires quick action more.

Native Americans have a great respect for older people as a fountain of experience and knowledge. In Anglo culture, on the other hand, old people are often ignored and considerable effort is expended to delay the aging process. The Lakota Sioux believe that one cannot speak from ignorance and that wisdom comes only with age, usually more than 60 years—an age at which Anglo culture starts to retire and discard its citizens. To show respect for their elders, younger people avert their eyes. It would be a sign of disrespect to look directly into the eyes of an older person. Native Americans' respect for age is also reflected in their practice of caring for old people until they die. They consequently have little or no need for nursing homes.

Native Americans tend to create and maintain more intergroup relationships. They encourage strong ties to clan members beyond one's immediate family. Many non-Native Americans, however, consider the biological family to be most important and generally limit their most important relationships to this group.

Native Americans tend to share their wealth. They have little sense of personal ownership. In contrast, wealth in the Anglo culture is a means of obtaining status and power. The value of generosity and sharing springs from the Native American belief that the earth is the mother from whom we all come. The land and the food to be found on it, therefore, belong to all. Among the Lakota there is a custom of giving away all one's possessions in order to honor someone else. Paradoxically, giving or sharing with the idea of getting honor in return destroys the essence of sharing. For this reason, when someone does something for you out of kindness, without being asked, it is very rude to thank the person, which would be tantamount to paying for the generosity.

Native Americans believe in achieving a balance with nature. Consequently, they pay attention to nature's signals and adapt themselves accordingly. The Anglo culture, however, constantly searches for new ways to control and master the elements around us and tends to indiscriminately consume the earth's resources with no thought of adverse affects. For the Lakota, getting along with nature means more than not misusing the earth. They believe that the Great Spirit is in all things and therefore all things deserve respect. Out of respect, the Lakota will tell others what they want to hear, never believing that their words are untruthful. They will also avoid telling someone what that person does not want to hear. This ethic is an obvious source of conflict when a teacher is trying to learn what actually happened in a particular situation.

Individual freedom is greatly prized among the Lakota and other Native American peoples. However, from their viewpoint, freedom means the right to make an appropriate choice. Above all else, appropriate choices are those that enable the group to survive. Even so, no one in the group has the right to force the choice of another individual. Traditional Lakota government was a true democracy, but those who did not agree with the decisions made were free to leave the group. The Lakota did not have overall leaders. Leadership depended on the situation and on the talent of the individuals involved. One person might be the best at hunting, another at making war. Even in war, no one was forced to participate. If someone wanted to get up a raiding party, only those who chose to go went along. In Anglo society, leadership is often inherited or granted rather than earned (Bennett, 1986).

The value system on which schools operate can differ significantly from that of Native American culture. Native American children experience considerable difficulty when their teachers fail to understand their culture and teach them in ways that coincide with their beliefs.

ASIAN-AMERICAN AND JEWISH-AMERICAN STUDENTS

Asian-Americans and Jewish-Americans have also experienced difficulties being assimilated into American culture. However, Asian-Americans and Jewish-Americans have experienced fewer problems than people of African or Hispanic descent because their work ethic is more similar to that of the dominant Anglo community. This ethic stands Asian- and Jewish-American children in good stead in the schools, where they often excel. Asian- and Jewish-Americans have also created an adequate economic base on which to establish themselves, usually in the form of small businesses born of economic necessity to support their own communities. Still, social and economic prejudice against both these groups in America today creates difficulties for children in school (Bennett, 1986).

Curriculum and Instruction for Minority Students

The curriculum of the public schools should include material about various minority groups. The history of these groups can be discussed, along with the contributions their members have made in the world. Textbooks, however, commonly ignore the contributions of minorities and focus almost exclusively on the accomplishments of Anglo community members. Individuals from the different minorities have indeed made significant contributions to American life in nearly all its aspects. Recognition of this fact would give minority students some sense not only of their collective American identity but also of their particular ethnic heritage. Ethnic studies should not be confined to special courses. It has been found that these courses are taken primarily by the members of the particular ethnic group studied. Instead, material currently covered in ethnic studies needs to become part of the general curriculum.

General emphasis on bilingualism is another significant way to provide a better learning environment for minority children and help the Anglo community be more accepting of cultural diversity. Although it has one of the most diverse populations in the world, the United States is one of the more parochial, even paranoid, nations as far as bilingualism is concerned. In America, the English language is considered the norm; learning other languages is thought to be unnecessary, wasteful, divisive, or unpatriotic. Bilingualism is usually associated with minority status and with an inability or an unwillingness to be assimilated. The possibility that English could fruitfully co-exist alongside other languages is considered impossible. In most other nations of the world, however, knowing a second—or even a third—language is a prerequisite for active societal involvement and for daily communication, both public and private. In such countries, bilingualism is promoted and supported by the state and its public institutions (Walsh, 1991).

It is important that teachers provide all children, particularly minority children, learning experiences that suit their learning style. Both ethnicity and socioeconomic status appear to be important factors in learning style differences. Most minority students tend to be field-sensitive learners: They prefer that teachers use more personal, conversational techniques and provide instruction in groups where social interactions are prevalent. Anglo and Asian-American children may find field-independent teaching more to their liking, a teaching style that capitalizes on students' inclination to achieve at a high level and compete among themselves.

African-American, Hispanic, and Native American children are more likely to be motivated to learn in a cooperative learning environment (Slavin, 1983). However, the orientation of most traditional classrooms in America emphasizes competition and individual achievement. These demands can be stressful for minority children faced with the necessity of competing to be successful while the expectations of their culture, which they have certainly internalized, dictate otherwise. Cooperative learning has been shown to make phenomenal improvements in relationships among members of different ethnic groups in desegregated schools. After the introduction of cooperative learning, race tends to be eliminated as a criterion for friendship among participants. In addition, students who participate in cooperative learning reach higher levels of achievement. They also engage in less off-task behavior and create fewer discipline problems (Slavin, 1986).

Role-playing is also an effective method of teaching minority children, particularly Puerto Rican students. Students are asked to pretend that they are another person or that they are involved in various situations; they are then instructed to act accordingly. Attitudes and values can be explored more dramatically and validly in this way. This approach first and foremost allows minority students to construct, assume control over, and then take ownership of the curriculum. It also helps them to become more attentive to the various voices in the classroom and to recognize differences and similarities among them. It gives them a sense of worth about themselves and their culture and language and an ability to recognize the sources of tension and pressure around them and how to diffuse or lessen them (Walsh, 1991).

Eliminating Gender Bias

Gender bias is a significant problem for children of all ethnic backgrounds, even those in the Anglo community. Gender itself is not the basic problem but rather the traditional roles associated with gender. Down through time, the roles of men and women have usually been well-defined and culturally ingrained. The assignment of roles was based in part on the physical makeup of the sexes. Men, on the whole, were better equipped for hunting. Women, who alone were able to bear children, began to tend to responsibilities closer to home. Over the centuries women came to be considered physically and intellectually inferior to men. They were generally thought incapable of performing professional and administrative work, and they were denied access to manual labor that required significant strength. In recent years, this view has begun to change. Many jobs that formerly required greater physical strength now can be performed by anyone having the skill to operate labor-saving equipment. It has also been shown that women's natural intellectual capacity is no different from that of men.

Although they are the intellectual equals of men, women in the work force still find themselves employed at lower-paying jobs with less responsibility than men. Often the differences in work opportunities and pay are a function of prejudice. Even though women make up an increasing percentage of the work force, they are still not seen as breadwinners. Sometimes the low-paying jobs taken by women are those they have selected and for which they have prepared themselves. Traditionally, the positions of elementary school teacher, nurse, and secretary are filled by women. Women are less frequently involved in higher-paying and more prestigious jobs in medicine, law, and science. Why do women select lower-paying, less prestigious jobs? There are obviously a number of factors, but one primary influence is cultural bias and its perpetuation in the schools. From the time children are very young, they are provided with gender roles and encouraged to follow them. The messages of parents and others in each child's environment have a virtually irreversible effect on the child's gender identity (Stockard & Johnson, 1980).

If women identify with the roles provided for them, they often accept lower expectations for themselves. For example, women are taught, subliminally and sometimes overtly, that they are somehow less capable than men of doing math or science. They tend to devalue their own potential and to assume that a man's career has greater importance than their own. Even when women can freely choose what to do in life, their choice is shaped by the existing social structure with all its expectations. This constraint is learned early and reinforced by most societal institutions. The outcome is that men perform the important functions in society and women are relegated to a supporting role (Weiler, 1988).

The schools generally perpetuate gender bias. In textbooks, for example, girls are seen as stereotypes—playing with dolls, giving tea parties, or working in the kitchen. They are frightened of animals and loud noises, ask the advice of others, and seek assistance in solving problems. Girls are often depicted as passive spectators, usually watching boys actively participate. In contrast, boys are shown engaged in important activities that prepare them for important careers. They save girls and mothers from danger. They solve problems and are sufficiently ingenious and creative to find the answers by themselves. Boys in textbooks are almost always shown being active—swimming, running, riding bicycles, playing ball, or unraveling mysteries (Gollnick, Sadker, & Sadker, 1982). Pictures of adults in various occupations are likewise biased. Textbook occupations for women are usually very limited. Women most often are shown in service occupations such as cafeteria worker, cashier, cleaning professional, dressmaker, librarian, nurse, teacher, or telephone operator. Occasionally there is a female physician. Men are found working in about six times as many different occupations as women (Women on Words and Images, 1975).

Interactions between teachers and students in the classroom are also biased. Boys are spoken to more frequently than girls in most science classes and are asked more higher-order questions (Becker, 1981). Boys are also praised more for the quality of their work whereas girls are praised for being neat. Teachers tend to give boys instructions on how to complete their science projects; they are more likely to show girls how to actually do the project or even to do it for them. In addition, boys receive more attention in the classroom than girls in the form of praise, criticism, remediation, and expressions of acceptance (Sadker & Sadker, 1985).

Teachers must recognize and avoid these double standards so that their female students can participate fully in the classroom and prepare for a greater variety of occupational possibilities. Textbooks need to show females in more challenging and prestigious roles. The curriculum should include contributions made by women and introduce students to the writings of both women and men. These measures and others may help to begin eliminating the gender bias so prevalent in the schools.

SUMMARY

Good discipline depends to a great extent on how successful teachers are in relating to their students. Teachers who have fostered good teacher-student relationships have fewer discipline problems. Several significant factors can promote better teacher-student relationships. The first is good communication skills. Communication involves both sending and receiving messages. Students need to receive messages that they are cared for and appreciated. They need to express their feelings to understanding teachers who take the time necessary to help them analyze their feelings.

A second factor is autonomy. Student-teacher relationships are greatly enhanced when students feel free to make important decisions and when they are taught how to make their own decisions responsibly. Students' needs can more appropriately be met when they have a significant role in deciding what they will do in school.

Good self-concept is perhaps the most important factor in developing student-teacher relationships and in promoting achievement and good discipline. The role of the teacher in encouraging the development of students' self-concept is strategic. Teachers who provide more opportunities for students to cooperate instead of compete in the classroom will foster more learning and reduce the incidence of poor self-concept and discipline problems.

Teachers must learn to interact successfully with children of different cultures. Failure to do so can significantly diminish the effectiveness of their teaching. Teachers must also avoid gender bias if they want all their students to have a full range of possibilities in their lives.

CENTRAL IDEAS

1. Improving student-teacher relationships will improve classroom discipline.
2. Good student-teacher relationships are built upon effective communication, which allows students to feel accepted and important.
3. Teachers create discipline problems by promoting poor self-concept development among their students.
4. Failure-prone students have developed elaborate schemes to get through school without exposing their true ability to public scrutiny. They arrange their own failure, which is more acceptable to them than trying their best and failing.

5. Overstriving students are driven to succeed in order to prevent the possibility of failure. Teachers unintentionally raise the specter of failure for them by continually expecting more of them.

6. Rather than provide success experiences for failure-prone students, teachers need to help them learn how to evaluate their own performances.

7. Cooperative learning may be a useful way to help overstriving students reduce their unreasonable expectations of themselves.

8. Teachers can bolster their credibility and increase positive communication with inner-city African-American students by learning the games of ribbing, jiving, and playing the dozens.

9. Teachers can help African-American and Hispanic children learn more effectively by providing cooperative learning opportunities for them and by engaging them in role-playing.

10. Teachers can enhance the potential of all their students by eliminating gender bias from their classrooms.

QUESTIONS AND ACTIVITIES

QUESTIONS TO CONSIDER

1. What can be done to ensure that students' developing self-esteem is not adversely affected in the schools?

2. What decisions are typically made at school in which students could take part?

3. What can teachers do to improve their communication skills in school?

4. What specific changes in curriculum and instruction will help minority students and females achieve recognition and acceptance as well as academic success?

CLASSROOM ACTIVITIES

Break the class into groups of three students. Have one student act as a student, the second as the teacher, and the third as an observer.

1. Use role-playing to simulate the following situations, which ensue when the student makes the indicated remark. In each situation, make sure that the student has in mind an underlying emotion that is not explicitly stated.

   a. "I hate you and I hate your class! How did you ever become a teacher?"

   b. "I'm not learning anything in this class."

   c. "This class is too hard. There is way too much homework."

2. Have the teacher in each group help the student prepare a solution for the following problems. Have them prepare a set of assumptions and criteria, which they then will apply in solving the problem.

a. whether to study a unit on practical chemistry or take a more theoretical approach

b. what to do when a girlfriend or boyfriend you have gone steady with for a year decides to end the relationship

STUDENT APPLICATIONS

Prepare a description of how in your own teaching you might avoid the devastating effects school often has on students' self-concepts. Include provisions for dealing with special problems posed by differences in ethnicity, economic class, and gender.

REFERENCES

Aronson, E., & Carlsmith, J. M. (1962). Performance expectancy as a determinant of actual performance. *Journal of Abnormal and Social Psychology, 65*, 178–182.

Aspy, D., & Roebuck, R. (1977). *Kids don't learn from people they don't like.* Amherst, MA: Human Resources Development Press.

Becker, J. R. (1981). Differential treatment of females and males in mathematical classes. *Journal of Research in Mathematical Education, 12*, 40–53.

Bennett, C. I. (1986). *Comprehensive multicultural education: Theory and practice.* Boston: Allyn and Bacon.

Birney, R. C., Burdick, H., & Teevan, R. C. (1969). *Fear of failure.* New York: Van Nostrand.

Brophy, J., & Evertson, C. (1976). *Learning from teaching: A developmental perspective.* Boston: Allyn and Bacon.

Brown, H. R. (1969). *Die nigger die!* New York: Dial.

Christian, C. C. (1978). The acculturation of the bilingual child. In F. Cordasco (Ed.), *Bilingualism and the bilingual child* (pp. 160–165). New York: Arno Press.

Cleaver, E. (1968). *Soul on ice.* New York: Ramparts.

Covington, M. V., & Beery, R. G. (1976). *Self worth and school learning.* New York: Holt, Rinehart and Winston.

Curwin, R. L., & Mendler, A. N. (1988). *Discipline with dignity.* Washington, DC: Association for Supervision and Curriculum Development.

Foster, H. L. (1986). *Ribbin', jivin', playin' the dozens.* Cambridge, MA: Ballinger.

Ginott, H. (1971). *Teacher and child.* New York: Macmillan.

Gollnick, D. M., Sadker, M., & Sadker, D. (1982). Beyond the Dick and Jane syndrome: Confronting sex bias in instructional materials. In M. Sadker & D. Sadker (Eds.), *Sex equity handbook for schools* (pp. 60–95). New York: Longman.

Gordon, M. M. (1964). *Assimilation in American life: The role of race, religion and national origins*. New York: Oxford University Press.

Jones, V. F., & Jones, L. S. (1986). *Comprehensive classroom management* (2nd ed.). Boston: Allyn and Bacon.

Levine, D. U. (1988). Teaching thinking to at-risk students: Generalizations and speculation. In B. Z. Presseisen (Ed.), *At-risk students and thinking: Perspectives from research* (pp. 117–137). Washington, DC: National Education Association and Research for Better Schools.

Martire, J. G. (1956). Relationships between the self-concept and differences in the strength and generality of achievement motivation. *Journal of Personality, 24,* 364–375.

Morrison, A., & McIntyre, D. (1969). *Teachers and teaching*. Baltimore: Penguin.

Purkey, W. W. (1970). *Self-concept and school achievement*. Englewood Cliffs, NJ: Prentice-Hall.

Ramirez, M., & Price-Williams, D. R. (1976). Achievement motivation in children of three ethnic groups in the United States. *Journal of Cross-Cultural Psychology, 7,* 49–60.

Sadker, D., & Sadker, M. (1985). Is the O.K. classroom O.K.? *Phi Delta Kappan, 55,* 358–361.

Saville-Troike, M. (1980). Cross-cultural communications in the classroom. In J. E. Alatis (Ed.), *Current issues in bilingual education: Georgetown University roundtable on language and linguistics* (p. 354). Washington, DC: Georgetown University Press.

Slavin, R. (1983). *Cooperative learning*. New York: Longman.

Slavin, R. (1986). *Using student team learning* (3rd ed.). Baltimore: Johns Hopkins Team Learning Project, Center for Research on Elementary and Middle Schools.

Stockard, J., & Johnson, M. M. (1980). *Sex roles: Sex inequality and sex role development*. Englewood Cliffs, NJ: Prentice-Hall.

Walsh, C. E. (1991). *Pedagogy and the struggle for voice: Issues of language, power and school for Puerto Ricans*. New York: Bergin and Garvey.

Weiler, K. (1988). *Women teaching for change: Gender, class and power*. South Hadley, MA: Bergin and Garvey.

Weiner, B., & Kukal, A. (1970). An attributional analysis of achievement motivation. *Journal of Personality and Social Psychology, 15,* 1–20.

Weiner, B., & Peter, N. V. (1973). A cognitive-developmental analysis of achievement and moral judgements. *Developmental Psychology, 9,* 290–309.

Women on Words and Images. (1975). *Dick and Jane as victims: Sex stereotyping in children's readers*. Princeton, NJ: Author.

15

Managing the Classroom

OBJECTIVES

This chapter is designed to help you
1. begin the school year in a way that will help promote better classroom management
2. learn how to become better acquainted with students and thereby enhance teacher-student relationships
3. manage time and establish classroom routines that contribute positively to classroom management
4. use the skills necessary to increase the amount of time students remain on-task
5. arrange the physical environment of the classroom so that it enhances learning and helps prevent discipline problems

Introduction

▼   When the bell rang, a few students were at their desks while others milled around the classroom socializing with their friends. Several students were in the hall outside the classroom door trying to juggle a kick-sack with their feet. Mr. Orme called for attention and implored the students out in the hall to come in before they were marked tardy. Mr. Orme's request had little effect, so he began to call out the names of students who were not in their seats. When someone failed to answer, Mr. Orme made inquiries about why that student was not in class. When he was satisfied that he had an accurate record of attendance, he hung the office notification form on a nail by the door. Some students were still out of their seats when he announced that he was going to pick up the previous night's homework. He made his way slowly around the room while students shuffled through their notes trying to find the requisite assignments. After he had finished collecting all the homework, he took a pile of papers from his desk and began handing them out one by one, calling out individual students' names as he did so. When this task was completed, Mr. Orme announced that the class would be starting chapter 12 that day and asked how many students had remembered to bring their books. This question was met with groans and requests to retrieve books from hall lockers. Mr. Orme confessed that starting chapter 12 was a change from what had been previously assigned, but he maintained that students should bring their books to class routinely anyway. This pronouncement was followed by a long lecture about responsibility. All the while students continued to talk in various places around the classroom. Fifteen minutes of class time had now passed and the day's lesson had still not begun. Strain showed plainly on Mr. Orme's face, and his voice registered his anger. Finally, in frustration he sent three students to the principal's office as a warning to the rest of the class to settle down and go to work.

This example illustrates the difficulty teachers experience when they fail to properly manage time in their classrooms. Many discipline problems can be avoided by properly managing the classroom environment and timing various classroom events so that students are meaningfully involved in learning. Without realizing it, Mr. Orme himself exacerbated the discipline problems by not getting his class immediately involved in productive work and by not using economical procedures for taking roll and passing out and receiving class assignments. Mr. Orme could have forgone the lecture on responsibility and the referral of students to the principal's office had he been better organized beforehand and created various routines to handle the day-to-day classroom operations efficiently and effectively. Unfortunately, poor handling of classroom routines not only takes up valuable instruction time, but it also encourages students to misbehave. Most teachers are unaware of the extraordinary amount of instructional opportunity lost as a consequence of poor time management. In one study, it was discovered that 57% of an instructional hour was taken up by in-class and out-of-class distractions such as announcements and various other intrusions. Additional time was lost because of poor attention due to ineffective management skills. On the average, only 19 minutes and 48 seconds of an entire instructional hour was effectively used for learning (Latham, 1985).

Beginning the Year

Getting off on the right foot with a class can make a big difference in the entire year. There are some tasks and behaviors that should unquestionably be avoided. Other activities can greatly enhance learning and help prevent discipline problems. Perhaps the most important day of the school year is the first one. Teachers ordinarily use this time to pass out books and take care of other essential business. However, there are other activities that should take precedence over these business matters during the first few days. The first day is a particularly good time for teachers and students to get acquainted and for students to learn about one another.

GETTING ACQUAINTED

Students can get acquainted with their teachers in several different ways. For example, teachers may teach their best lesson on the first day of class. Students can thus get a fairly good idea of what they may reasonably expect from their teachers. Another way for teachers to introduce themselves to students is to give some type of performance or display of their talents. Art teachers can paint or draw a portrait of one of their students while other students watch; they can also place examples of their artwork around the room. Music teachers may give a concert, either vocal or instrumental, or teach students some entertaining songs. Drama teachers can do a reading from a play, enlisting the help of more experienced students to help demonstrate the kinds of skills new students might be expected to acquire. Science teachers may talk about their own research with their students. English teachers may share examples of their writing. The purpose of these first-day activities is to help students gain a perception of their teachers as acceptable human beings with talents and skills, including considerable teaching ability. Students should conclude that they will be having a very enjoyable experience spending a year with their teachers.

Many teachers find it useful to have their students get acquainted with one another, particularly when they plan to have students working together in groups. Sometimes teachers invite students to play get-acquainted games or tell the class something about themselves. One teacher has been successful in getting to know her students by having them break into pairs and talk to each other extensively about themselves; then one member of the pair tells the rest of the class about the other.

Another teacher plays a game called Passing a Face. Students are arranged in groups of about ten students. One member of each group is instructed to make a face at another person in the group. This individual then tries to alter the facial expression slightly before passing it on to the next person. This progression goes on until the last person makes a face at the person who started the game. The teacher can join in this game, too. After it has been completed, questions can be asked about the experience: "How did you feel while you were playing the game?" "What was difficult about the game?" "Whose expression did you like the best?" Games of this kind help break the ice and reduce the natural uneasiness students may feel as they begin a school year. Such games also help students see their teachers as human beings (Lemlech, 1988).

Some teachers have their students divide into groups to write a class song. This assignment can take the form of a contest: The winning composition will be the theme song for the class. The song may then be sung on various occasions throughout the year.

Teachers obviously need to know the names of their students. Students also need to know one another's name. Sometimes students are already well acquainted with one another. At other times, such as the beginning of junior high or high school, there may be many unfamiliar classmates. One way to practice names is to arrange the class in a long line around the room. If the name of the first person in the line is John, he simply announces that fact to the person next to him. Ruth, the next person in the line, points at John and says, "Your name is John, my name is Ruth." This procedure is continued until the last person in the line has named herself or himself; then that person must name all the other students in the line. After this first round, the person at the back of the line goes to the front and the whole procedure is repeated. The game continues until all the students and the teacher can name everyone in class. (Teachers may also want to employ a seating chart for a few weeks until they are sure that they know every student's name.)

Getting to know students is more than learning names. Teachers also need to become familiar with their students' likes and dislikes, favorite activities, and learning preferences. One way to obtain such information is to ask each student to fill out a card and list hobbies, school activities, interests, work experience, and so forth. This information may help teachers better understand their students and can stimulate class participation and the development of better student-teacher relationships. In the case of students at the secondary level, it is also important to know whether they plan to attend college after graduation and what vocational plans they have. This information is helpful to teachers in determining the kinds of experiences students in their class will benefit from most.

Teachers also need to communicate whatever expectations they may have. Students need to know such things as whether homework will be assigned on weekends, whether unannounced quizzes will be given, whether reports will be oral or written, whether the format of the class is primarily lecture or discussion or independent study, whether there will be group projects, how much reading will be expected, and how they will be evaluated. Students need to know what to expect from their teachers and how it will contribute to their education.

ESTABLISHING RULES

Rules need to be established in every classroom. If they are not, misbehavior can be anticipated. Although rules are essential, they do not necessarily have to be determined exclusively by the teacher. Students can be significantly involved in determining rules as well as consequences for rule infractions. This activity is one of the single most important goals to accomplish during the first few days of class. It is probably a good idea to take care of this important task soon after you have given your students some idea of what to expect from you as a teacher. Rules may require several days to establish if students are involved. Otherwise, one class period may be all that is necessary. Whichever approach you choose, it is wise to post the rules and provide a copy to each student. Some teachers even send a copy of the rules home to parents.

If teachers decide to allow students to help determine rules, it is important to let them know that the rules they make must reflect the more general rules that have been established by the school or school district. For example, if the school has a rule against gum-chewing, the class should not be allowed to make an exception. Teachers may also want to temper the consequences students decide to impose on those who break the rules. Some of these consequences may not be in the best interest of students and their learning. Others may even create legal problems for the school.

Time Management

Managing time in the classroom in order to keep students on-task is an important factor in maintaining good discipline. One problem teachers face is that of determining how much time they will allot for each of the planned classroom learning activities. Sometimes teachers make this decision in terms of their own interests. They make little effort to determine either the interests of their students or the amount of instruction time appropriate to their students' current level of proficiency. Teachers must balance the curriculum to meet the diverse needs and interests of students. Teachers, of course, have a professional and ethical obligation to teach those subjects and concepts their students need most. Taking into account students' interests and needs, teachers must ask themselves what learners need to know and how much time will be required for them to achieve an acceptable level of competence. How much time can be profitably spent on different topics without contributing unnecessarily to the boredom of students who have only a marginal interest in the subject? This decision is almost always a judgment call for teachers. The only rule of thumb is that as much time should be taken as students need in order to benefit most from the activities.

After time has been allocated for various topics of study, teachers must concern themselves with making sure that students remain engaged and on-task. Keeping students on-task is not just a matter of making sure that they are working; they must be meaningfully involved in learning. Therefore, so-called busywork should be avoided. The only sure way to avoid giving busywork is to be sure that students are consulted about what they learn. In addition, students should experience a reasonable level of success. Unsuccessful students will not remain on-task for long. Their minds will wander, and what they decide to put effort into will in all likelihood create discipline problems.

ESTABLISHING ROUTINES

One essential time management task is the establishment of classroom routines. Tasks such as taking attendance, making announcements, distributing materials, and collecting students' work need to be turned into routines so that they do not waste time or cause disruptions. Ways also need to be devised for moving from one activity to another and for deciding what to do when students need to go to the office, get something from their locker, or take a restroom break. All these activities can be handled with a routine that does not take the time or the attention of the teacher away from the instructional process.

A lot of time is commonly wasted at the beginning of a class period or school day. Ordinarily teachers use this time to take attendance, collect homework, deal with absences from the previous day, get a lunch count, and make announcements. In many schools, announcements are confined to the first and last period of the day; in others, interruptions can be expected over the public address system at any time during the day. It is far better to be able to anticipate those times when announcements will be made and plan accordingly.

The other housekeeping duties that ordinarily take place at the beginning of a period also have to be routinized. Assigning students as helpers to handle routine tasks allows the teacher to spend the time making sure that class members start their work and are not involved in disruptions. Another effective way of handling housekeeping routines is to do them during class activities that are scheduled to begin as soon as students arrive. If these activities are designed to start as soon as the bell rings, or even before, less time will be lost and fewer discipline problems will develop. Students may be routinely directed to attend to instructions on the chalkboard or overhead projector screen. These instructions may inform them to review some material, begin working on an advance organizer for the current lesson, solve a puzzle, or engage in some enjoyable activity. While students are working, the teacher and student helpers can complete the various administrative tasks.

One helpful routine is to have students place their homework and other assignments in appropriately marked baskets located near the door. The teacher then does not have to deal with this daily chore. Corrected papers and tests can also be distributed in a similar manner. In some cases, students have small mailboxes into which teachers can put all materials that are to be returned to them. If this approach is impossible, the aid of student helpers may be enlisted to pass out papers at the beginning of class, especially if the teacher wants to go over the material during class. If mailboxes are used to distribute materials, thought should be given to their location. It is unwise to place them where students have to line up to retrieve their materials.

Activities such as going to the restroom, using the pencil sharpener or drinking fountain, going to learning centers, using computers, working on projects with other students, and going to the library, the cafeteria, the main office, the nurse, or the counselor all require the establishment of routines. In most schools, movement in the hallways during class time is carefully regulated. Students are generally not allowed in the hall without permission. Teachers need to create a system so that they do not have to respond endlessly to students' requests to be excused from class. In many classrooms, a hall pass is provided for this purpose. Rather than sign individual passes, teachers may direct students to take turns using a single hall pass as necessary to conduct their business outside the classroom. This routine allows students to regulate themselves unobtrusively. The one problem that may occur is that a few students will monopolize the hall pass. But this problem can also be regulated by students. A hall pass monitor can be assigned to check the frequency and duration of hall pass use. In this way fairness can be achieved without excessive intervention by the teacher.

MAKING CLEAR ASSIGNMENTS

The way in which teachers make assignments also has the potential for wasting time and promoting discipline problems. Nearly all teachers have had the experience of making assignments only to receive a request a moment later to repeat them. Sometimes several students will make this request for each assignment. Nevertheless, it is not uncommon to discover the next day that one or more students misunderstood the assignment. Repeating instructions for assignments several times should be avoided. In the first place, some students use this ritual as a way to manipulate their teachers. Second, those students who understood the assignment the first time are understandably bored and perplexed by repeated explanations. Some teachers solve the problem by writing assignments on the board or passing out an assignment sheet to each student. Some use overhead transparencies. Others post long-term assignments on the bulletin board. Many teachers, however, make the mistake of giving all assignments orally. Unfortunately, oral assignments are easily misinterpreted and forgotten. If children are unprepared or complete their assignments inappropriately, they can always claim that they did what they thought you said. Written instruction helps prevent this problem. Probably the most effective method of making assignments is to provide students with written instructions along with verbal explanations. With this method most misinterpretations can be corrected immediately. Many children have a difficult time understanding and following written instructions without verbal explanations. Yet they need written instructions to refer to later in case they forget something. If after giving verbal and written instructions the teacher requests one or two students to explain what they think the assignment is, any lingering confusion can be cleared up. This process is markedly different from the practice of some teachers who say to their students, "I'm only going to give this assignment once. If you don't get it, that's tough."

DISTRIBUTING MATERIALS

Slowdowns and disruptions can also be caused by the inefficient distribution of learning materials. Most classrooms have large supplies of books and magazines, art supplies, and laboratory and audio-visual aids of various kinds. These instructional materials often need to be passed out or collected sometime during the class period. This distribution can waste time and create disruptions. To avoid such aggravation, the materials should be strategically located so that their distribution creates as few problems as possible. Procedures for distribution should be established. For example, if reference books need to be passed out, book monitors can be selected to supply them for the students in their row. This procedure helps teachers avoid the congestion and potential scuffling that may occur when the entire class tries to retrieve or return their books at the same time.

ENDING THE LESSON

Most teachers have experienced the inevitable book-closing and paper-rustling that occurs just before the bell rings as students ready themselves to leave the classroom. This flurry of activity prompts many teachers to cut short their lessons and to mumble last-minute instructions, which few students hear. This transition too can be more effectively managed with the establishment of a routine all students understand and are willing to follow. This time should be used productively by the teacher. Perhaps it can be a time when lesson objectives are reviewed and last-minute instructions for assignments are given. Students can be informed that if they work until told to stop, they will be dismissed on time. Teachers should then make sure to finish with all instructional activities before the bell rings. If this procedure is routinely followed, students will not feel compelled to provide cues to teachers that it is time to start winding up the lesson.

Pacing

If students are to learn effectively, learning activities must be appropriately paced. However, pacing is a very difficult and complex task. Because students have different learning needs and interests as well as abilities, there is a wide variation in the time it takes them to understand what is being taught or to complete assignments. Some students are able to grasp a concept or master a skill quickly, whereas others are unable to learn it at all in the time allotted. If it is not necessary for students to learn the same things in about the same length of time—for example, if instruction is individualized and self-paced—this diversity poses no problem. If, however, all students need to learn the same material at the same time, pacing is critical.

One method teachers can use to gauge instruction is to find several students in the class, a reference group, who can provide them cues about the appropriateness of the classroom pace. This reference group can be asked questions about the concepts being taught; from their responses teachers can make judgments about the general level of understanding. They can also observe various nonverbal cues. Teachers may look for puzzled expressions on the faces of specified students. If high-achieving students look puzzled, the teacher knows that nearly the whole class is likely to be lost. Boredom can also give an indication of poor pacing. The pace is usually too slow when a significant proportion of the class starts looking out the windows, thumbing through their books, or poking and talking to one another.

The question is: What is an appropriate pace? If you go too slow, the more able students get bored. If you go too fast, the less able members of the class get lost. How do you please the most students—or displease the fewest? Savage (1991) recommends choosing a pace that is appropriate for about 75 percent of the class. This pace, he explains, will be a bit slow for the more able learners, but it will keep the lesson moving along and provide success for a majority of the students. Students who are unable to keep pace will require some additional help. Perhaps periods of time could be set aside specifically for this group. If time is reserved for some students, teachers should be careful not to stereotype them. Their lack of success is probably a result of self-concept problems that developed in other classrooms where their inabilities received too much attention.

Maximizing On-Task Behavior

As Kounin (1970) and his colleagues found out, it is far easier to prevent discipline problems than to deal with them once they occur. Successful classroom managers, they found, used several strategies to ensure students' continued involvement in instructional activities. Successful teachers were better prepared and organized and able to guide their students smoothly through their learning activities. These teachers also had a greater awareness of what was happening in the classroom and could communicate this awareness to their students. These teachers were better able to teach interesting, stimulating lessons and to employ techniques that individualized instruction and appealed to the interests of students. Most of these strategies encouraged students to stay on-task and become productive learners.

Several well-documented practices can be used to maximize on-task behavior.

STIMULATING STUDENTS' INTEREST

Maximizing on-task behavior depends on maintaining students' attention. One way to maintain students' attention is to use the introduction to a lesson to stimulate their interest and get them involved. Start the lesson with a highly motivating activity. Often lessons create interest and help maintain students' on-task behavior if they begin with an overview of how the topic is related to issues the children consider important. Waiting to start a lesson until such distractions as extra books, papers, and toys have been removed and everyone is paying attention also promotes on-task behavior.

Another way to maintain students' attention is to ask them questions. In a question-and-answer session, teachers should ask the question before calling on a student to answer it. Students who answer questions should be selected at random so that they do not know when they will be expected to make a response. It is also wise for teachers to wait a few seconds after asking a question and getting no response before calling on another student or answering the question themselves. Often students pretend not to know the answer if they realize that the teacher habitually waits only a very short time before asking other students to answer the question. A pause of at least 5 seconds after asking a question should be routine. A pause of as much as 10 seconds may sometimes be appropriate. Incredibly, the average time teachers wait for students to respond to their questions is a mere 0.9 second (Rowe, 1974).

Another way to maintain students' attention is to ask them to respond to their classmates' answers. In the typical classroom, students believe that the only worthwhile information is that provided by the teacher. Students' responses are considered unimportant, especially for test purposes. It would be rare, but very worthwhile, for students to record the responses made by classmates in their notes.

Students' attention can be expected to improve if teachers avoid mimicry, the practice of parroting back a student's response and following it with a short reinforcing statement. Typically a teacher-student interchange begins when the teacher asks a question. The student gives a response, which the teacher mimics and then reinforces. For example, the teacher may ask, "What is 2 times 2?" The student responds, "4." The teacher says, "4. That's correct. Good response." Ordinarily most student-teacher recitation sessions consist mainly of numerous repetitions of this question-response-acknowledgment cycle. Research has demonstrated that this pattern greatly reduces inquiry by students in the classroom. In addition, the length and quality of students' responses is greatly reduced (Edwards, 1980).

GUIDING STUDENTS' LEARNING

Effective seatwork is an essential ingredient in keeping students on-task. It is easy for children to get distracted once seatwork begins, often because they have made poor transitions from preceding learning activities and seatwork. To make transitions properly, students must know precisely what to do and have the necessary materials readily available. Once students begin their work, it is critical to monitor them.

Students sometimes fail to work consistently on an assignment until it is completed because they have no clear concept of how their work is related to previous learning, what procedures they should follow in completing the work, or how it will be evaluated. Teachers should give instructions that tell students exactly what they will be doing and how this activity relates to what they have done before. Students also need to know how to obtain assistance, what to do when the work is completed, and how much time the learning activity is likely to take. In addition, students need to know that they will be held accountable for the quality of their work.

To remain on-task, students need to know how they are doing. They need immediate and specific feedback about how they are performing so that they can make quick adjustments. The teacher needs to provide students with the information they need to continue their work successfully. One mistake teachers often make is spending too much time with too few students. Jones (1987) indicates that when teachers supervise seatwork, they ordinarily ask students where they are having difficulty. They then proceed to show students where they are making mistakes. This process takes so much time that teachers do not get around to all students who need help. Jones recommends that each of these help sessions be shortened. He suggests that teachers avoid lengthy explanations; instead, they should give students a short prompt to help them solve the next part of the problem they are working on and then move on to the next student. In this way teachers are able to get around the room and help more students, thus keeping the entire class working. Otherwise, students tend to get distracted.

MINIMIZING DISRUPTIONS

Students find it difficult to remain on-task if their teachers handle class disruptions ineffectively. Teachers need to demonstrate "withitness" in their classrooms—knowing what is going on in the classroom at all times. They also must know how to target the most disruptive behaviors first and use proper timing in correcting them. If teachers are late in making their desists or focus attention on less serious problems before solving more significant ones, they will be unable to maintain proper classroom control. In addition, they must be able to demonstrate skill in "overlapping"—handling several situations simultaneously. A teacher may, for example, have to redirect one student while continuing to help another solve a problem (Kounin, 1970).

Managing the Physical Environment

Research has shown that the physical arrangement of classrooms contributes to the amount of learning that takes place in them. Furniture must be arranged to accommodate the instructional program. Consequently, the physical arrangement of the classroom must be flexible enough so that adjustments can be made for individual work, group work, and total-class activities. Space must be properly arranged to accommodate the traffic patterns of the teacher and students. Classrooms should not only be functional; they should also be aesthetically pleasing and comfortable.

THE ACTION ZONE

Adams and Biddle (1970) found that when classrooms were arranged with the students' desks in rows, the front and center of the classroom constituted an "action zone" where greater student-teacher interaction took place and where students were more successful academically. They found that students sitting in the action zone participated more in class, demonstrated better on-task behavior, had better attitudes, and attained higher achievement levels. Students who sat outside the action zone had lower self-esteem and felt threatened by proximity to the teacher. By sitting in the periphery, they succeeded in getting called on less often, thus reducing their risk of failure. Teachers tended to monitor them less frequently and allowed them to be less involved in all class activity. There is some evidence that students with a poor self-concept can have more positive experiences when they are assigned seats in the action zone (Dykman & Reis,

1979). Students who have difficulty staying on-task may also benefit from being in the action zone. Because students who are in the action zone receive more constructive feedback and have higher achievement levels, they experience greater feelings of competence and attain more intellectual growth.

Because the action zone is defined by proximity to the teacher, it can be changed at will by the teacher. When the seating is properly arranged, teachers can shift the action zone to almost any place in the classroom. Teachers therefore need to arrange the seating in such a way that they can decide at any time which class members to include in the action zone. Shifting the action zone should entail no more than a quick movement by the teacher to a different location in the room.

STUDENTS' SEATING

How students' desks are arranged is important not only to the movement of the teacher through the classroom but also to the creation of specific learning configurations. There is no one best way to arrange students' seating. Different seating arrangements influence behavior in different ways. It is the teacher's task to ensure that the seating arrangement employed provides optimum conditions for the kind of learning intended. Desk arrangements provide the major framework for shaping student-teacher interactions and the learning that results.

Weinstein (1979) indicates that organizing desks such that student-to-student interaction is limited to two or three students leads to higher on-task behavior, less off-task movement, and less loud talking. According to Rosenfield, Lambert, and Black (1985), students maintained greater on-task behavior and paid closer attention in discussions in which they were seated in a circular pattern. However, more students also spoke out of turn. Obviously sitting in a circle enhances students' spontaneity. Students seated in rows, on the other hand, were more likely to withdraw from discussions and engage in more off-task behavior. Students arranged in clusters were less spontaneous than those arranged in circles, but they still maintained a good deal of on-task behavior.

Teachers should create seating arrangements that correspond to their instructional intentions. If, for example, they wish to limit students' interaction and promote independent work, seating by rows would be appropriate. If they want students to initiate discussion, a circle arrangement would be best. Clusters may be the arrangement of choice when ordered participation is desired.

Good and Brophy (1986) report that students in a fourth grade classroom who were seated at rectangular tables to do a creative writing assignment experienced difficulty in completing the assignment. Apparently it was hard for children to work on an independent assignment when every time they raised their heads they were looking into the eyes of their peers. This arrangement facilitated discussion, but it greatly inhibited the actual writing process.

Glasser (1977) made a study of the physical design of open classrooms. He found that classroom boundaries were necessary for students to engage in activities without interfering with one another. Teachers may find it necessary to partition off areas of their classrooms to serve different purposes. Book shelves and filing cabinets are useful for this purpose, as are movable dividers. Figure 15.1 illustrates an elementary classroom designed for different types of work, partitioned off to provide some degree of

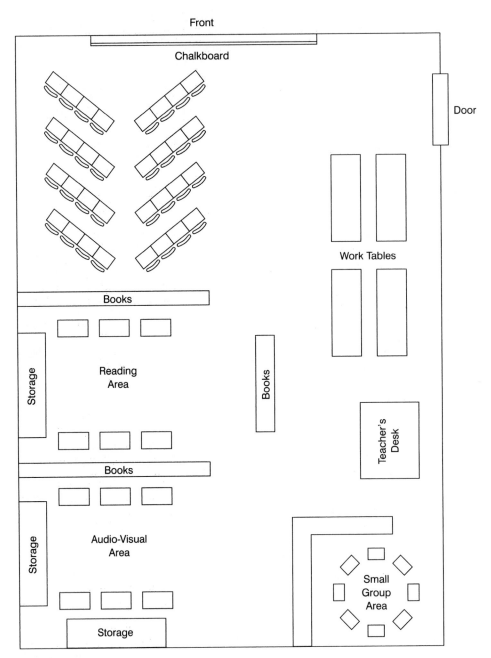

FIGURE 15.1
A flexible classroom arrangement.

privacy. Notice that the teacher's desk is located where all areas of the classroom can be simultaneously monitored. Conceivably some students could be finishing assigned seatwork while others are engaging in laboratory work, doing small-group work, watching films, or reading. This arrangement provides the kind of flexibility necessary to accommodate the needs of students and the instructional strategies of teachers.

CLASSROOM ENVIRONMENT

Classrooms should be exciting, comfortable places to be. No classroom should be ugly or forbidding. Instead, the classroom environment should produce feelings of security and warmth. Because the classroom environment has a direct impact on children, the teacher has the important responsibility of creating pleasant surroundings that emphasize learning. According to Weinstein (1979), studies have shown that as the quality of the classroom environment deteriorates, teachers become more controlling and less friendly and sensitive. Students become correspondingly less involved and engage in more conflicts with peers. Students in unattractive classrooms experience more feelings of fatigue and discontent.

What can teachers do to improve the learning environment? Providing more comfortable furniture is one thing that may be done. A couple of overstuffed armchairs and a few bean bag chairs appropriately placed would help. Some reading lamps and live plants and pictures can also make the classroom more comfortable. Bulletin boards on which questions to be investigated are posted provide intellectual stimulation. Books and magazines can be placed in strategic places in the room as well. Books discarded by local libraries can be picked up for a few pennies. Many of these books are still valuable and can serve as additional learning resources for students.

Creating efficient traffic patterns is also a critical factor in arranging classroom furniture. Jones (1987) suggests several arrangements that allow teachers easy, quick access to all areas of the classroom (refer to Figure 10.1). Teachers need to be able to move from one location to another without having to retrace their steps or move around various obstacles.

The location of the teacher's desk is also a consideration. In many classrooms the teacher's desk is located at the front of the room. However, this is probably the worst possible location (Savage, 1991). A much more suitable location is a corner in or near the back of the room. Here teachers can conduct business with individual students in greater privacy, and students can share their feelings with teachers with less risk of embarrassment. In addition, if the teacher is in the back of the room, students are less aware of when they are being closely monitored. More on-task behavior can be expected under these conditions.

Background music can also improve classroom ambience. Soft music in the background can aid learning and may even improve academic performance (Charles, 1983). Music can be used to create a sense of relaxation and to block out various distractions. It can also be used to create a learning set—that is, classroom conditions arranged in such a way that students want to begin learning immediately. One elementary teacher used a piece of music called *Popcorn* to enhance a lesson on poetry one day. While the children were out for recess, this enterprising professional placed three or four popcorn poppers around the room. Just as the children were coming in from recess, the poppers began emitting an unmistakable sound and an irresistible aroma. Meanwhile, *Popcorn* played softly in the background. As the students took their seats, they were instructed to go to work immediately writing a poem about popcorn. As they worked, their little bodies moved with the music while their teacher moved around the room depositing little piles of popcorn on their desks. The children's poems were so extraordinary that the teacher's eyes filled with tears as she read them.

▼

SUMMARY

Successful classroom management can go a long way toward preventing discipline problems. It is far better to prevent discipline problems than to solve them once they occur. Effective classroom management begins on the first day of class. Because good first impressions are so important, teachers may plan to teach their best lesson of the year on that day. Afterward, classroom rules should be established. Then teachers and students can take part in get-acquainted activities. Teachers need to know the names of their students and get some idea of their interests and favorite extracurricular activities. All this groundwork needs to be laid before such mundane tasks as passing out books are undertaken.

A critical part of classroom management is time management, the establishment of routines that economize classroom operations. Better discipline can be expected when books and papers are passed out and collected efficiently.

Children need to make the best use of their time and maintain their concentration on learning if they are to achieve the most from their school experiences. The more time spent studying, the greater the potential for learning. Time on-task can be enhanced by maintaining students' attention, giving clear instructions, presenting stimulating lesson introductions, making proper use of questioning strategies, carefully monitoring students' seatwork, providing timely and specific feedback, and managing disruptions effectively.

The physical environment of the classroom contributes a great deal to students' comfort and learning. The arrangement of students' seating should allow teachers to move the action zone wherever they desire. It should also help teachers maintain control. Different seating arrangements should be used depending on the kind of learning activity. The classroom can be made more pleasant for students with the addition of comfortable furniture, better lighting, more interesting bulletin boards, supplementary learning materials, and other amenities. Improving the classroom environment will improve students' learning.

CENTRAL IDEAS

1. The first day of class is usually the most important day of the school year. It should be filled with learning activities that promote a positive image of the teacher.

2. To properly manage a classroom, teachers need to know their students well—not only their names but also their interests and favorite activities. Teachers can use this information to foster more positive relationships with their students.

3. All classrooms need rules. Students may or may not be involved in determining the rules. Students should help make the rules if the goal of the teacher is to help them become more self-governing.

4. If students are engaged in common learning experiences, teachers need to properly pace instruction so that the greatest number of students receive the greatest benefit. Instruction that is given at too slow a pace bores the more able students, and the less able students become lost when the pace of instruction is too fast. Teachers must try to find a pace that accommodates both groups.

5. Classroom routines such as collecting and passing out papers must be managed so that little time is lost and students do not become distracted.

6. Proper classroom management involves keeping students on-task. When students are allowed to be distracted, discipline problems occur.

7. Seating in the classroom should provide maximum flexibility for teachers. They should be able to move quickly to any place in the classroom to maintain control or adjust learning conditions.

8. The environment in the classroom does make a difference in the achievement as well as the comfort of students.

QUESTIONS AND ACTIVITIES

QUESTIONS TO CONSIDER

1. What issues need to be resolved in creating classroom rules?

2. How can teachers get the resources they need to create a stimulating and comfortable atmosphere in their classrooms?

CLASSROOM ACTIVITIES

1. Have the class develop a list of routines for managing the various tasks and conditions in classrooms that can become management problems.

2. Create a diagram of a classroom. Have students position various items of furniture in appropriate places to enhance learning and provide proper classroom control.

STUDENT APPLICATIONS

Create a comprehensive statement about how you can become an effective classroom manager. Discuss what you could do during the first few days of class to improve student-teacher relationships and to provide an image of yourself as a competent teacher. Explain what you plan to do about classroom rules. Outline the routines you plan to use in managing your class. Sketch some the furniture arrangements you would like to have in your classroom. Describe the ways in which you could make your classroom environment more comfortable and conducive to learning.

REFERENCES

Adams, R. S., & Biddle, B. J. (1970). *Realities of teaching: Exploration with videotape*. New York: Holt, Rinehart and Winston.

Charles, C. (1983). *Elementary classroom management*. New York: Longman.

Dykman, B., & Reis, H. (1979). Personality correlates of classroom seating position. *Journal of Educational Psychology, 71*, 346–354.

Edwards, C. H. (1980). The relationship between type of teacher reinforcement and student inquiry behavior in science. *Journal of Research in Science Teaching, 17*, 337–341.

Glasser, W. (1977). Ten steps in good discipline. *Today's Education, 66*(4), 61–63.

Good, T. L., & Brophy, J. E. (1986). *Educational psychology* (3rd ed.). New York: Longman.

Jones, F. H. (1987). *Positive classroom instruction*. New York: McGraw-Hill.

Kounin, J. S. (1970). *Discipline and group management in classrooms*. New York: Holt, Rinehart and Winston.

Latham, G. (1985, November 7). *Defining time in a school setting*. Presentation to PDK/UASCD Conference, Salt Lake City, UT.

Lemlech, J. K. (1988). *Classroom management: Methods and techniques for elementary and secondary teachers*. New York: Longman.

Rosenfield, P., Lambert, N., & Black, H. (1985). Desk arrangement effects on pupil classroom behavior. *Journal of Educational Psychology, 77*, 101–108.

Rowe, M. B. (1974). Reflections on wait-time: Some methodological questions. *Journal of Research in Science Teaching, 11*, 263–279.

Savage, T. V. (1991). *Discipline for self-control*. Englewood Cliffs, NJ: Prentice-Hall.

Weinstein, C. (1979). The physical environment of the school: A review of the research. *Review of Educational Research, 49*, 577–610.

Epilogue

Discipline problems are the most common difficulties you will experience in the classroom. Many of these problems are the result of social and family problems, but school policies and procedures—and sometimes your own attitudes and behavior—also contribute to them. In order to discipline your classes successfully, despite a host of personal and school-related problems, you need to determine for yourself the discipline approach that you believe is the most appropriate and then master its use.

The process of deciding on a discipline approach is not an easy one. You should not undertake it superficially. It is much too important a task. If you use your values to guide this process, the approach you finally decide on should be consistent enough with your beliefs so that you can make a relatively strong commitment to it. Without commitment to your values and corresponding educational philosophy, your teaching and discipline practices are likely to be disjointed and guided by trial and error.

Your task as outlined in this book is first to clarify your personal values and philosophy of education; in particular, you must decide how much control you believe is appropriate for you to exercise versus how much autonomy students should enjoy. You can then formulate criteria with which to evaluate various possible discipline theories. Eight different discipline models have been presented along with their assumptions so that you can examine the various possibilities in terms of their basic principles as well as practices. In considering which discipline approach to use, you are encouraged to provide for the functions of preventing discipline problems as well as correcting them and to select a model that can be applied on a schoolwide basis. Choosing an orientation—theory-based, eclectic, or shifting—is a critical part of deciding finally what discipline approach you believe is most acceptable.

Successful teaching requires you not only to maintain good discipline but also to apply good classroom management procedures. Good classroom managers use teaching activities that provide an appropriate level of autonomy for students and capitalize on students' interests. Cooperative learning includes opportunities for students to regulate their own learning and satisfy their interests, and it helps them avoid excessive competition. Excessive competition is a significant cause of poor self-concept, learning difficulties, and behavior problems. The problems culturally diverse students face in school can also be more adequately addressed through cooperative learning and other self-initiated experiences.

You can also enhance students' learning when you apply procedures that economize their time and maximize their on-task behavior. If you pace your lessons properly, use appropriate instructional techniques, organize the physical environment of the classroom, and establish classroom routines that help students avoid wasting time, you can make learning more efficient and profitable.

Modern school classrooms are dynamic social systems. Various features of classrooms make them unusually difficult places to manage without critical discipline and classroom management skills. At any time a multitude of potential disruptions can develop that, left unchecked, may interfere with your teaching and obstruct your students' learning. You must successfully cope with these complex situations so that learning will be unimpeded, and you must provide a stimulating learning environment without unnecessary distractions. Your job will not be easy. However, if you make a serious study of discipline and classroom management, you will be much better prepared to deal with problems and help students learn.

Audio-Visual Materials

FILMS

BEHAVIOR MODIFICATION

Title: Token Economy—Behaviorism Applied
Time: 20 minutes
Producer: CRM Films
Summary: A visit to a mental health center where a token economy is in use, with an introduction by B. F. Skinner. Description is given of treatment to help old people, young people, orphans, and others grow toward control of their socially unacceptable behaviors. Results show higher rates of rehabilitation. Some details of operating a token economy are outlined.

Title: Behavior Modification in the Classroom
Time: 24 minutes
Producer: University of California, Extension Media Center
           2223 Fulton Street
           Berkeley, CA   94720
Summary: Teachers using Behavior Modification to alter students' inappropriate behavior and daydreaming.

Title: Behavior Modification—Teaching Language in Psychotic Children
Time: 43 minutes
Producer: Prentice-Hall, Inc.
           Sylvan Avenue
           Englewood Cliffs, NJ   07632
Summary: The steps involved in teaching psychotic children the functional use of speech to curb self-stimulation and destructive behavior. The uses of rewards and punishment are discussed.

ASSERTIVE DISCIPLINE

Title: Assertive Discipline in Action
Time: 25 minutes
Producer: Film Images
Summary: The step-by-step procedure for adopting Assertive Discipline in an individual classroom and on a schoolwide basis.

LOGICAL CONSEQUENCES

Title: Individual Psychology in Counseling and Education: Part I. Rudolf Dreikurs
Time: 35 minutes
Producer: American Personnel and Guidance Association
              1107 New Hampshire Avenue
              Washington, DC   20009
Summary: An overview of Alfred Adler's concepts, dealing particularly with the role of emotions and the relationship of emotions to personal intentions. Emphasis is given to individual human potential.

Title: Individual Psychology in Counseling and Education: Part II
Time: 35 minutes
Producer: American Personnel and Guidance Association
              1107 New Hampshire Avenue
              Washington, DC   20009
Summary: A description of Adler's contributions to the concept of holism, focusing on the idea of social interest or the feeling of belonging. Emphasis is given to helping teachers and other school personnel understand the personality development of children.

Title: Individual Psychology: A Demonstration with a Parent, a Teacher and a Child: Parts I and II
Time: 70 minutes
Producer: American Personnel and Guidance Association
              1107 New Hampshire Avenue
              Washington, DC   20009
Summary: Applications of Individual Psychology with a troubled child. Explanations of the approach are given.

TRANSACTIONAL ANALYSIS

Title: Games We Play in High School
Time: 29 minutes
Producer: Media Five
              3211 Cahuenga Boulevard West
              Los Angeles, CA   90068
Summary: Description of games students and teachers play in the classroom. Basic concepts of Transactional Analysis are described in relation to improving discipline in the schools.

Title: The OK Classroom
Time: 29 minutes
Producer: Media Five
           3211 Cahuenga Boulevard West
           Los Angeles, CA   90068
Summary: Discussion of the special meanings of the terms Parent, Adult, Child, Transaction, Strokes, Life Positions, and Games. Examples are given of the theory in action.

Title: Transactional Analysis
Time: 30 minutes
Producer: University of California, Extension Media Center
           2223 Fulton Street
           Berkeley, CA   94720
Summary: The use of Transactional Analysis in management. Interviews are used to dramatize the use of Transactional Analysis in dealing with game-playing.

Title: Transactional Analysis
Time: 70 minutes
Producer: Human Development Institute
           20 Executive Park West, NE
           Atlanta, GA   30329
Summary: Illustration of the use of Transactional Analysis in a group. Berne's goal is shown to be helping people exhibit game-free behavior.

REALITY THERAPY/CONTROL THEORY

Title: Class Meeting on Class Meetings
Time: 28 minutes
Producer: Media Five
           3211 Cahuenga Boulevard West
           Los Angeles, CA   90068
Summary: Demonstration of the dramatic results class meetings can produce as sixth graders think about questions, listen to others, and search for reasonable alternatives to problems.

Title: The Reality Therapy Approach
Time: 29 minutes
Producer: Media Five
           3211 Cahuenga Boulevard West
           Los Angeles, CA   90068
Summary: Teachers using Reality Therapy concepts. The seven steps of Reality Therapy are shown.

Title: Dealing with Discipline Problems
Time: 29 minutes
Producer: Media Five
           3211 Cahuenga Boulevard West

Los Angeles, CA   90068

Summary: A model school where Glasser's concepts of Schools-Without-Failure are used. Teachers apply Reality Therapy in everyday practice.

Title: The Reality of Success
Time: 28 minutes
Producer: Media Five
                3211 Cahuenga Boulevard West
                Los Angeles, CA   90068

Summary: Outline by Glasser of five steps for achieving effective discipline in the schools.

Title: Roles and Goals in High School
Time: 29 minutes
Producer: Media Five
                3211 Cahuenga Boulevard West
                Los Angeles, CA   90068

Summary: Schools-Without-Failure concepts. Teachers use Reality Therapy in role-playing situations.

Title: The Glasser Up-Date
Time: 30 minutes
Producer: Media Five
                3211 Cahuenga Boulevard West
                Los Angeles, CA   90068

Summary: A revised approach to Reality Therapy. The way in which undesirable behavior can be eliminated is highlighted.

Title: Reality Therapy in High School
Time: 29 minutes
Producer: Media Five
                3211 Cahuenga Boulevard West
                Los Angeles, CA   90068

Summary: Reality Therapy in use. The effects of Reality Therapy on the total school climate are emphasized.

Title: What Is Discipline Anyway?
Time: 30 minutes
Producer: Media Five
                3211 Cahuenga Boulevard West
                Los Angeles, CA   90068

Summary: Differentiation of discipline from punishment. Alternative methods of discipline are explored.

B

Preferred Activities:
Suggested References

	Elementary	Middle Grades	High School
Games of the World by Frederic Grunfeld: Ballantine Books	•	•	•
Thinking Games by Carl Bereiter and Valerie Anderson: Scholastic Book Services	•	•	•
Rainbow Activities—50 Multi-Cultural Human Relation Experiences: Creative Teaching Press	•	•	
The Great Perpetual Learning Machine by Jim Blake: Little, Brown and Company	•		
Kids' Stuff: Book of Math for the Middle Grades by Marjorie Frank: Incentive Publications	•		
Bag of Tricks—Instructional Activities & Games by Janet Blake: Love Publishing Co.	•		
The Kids' Diary of 365 Amazing Days by Randy Harleson: Workman Publishing Company	•	•	
Teacher's Gold Mine by Dorothy Michener: Incentive Publications	•		
Word Games by Joanadel Hurst: Word Games	•	•	
Mad Libs by Roger Price: Price, Stern, Swan Publishers	•	•	•
Frisbee by Stancil Johnson: Workman Publishing Company	•	•	•
The Cooperative Sports & Games Book by Terry Orlick: Pantheon Books	•	•	
Everybody's a Winner by Tom Schneider: Little, Brown and Company	•		

	Elementary	Middle Grades	High School
The Spice Series: Educational Services Spice (Primary Language Arts); Anchor (Intermediate Language Arts); Probe (Science); Plus (Math); Spark (Social Studies); Create (Art); Action (Physical Activities); Stage (Dramatics); Rescue (Remedial Reading); Pride (Black Studies); Launch (Early Learning); Flair (Creative Writing); Note (Music); Eco (Ecology); Prevent (Safety).	•	•	•
The New Games Book by Andrew Fluegelman: The Headlands Press	•	•	•
Turn-Ons/185 Strategies for the Secondary Classroom by Stephen Smuin: Fearon, Pitman Publishers			•
The Great American Book of Games by Ferretli: Workman Publishing Company	•	•	
Until the Whistle Blows by Hall, Sweeney & Esser: Goodyear Publishing Company	•	•	
Skillstuff/Reading by Imogene Forte: Incentive Publications	•		
Mathematics Games for Classroom Use by Norma M. Molina: Silver Burdett	•	•	
Games to Grow On by Carol Winner: National Institute for Curriculum Enrichment (Math)	•	•	
Math Sponges: Enriching Ways to Soak Up Spare Moments, by Leigh Childs and Nancy Adams: National Institute for Curriculum Enrichment	•		
Big Book of Board Games by Laura Palmer: Troubador Press	•	•	

	Elementary	Middle Grades	High School
Play the Numbers: Math Games of Chance by Kay Zmudka, Sharon Barr, Jean McDermott and Thomas Wickham: Skakean Station	•		
Teacher's Treasury of Classroom Reading Activities by Mary Jo Lass-Layser: Parker Publishing Company	•	•	
Blackboard Games by Leslie Landin and Enoch Dumas: Scholastic Book Services	•	•	
Mathematical History: Activities, Puzzles, Stories and Games by Merle Mitchell: National Council of Teachers of Mathematics		•	
The Wonderful Word Book by Don Wolfson: Xerox Education Publications		•	•
Recylopedia by Robin Simons: Houghton-Mifflin Company (how to make games, crafts, and science experiments out of recycled material)	•	•	
The Beautiful Naturecraft Book (26 Contributing authors): Sterling Publishing Company	•	•	
The Kids' Arts and Crafts Book: Nitty Gritty Publications	•	•	
A Handbook of Arts and Crafts for Elementary and Junior High School Teachers by Willard F. Wankelman, Phillip Wigg, and Marietta Wigg: Wm. C. Brown Co.	•	•	
Games by Frank W. Harris (49 games to encourage cooperation): Frank W. Harris, 14597, Detroit, MI 48223	•	•	

Source: From Jones, F.H. (1987). *Positive Classroom Discipline.* New York: McGraw-Hill Book Company.

Index